Care and Agency

Rutgers Series in Childhood Studies

The Rutgers Series in Childhood Studies is dedicated to increasing our understanding of children and childhoods throughout the world, reflecting a perspective that highlights cultural dimensions of the human experience. The books in this series are intended for students, scholars, practitioners, and those who formulate policies that affect children's everyday lives and futures.

Series Board

Stuart Aitken, geography, San Diego State University

Jill Duerr Berrick, social welfare, University of California, Berkeley

Susan Danby, education, Queensland University of Technology

Julian Gill-Peterson, transgender and queer studies, University of Pittsburgh

Afua Twum-Danso Imoh, sociology, University of Sheffield

Stacey Lee, educational policy studies, University of Wisconsin-Madison

Sunaina Maira, Asian American studies, University of California, Davis

David M. Rosen, anthropology and sociology, Fairleigh Dickinson University

Rachael Stryker, human development and women's studies, Cal State East Bay

Tom Weisner, anthropology, University of California, Los Angeles

Care and Agency

The Andean Community through
the Eyes of Children

JEANINE ANDERSON AND
JESSACA B. LEINAWEAVER

RUTGERS UNIVERSITY PRESS
NEW BRUNSWICK, CAMDEN, AND NEWARK, NEW JERSEY
LONDON AND OXFORD

Rutgers University Press is a department of Rutgers, The State University of New Jersey, one of the leading public research universities in the nation. By publishing worldwide, it furthers the University's mission of dedication to excellence in teaching, scholarship, research, and clinical care.

Names: Anderson, Jeanine, author. | Leinaweaver, Jessaca B., author.
Title: Care and agency : the Andean community through the eyes of children / Jeanine Anderson and Jessaca B. Leinaweaver.
Description: New Brunswick : Rutgers University Press, [2024] | Series: Rutgers series in childhood studies | Includes bibliographical references and index.
Identifiers: LCCN 2023054364 | ISBN 9781978840737 (paperback) | ISBN 9781978840744 (hardcover) | ISBN 9781978840751 (epub) | ISBN 9781978840768 (pdf)
Subjects: LCSH: Children—Social aspects.
Classification: LCC HQ767.9 .A52 2024 | DDC 305.23098—dc23/eng/20240515
LC record available at https://lccn.loc.gov/2023054364

A British Cataloging-in-Publication record for this book is available from the British Library.

Copyright © 2025 by Jeanine Anderson and Jessaca B. Leinaweaver

All rights reserved

No part of this book may be reproduced or utilized in any form or by any means, electronic or mechanical, or by any information storage and retrieval system, without written permission from the publisher. Please contact Rutgers University Press, 106 Somerset Street, New Brunswick, NJ 08901. The only exception to this prohibition is "fair use" as defined by U.S. copyright law.

All photos were taken by members of the authors' field team.

References to internet websites (URLs) were accurate at the time of writing. Neither the author nor Rutgers University Press is responsible for URLs that may have expired or changed since the manuscript was prepared.

♾ The paper used in this publication meets the requirements of the American National Standard for Information Sciences—Permanence of Paper for Printed Library Materials, ANSI Z39.48-1992.

rutgersuniversitypress.org

For the children of Yauyos—and for three children who joined
our family groups during the gestation of this project,
Elías, Tomás, and Leo

CONTENTS

1	Care, Community, and Children: A View from the Andes	1
2	Knowing Children	21
3	Intimate Contexts of Care	41
4	Economies of Care	58
5	Ecologies of Care	78
6	Practices of Care	91
7	The Limits of Care	108
8	Care and Flourishing	122
9	Conclusions	138

Acknowledgments	153
Notes	157
References	167
Index	187

Care and Agency

1

Care, Community, and Children

A View from the Andes

This is a book about children and care: the webs of care children are enmeshed in, their strong and weak points, their gaps, and children's protagonism within those webs. Children have overlapping roles in the organization of care: they are caregivers and care receivers, they are observers and critics of themselves and other participants, they are inheritors of norms and customs who are also capable of rejecting, modifying, and replacing them. The research behind this book was designed to register care from multiple perspectives, involving multiple actors, and in multiple relationships and settings. It started from the premise that children are agents within circuits of care, in many ways fully the equals of adults. Like the efforts of adults, those of children may be successful or may fall short. The research was also carried out in the awareness that caregiving and care receiving take many forms, even in what appear to be traditional, relatively homogeneous, small communities. Some of the diversity brought to care by children springs from their condition as learners on developmental paths that lead to their gradual appropriation—more or less critically, more or less comprehensively—of the understandings about care that distinguish their communities of birth and residence.

The book describes and analyzes the organization of care in rural towns in the Andes Mountains of Peru. This is an especially propitious place to study caring and its vicissitudes. As one of the few high-altitude environments permanently settled by human beings, it is particularly demanding. Andean people have carefully managed natural resources for centuries. They are also renowned for having developed resilient institutional structures: strong community governance, rules of cooperation and exchange, collective identities, and mechanisms for defense against outsiders, including, on occasion, the ministrations of the Peruvian state. A repertory of strategies and specialists exists to care for the elderly, sick, and disabled. Yet something of a shadow hangs over childcare and child-rearing in the Andes. Peruvian social thought contains a deeply conservative strand that attributes the country's political and economic difficulties to its indigenous

1

population and locates Andean peasants at its roots.[1] According to a recurring line of thought among some urban Peruvian elites, Andean child-rearing is responsible for school failure, stunting, depression, and the difficulties of integration in mainstream society. Unsympathetic observers report what seem to be high levels of corporal punishment, exaggerated demands for children's labor, and premature entry of adolescents into work or marriage. It is a common trope in the entire Andean region that traditional practices more generally (as Allen 2002 has argued for coca-chewing) hinder national development. A wide body of systematic research rejects these ideas. Nonetheless, stereotypes persist in the minds of educators and policymakers, animating prejudices against Andean parental practices.

Living was never easy under the conditions of the Andes. Today the region is under even more duress from population loss, climate change, and new forms of resource extraction. Political marginalization is a long-standing reality. In Peru, as in many other nations of the Global South, the state can shortchange its rural population with impunity (Collier 2007). Rural people do not receive an equitable share of the capacities for care (Gonzáles de Olarte and del Pozo 2018). Swept up by waves of migration, caretakers disappear into global care chains (Pérez Orozco et al. 2008; Leinaweaver 2010a). These and other factors, exacerbating rural poverty, limit what care can be given while making its delivery ever more urgent (Figueroa 2000).

In this book, we relate local ideas and practices of care to the ecological, economic, social, and political context. Set in the rural province of Yauyos, the research explored carework that takes place in households, extended families, schools, and neighborhoods; in shops, parks, plazas, and municipal offices; on farms and herding lands. Compared to much of the literature on childhood in non-Western societies, our study was large, ambitious, and radically ethnographic. We wanted to learn how humans, plants, animals, water, earth, and mountains converge in an ecosystem of care that ultimately determines the fortunes and flourishing of the youngest participants. This introduction sets out the questions that guided our research in Yauyos and the theoretical concepts that underlay them. The research and analysis involved a dozen student field-workers, six towns, a comprehensive training, and an extensive and time-intensive process of analysis. (Methodological details are provided in chapter 2.)

Research Questions and Theoretical Framework

We chose to organize the study in Yauyos around two concepts: care and agency. These are among the newer and richer concepts in the social science portfolio, and they are still undergoing active debate. Care has elements that are visible and translate easily into empirical descriptions, whether these be household tasks exhaustively dissected in ads for detergents and cleaning aids, the protocols provided to nurses and other professional caregivers, or actions and attitudes that people readily label as "caring." Agency is less immediately recognizable. It can be known inductively, by getting into actors' minds and understanding how they construe their options for choice and initiative in any given situation. So it is that the chapters of the book are structured around care as it appears in different domains of life in Yauyos. Agency comes to the fore in our conclusions, in which we evaluate how children understood their own interests and how much initiative they actually exercised.

Care

The label "care" marks a vast and complex domain, inviting many different approaches. One is health, welfare, and livability. Tronto (1993, 103) defines care as "everything we do to maintain, continue, and repair our 'world' so that we can live in it as well as possible." Clearly, another theme is that of work: care involves activities and labors of a particular kind (see Thomas 1993). Boris and Parreñas (2010, 1) speak of "labors, both paid and unpaid, that sustain the day-to-day work that individuals and societies require to survive—and flourish." Glenn (1992, 1) adds the notion of relationships in speaking of an "array of activities and relationships involved in maintaining people, both on a daily basis and intergenerationally." Other theorists define the concept of care by naming its associated concepts. Hughes (2002, 119) locates it in a field of "cluster concepts" that include obligation, dependency, responsibility, friendship, duty, reciprocity, and trust. Tronto (1993, 3) associates it with "attentiveness, responsibility, nurturance, compassion, meeting other's needs."

Buch, in a review article (2015), notes the multiple origins of inquiries into care within anthropology, including kinship studies, ecological systemics, and reconstructions of "primitive" economics (Sahlins 1972). She argues for the necessity of maintaining a polysemic view. In line with the discipline's historical strategy of linking ethnographic description to cultural interpretation, care appears as a set of everyday practices generated by, and generating, moral norms and expectations (Thelen 2015; Yarris 2017; Amrith and Coe 2022). These practices are often grounded in relations of kinship, however defined in diverse human societies (Alber and Drotbohm 2015). As Borneman (2001, 11) shows, although kinship entails obligations of care among related others, care is, in a strong sense, productive of kinship (see also Yeates 2009).

Care can be approached through the roles involved: caregivers and care receivers, those who deny or refuse care, judges, and onlookers. Relations of care are created by persons acting on their perceived interests, understandings of their rights and obligations, and their vision of the moral order that prevails in the world. All this signals a dynamic process. Care is often associated with dependency and with the presumed incapacity of certain categories of people to care for themselves: children, the sick, the disabled, the elderly. Adults care for children with the objective of making them capable of caring for themselves (Ruddick 1984; Feder Kittay 2019). They in turn subsequently care for their former caretakers in long cycles of reciprocity between generations.

The focus on care-as-work has inspired a plethora of descriptions of daily life in a wide variety of world settings. These serve to correct earlier versions that made housework and intimate care invisible or portrayed them as simple and repetitive, relegated to the trackless territory of "social reproduction." Landmark studies show in intricate detail the activities involved in cooking and feeding the family (DeVault 1991), housework (Horsfield 1998), childcare (Spray 2020; Hondagneu-Sotelo 2001), elder care (Dossa and Coe 2017; Lamb 2000), and health care (Mol 2008). Case studies from Latin America contribute nuance on themes ranging from feeding the family (Weismantel 1988 for Ecuador), to time use in housework (Aguirre and Batthyány 2005 for Uruguay; Beltrán and Lavado 2015 for Peru), to childcare in indigenous groups (Ames and Padawer 2015; Flores 2010; Anderson 2016), to institutional elder care (Zegarra 2022 for Peru; Aguirre and Scavino 2018 for Uruguay), to the absence of health care (Scheper-Hughes 1992 for Brazil).

Care is deeply implicated in hierarchies of value, and it is profoundly inflected by gender. Women do most of the caring labor in contemporary societies, and many caring professions are highly feminized: for example, nursing, teaching, social work, psychotherapy, home health care, and esthetics. Housework and family care, according to dominant Western ideology, are freely performed by wives and mothers for "love." Even when these activities are remunerated, they are strongly female identified, as occurs with domestic workers (Ray and Qayum 2009). Feminist scholars decry the social devaluation of care, even as they struggle to disentangle it from hierarchical gender relations entailing dominance and subordination (Batthyány 2020; Montaño and Calderón 2010; Babb 2018). Keeping the community alive and running smoothly involves tasks that tend to be assigned to less powerful social actors. As Tronto notes (1993, 146): "By its very nature, care is rarely an activity engaged in by equals." Buch (2015, 279) argues that care is both "a form of moral, intersubjective practice and a circulating and potentially scarce social resource," requiring an approach that "neither romanticizes care as separate from political economy nor reduces care to power altogether."

Multivocal as a concept, the practice of care breaks down the boundaries between disciplines and intellectual perspectives. Zelizer (2005, 20–26) argues against the separation of "hostile worlds": the social from the economic, intimate relations from monetary transactions. Care inevitably involves resources and a material dimension. Its performance is partially codified in laws that have clear economic effects: laws of inheritance, negligence, medical malpractice, fraud and breach of contract, elder abuse, child endangerment, wrongful death, and more. Tronto (1993, 10) emphasizes the breakdown of the public/private "moral boundary." Performing care for strangers or under contractual arrangements tends to induce an attitude of empathy, even overcoming the initial resistance of the caregiver (Glenn 2010; Hondagneu-Sotelo 2001).

Boundary issues also haunt the question of who is obligated to provide care. The United Nations Entity for Gender Equality (UNWomen) promotes a line of research on the international distribution of care resources and care providers. It is structured around the figure of a "diamond" whose four points are the state, the private sector, philanthropic and nongovernmental institutions, and families and communitarian groups. Community care can incorporate neighbors, volunteers in community services, and women's organizations as advocates (Henríquez 2005; Bornat et al. 1997). Charitable care, provided by local organizations or churches, may be under-resourced and noncontinuous. In Peru, such initiatives have often replaced the state in providing services and alleviating poverty (Portocarrero and Sanborn 2003; Luttrell-Rowland 2023, 52–54). Large institutional care providers influence national policies and international relations, even as they expose profound inequalities in the contemporary world. Philosophers Appiah (2010) and O'Neill (2000), among others, meditate upon the limits of human empathy and solidarity. The ambiguities at play can be seen in the politics of immigration and humanitarianism (Ticktin 2011) and in the recruitment of caregivers (doctors, nurses, childcare workers, teachers, cooks, and cleaners) from the Global South to service developed economies (Yeates 2009; Pérez Orozco et al. 2008).

While care among strangers is an important topic when considering whole nations such as Peru, most care takes place in spheres of intimacy where the internal states of caregivers and receivers are relevant. We follow Zelizer (2005, 14–20) as she locates intimacy by applying three criteria: knowledge, hands-on attention, and trust. It does not always entail "warm emotions" or even face-to-face contact. Knowing someone intimately facilitates care that is responsive to that individual's unique needs. Moral philosophers link care to practices of responsibility and virtues such as generosity and selflessness (Walker 1998, 93–94). Tronto (1993, 104) calls for a new morality—a care ethic—that emerges, not from impersonal, rational autonomy, but out of "emotion, daily life, and political circumstance." She stresses the importance of the "disposition" of actors to participate in relationships of care.

Wherever we start, with whatever domain or modality of care, the discussion moves between daily minutiae and transcendent values. Caretaking highlights the interdependence of all human beings; every person gives and receives care, in different measures, at different points in their lives (Nussbaum 1995; Walker 1998). Nussbaum (1993, 246) links care to human development and the capabilities approach that she is identified with, together with Amartya Sen and numerous collaborators. Concerns for bodily integrity, the search for understanding, recognizing infancy as conditioning later experiences, practical reason born out of the drive to control one's own life and conduct, affiliation (including "social association of a playful kind"), and humor (Nussbaum 1993, 263–265) are all "virtues" that can be promoted and facilitated through acts of care. Care is forward-looking in its pursuit of higher states of autonomy, welfare, and happiness for receivers and providers. In that sense, it embodies hope and trust: the assurance that others will fulfill their roles in reciprocal relations of care (Mattingly 2010; Mattingly and Jensen 2015). The evaluative approach to care opens a Pandora's box of complicated concepts, all of which are culturally inflected (Lear 2006; Anderson 2020). Currently, ideas of flourishing in Latin American appeal to the concept of "buen vivir" ("sumaq kawsay" in Quechua), or "living well:" an Indigenous-inspired proposal that calls for an authentic and respectful relation with the environment and a recovery of the cooperative traditions of the Andes (Albó 2019; Quijano 2011).

This scholarship has served us as inspiration through the pages of our book. We align with Tronto (1993, 103) when she speaks of the world of care as including "our bodies, our selves, and our environment, all of which we seek to interweave in a complex, life-sustaining web," but we follow our research subjects in incorporating an even broader roster (animals, spirits, natural features) who participate in the rural context we examine. We further diverge in the focus on children not as passive receivers of care but as actors and caregivers. Our ethnographic approach reflects our acceptance of how actual lived experiences of caregiving and receiving are historically contingent, messy, unruly, invented day by day as circumstances permit and as caretakers sort out competing demands (Seaman, Robbins, and Buch 2019; Mol 2008; Mol et al. 2010).

Agency

Diagnosing children's involvement in systems of care requires that we recognize their capacity to influence the circumstances of their lives. Our research takes its place within a contemporary current in childhood studies that views children as social actors in their own right (Moran-Ellis and Tisdall 2019; Hammersley 2017; Frekko et al. 2015; James and Prout 1997; Greene and Hogan 2005; Lancy 2008). This perspective upends classical visions of early socialization as dominated by adults. It directs attention to children's activities, choices, narratives, and relationships with other children. The approach accords well with contemporary social scientific emphasis on practice (Schatzki et al. 2001; Ortner 2006). It rejects any universality of "childhood," recognizing instead that childhood is socially constructed in particular historical and cultural contexts (Rodríguez and Mannarelli 2007; Zelizer 1985).[2] It positions those children who seem to be creating their own societies and life paths as purposeful, not aberrant: street children, children in gangs, child breadwinners, and children becoming heads of family at an early age. Ortner (2006), whom we follow closely in developing our perspective, has connected theories of practice to notions of "strategies," "life projects," and "serious games"—this last being a particularly interesting metaphor in a discussion of children.

Agency is the key concept that unlocks this domain. Every human is endowed with agency to one degree or another; it is a feature of personhood. Yet agency is difficult to recognize unambiguously in people's actions. Ortner (2006) analyzes two conditions that must be considered. The first involves intentionality. Agency "is best seen . . . less as a psychological property or capacity unto itself, and more as a disposition toward the enactment of 'projects'" (Ortner 2006, 152). Often it can be equated to having consciously held goals, yet this may not always be the case, especially where children are concerned. They may not have the maturity nor have accumulated sufficient social experience to be able to articulate, even to themselves, the "projects" they have or calibrate the effectiveness of the strategies they employ in attempting to achieve them. Intentional action can be understood in opposition to following routines or taking orders; it involves acting creatively. Again, in relation to children, it rejects obedience in favor of initiative and responsibility.

As a second condition, context matters. Agency is always exercised within the social, cultural, and political structures that characterize particular societies. The "games" people play—of gender, dominance, prestige, material success, and others—are defined, channeled, and given meaning by preexisting values and social arrangements that resist modification. In this way Ortner seeks to ensure that power is fully incorporated into her account, both the power of individuals to further their projects and the power of more dominant actors, and sedimented structures, to constrain and frustrate them. The study of agency consists in "laying bare what (each society's) cultural games are, about their ideological underpinnings, and about how the play of the game reproduces or transforms those underpinnings" (Ortner 2006, 152). "The agency of projects . . . is . . . about people playing, or trying to play, their own serious games even as more powerful parties seek to devalue and even destroy them" (Ortner 2006, 147).

The literature gives us ample reason to center the concept of agency in our investigation of rural Andean children (Leinaweaver 2007a, 2010b; Ames 2013b; Bolin 2006). Even as it facilitates an understanding of children's own interests and autonomy, it sensitizes us to the power adults wield over children, and to the power that urban Peruvians wield over rural Peruvians; perhaps not to destroy but certainly to devalue their very serious games (figure 1.1).

The Andean Community

In setting our research in rural areas of the Andes, we inevitably engaged with ongoing conversations about the "Andean community" and "Andean culture." One of the challenges we set for ourselves was considering contemporary rural Andean towns in light of the characteristics of Andean communities that hold across a large corpus of classical ethnographies. We would simultaneously be challenged to locate children in that corpus, a task made difficult by the short shrift that children are given in many classical texts. Our perceptions of the Andean community are undoubtedly distorted by the practice of relegating descriptions of children's roles, and even the activities of women, to a brief chapter on "life cycle" or "family." This, of course, is not a problem unique to Andean studies (Hirschfeld 2002; Montgomery 2009).

Efforts to characterize the Andean community date back to the earliest years of contact with the Spanish conquistadores in the 1500s. The Republic of Peru inherited many of the prejudices that underpinned the colonial regime and many

FIGURE 1.1. Serious games: schoolboys playing with tops.

of the laws that influenced the internal organization and external relations of the high-altitude villages with their indigenous inhabitants. A long process of exploitation and impoverishment set in, denounced by *indigenistas* (defenders of Peru's autochthonous peoples and languages) but unresolved by policymakers (Figueroa 2010; Parodi 2000; Gonzáles de Olarte and del Pozo 2018). One result was massive migration from the Andes to the coast, converting Peru from predominantly rural to predominantly urban by the 1960s (Matos Mar 2004; Amat y León 2012).

Even as they were experiencing profound changes, small communities in the Andes became a favored site for ethnographers (Bolton and Mayer 1977; Isbell 1985; Bourque and Warren 1981; Salomon 1982; Ferreira 2016). They sought to capture entire lifeways, from material culture to oral history to symbols and beliefs (Pajuelo 2000). These early anthropological studies were structured around a number of themes that encouraged the use of "controlled comparison" (Eggan 1954).[3] Kinship systems led the roster, and it became obligatory to include, in each new ethnography, a description of local kin terminology and an analysis of the work done by kinship and alliance in governing relations of reciprocity and exchange (Alberti and Mayer 1974). Agricultural practices, production systems, and risk management were another focus (Fonseca 1972; Bruschwig 1988; Earls 2006, 2008). Institutions of governance were also of interest, especially as they could demonstrate relative autonomy from the national legal and political system (Bonilla et al. 1987; Keith et al. 1970; Mallon 1983). Researchers documented and attempted to interpret a richly populated supernatural world and a panoply of rituals and techniques for relating to it (Allen 2002; Weismantel 2003).

The often lyrical, seemingly timeless descriptions of these communities tended to obscure the tensions within them (Ferreira 2016; Starn 1991, 1994). Inequality, in the form of internal stratification and ethnic discrimination (Cotler 2021) coexisted with institutions that promoted integration: *compadrazgo* ("ritual kinship") and the annual fiesta cycle. People were torn between what they owed to their own family group (labor, resources, loyalty) and the demands of the community (Golte and de la Cadena 1986; Urrutia and Diez 2016; Lennox 2015). Gender violence indisputably occurred (Babb 2018; Bolton and Bolton 1975; Alcalde 2014). These tensions would become unavoidably visible by the time of the internal conflict set off by Shining Path, as described in chapter 2 (Starn 1991). But until then, the relative importance that researchers assigned to these contradictions depended in part on the stance they took with respect to what Harris (2000) identified as long-termism (emphasizing processes, continuities, and "culture") versus short-termism (emphasizing contemporary events, change, political oppression, and resistance).

Misunderstanding the Andean community led to development efforts that failed to reach their lofty goals (Pribilsky 2009; Babb 1985; Asensio 2023). While earlier approaches to studying communities comparatively were oriented to creating an orderly ethnographic register, more recent applications of the strategy sought to explain the fortunes of rural populations under the conditions of liberal and increasingly neoliberal Peru. Here, the comparisons isolated the factors that appeared to promote development and "progress" in some communities while others lagged behind.[4]

Children were not a subject for "controlled comparison" in Classic Period studies of Andean villages. Ferreira, editor of *A Return to the Village* (2016), presents a fascinating collection of reminiscences and second thoughts by several of the authors of fundamental texts on Andean villages.[5] Children flit in and out of the background of the various contributions like so many rare species of butterfly. They "mob" the anthropologist perched on a hillside doing drawings of the town below (Colloredo-Mansfeld 2016, 154). They make doll play out of a videotaping session designed by the anthropologist to illustrate traditional rituals (Isbell 2016, 51). They participate in three-generational storytelling sessions presided over by grandparents (Allen 2016, 88, 89). They cause concern to the anthropologist charged with protecting the community's cultural patrimony—ancient quipus—from any mishandling (Salomon 2016, 178). They follow the anthropologist around with "stories and riddles" (Platt 2016, 210). The challenge is to recognize such children as more than bit players. In anticipation of more detailed discussions to come, we can briefly sketch some answers to the questions: What is the vision they leave us with? And what are the issues they raise?

Children are clearly desired, and they are fully integrated into village life. They share many activities with adults, but they also have a great deal of autonomy. They associate with multiple caregivers, and they are encouraged to accept a variety of caretaking arrangements that may put them in the custody of relatives, godparents, and employers for periods of time. Childhood is a time of active learning: of daily household tasks, farming, buying and selling, and ritual practices. Children are connectors between generations and, as such, are made to feel the inheritance they will receive and the obligations that creates. Parents have aspirations for their children that presuppose long-term relationships of reciprocity. Much turns on the idea of "respect": parents must respect their children, and children must learn to feel, and to demonstrate in culturally appropriate ways, respect for their caregivers and elders.

The literature amply shows how children become involved as economic actors early on. The youngest work alongside their parents, but they are expected to take solo responsibility for a wide range of tasks as they grow, in a complicated mix of initiative and obedience. Punishment is swift for errors or laziness yet controversial as a norm. Children are endowed with instruments, resources, and capabilities for implementing their projects. Many are precocious adults, called upon to take over parental roles temporarily or permanently. At the same time, children have their own desires, needs, friendships, and understandings of their prerogatives. Many opportunities arise for conflict between adults' interpretations of the common good and children's observations and experiences of social life.

These attempts to characterize Andean childhoods point us in particular directions. They invite us to explore possible frictions between children's expectations for their future lives and the expectations of their parents, especially under the conditions of the twenty-first century. They call us to enter children's mental and emotional worlds and to examine the identities they harbor growing up in a region still within the indigenous orbit. They suggest the ongoing relevance of rural poverty and disadvantage with respect to urban Peru. They confirm the usefulness of the two concepts we have taken as our guides: care and agency. Without exception, the literature on children in the Andes—small and select as it is—demonstrates their role.[6]

The Research Setting: Yauyos Province, Peru

In the Andean community archetype does not always match the lived reality. The research on which this book is based was carried out in six towns located in the Yauyos province in central Peru, part of the hinterland of the capital, Lima. The province coincides with the watershed of the Cañete River, which begins in the glaciers of the high Andes, at altitudes near 5,000 meters above sea level, and drops dramatically to empty into the Pacific Ocean 215 kilometers to the southwest.[7] Human habitation appears at altitudes around 4,000 meters in the form of herding communities, some occupied only seasonally. At successively lower levels are dozens of towns and villages with a mixed economic base: agriculture, stockraising, commerce, and services. While Quechua or Aymara are in daily use in other parts of the rural Andes, Spanish predominates in Yauyos. Some older residents speak Quechua, the language spread throughout modern day Peru, Ecuador, and parts of Bolivia, Argentina, and Chile by the Incas (Mannheim 1991). Jaqaru, a language related to Aymara, is spoken by a few elders in the community of Tupe.

Our study in Yauyos focused on six localities (figure 1.2). Five are district capitals and one is the capital of the province, also named Yauyos.[8] They vary in size

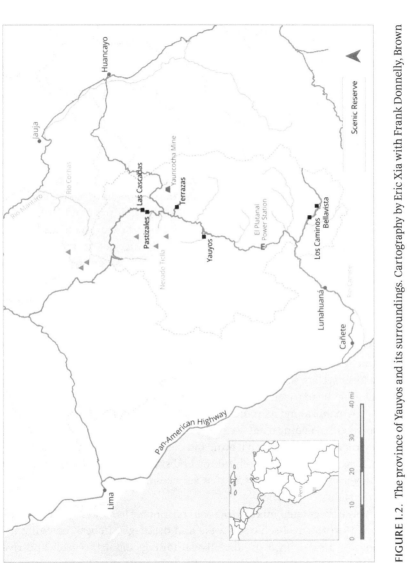

FIGURE I.2. The province of Yauyos and its surroundings. Cartography by Eric Xia with Frank Donnelly, Brown University Library, 2023.

from some 350 to 1,750 inhabitants. They lie at different altitudes, with over 1,000 meters separating the highest, Pastizales (3,600 meters above sea level) from the lowest, Los Caminos (2,500 meters above sea level). In between, in the area known as Nor Yauyos, are the towns we call Las Cascadas and Terrazas. In the southwestern part ("Sur Grande"), together with Los Caminos, is Bellavista. The capital, Yauyos City, lies roughly in the middle.

Like most anthropological work, ours is a study in communities, not of communities (Geertz 1973). We could not do the prolonged, multidisciplinary fieldwork that would have been required for a full portrait of the towns. Nonetheless, this section provides some basic information that should be helpful for understanding the following chapters.

The Environment

Humans have intervened directly in the ecology of the Andes over centuries, domesticating a wide range of plants and animals that are adapted to flourish in widely varying microclimates (Lennox 2015, 781). Humans have also caused harm to the landscape. Erosion is an ever-present threat, often triggered by the heavy rains of the periodic El Niño/La Niña cycles in the Pacific Ocean off the Peruvian coast but aggravated by human activity: road building, deforestation (thought to date from prehistoric times), overgrazing, and intensive cultivation (Gil 2013; ParksWatch 2003, 20).[9] Small farmers can make little capital investment in seeds, pesticides, or chemical fertilizers, and they depend on their herds for fertilizer.

Like the other great river systems that begin in the high Andes, the streams and lakes of Yauyos province are fed by glaciers and mountain springs. Yet glaciers are melting rapidly all along the Andes range (Glave and Vergara 2016; Carey 2005), with still uncharted effects on landscapes and communities (Pærregaard 2020). The Cañete River system serves many functions, some at cross-purposes with others (Gil 2013; Li 2015; Rasmussen 2015). It supplies drinking water and sanitation to dozens of settlements along its route and to the urban complex around the city of Cañete at its mouth. Feeding a network of canals, it supports agriculture, the larger part under irrigation. It sustains a fishing industry centered on trout and freshwater shrimp. It attracts tourism, from hiking and sightseeing to whitewater rafting and other adventure sports. As of 2010, it services one of Peru's most important hydroelectric plants, El Platanal.

The largely unregulated mixture of uses contributes to serious pollution of the river system. Most towns discharge sewers and drainage ditches, including from slaughterhouses, directly into streams. Illegal tailings enter the lakes and rivers from wildcat mines that are dispersed over the landscape as well as from large formal mining enterprises, extracting lead, zinc, copper, silver, and, until recently, coal. This intensifies during the rainy season when the rivers are turbulent and pollution is hard to detect (ParksWatch 2003, 8–9). Of the towns we worked in, this was most visible in Terrazas, where a large mine upstream compromises the water source. The town has ongoing lawsuits against the mine operators to stop the practices that jeopardize the health of the population, even as many men from Terrazas are employed at the mine and, under orders from management, may be the very ones implicated in the dumping.

The drainage systems on Peru's Pacific coast constitute complex ecosystems (Earls 2008; Alegría 2008). Lennox (2015) emphasizes the political factors—marginalization, impoverishment, neoliberal policies, and globalization—that exacerbate the threat coming from climate change. While Yauyos farm families increasingly incorporate "urban" foods and manufactures into their lives, they participate in the global economy primarily as consumers and only tangentially as producers. This contributes to their vulnerability and helps explain some of the further changes yet to be examined, especially population loss through out-migration.

Small-scale family farming, much of it oriented to subsistence, dominates the economy and social organization in Yauyos. It is the poorest of the five provinces that make up the Lima region and that exist in the shadow of the national capital. According to Agrarian Census data, three-quarters (73 percent) of Yauyos family farm units have insufficient assets (land, animals, productive infrastructure) to meet the nutritional needs of the family (Escobal and Armas 2015, 80). In Peru overall, one-quarter of the small family farms produce negative incomes and are thus subsidized by other income-generating activities of the families (Escobal and Armas 2015, 74).

Infrastructure and Its Deficiencies

Infrastructure comes at a high cost in mountainous environments like the Andes (figure 1.3). Peru has never invested the funds required to achieve universal coverage of its rural areas with potable water, sewers and drainage systems, waste management, and electricity. Investments in roads and health facilities have been shown to have notable impact on rural incomes (Escobal 2005; Meléndez and Huaroto 2014; Zegarra and Minaya 2007), yet most of the province of Yauyos is crisscrossed by dirt roads that can wash out completely in the rainy season.[10]

Basic services were absent or precarious in all of the localities of our study, even the provincial capital. All six towns had piped water that served the homes and businesses, but the water was not effectively treated, and the supply was not steady. Even the capital ran short of water at least once a week. Except for a few homes used as tourist lodgings in Nor Yauyos, people did not have water heaters or showers.[11] Children bathed in the streams, lakes, and irrigation canals. The same canals were used for washing clothes and for watering animals.

All of the towns were built on uneven ground. Stone-lined drainage ditches coursed through many sectors, and garbage and animal waste often got stuck in eddies. During rainy season the ditches were prone to overflow, and water ran freely down muddy unpaved streets. Sewer systems served only part of the

FIGURE 1.3. The mountainous setting.

population and were difficult to keep in working order. Many households improvised systems of waste disposal, which might include availing themselves of the facilities in the school if they lived nearby.

The authorities hired street sweepers for collecting garbage and transporting it to ravines on the edge of town to be feasted upon by vultures and the odd donkey. Burning garbage was a common practice, and the resultant airborne pollutants were augmented by the almost universal use of firewood as a cooking fuel. Propane gas was just arriving to the province, and it was expensive and not always available. "Come into my kitchen," a householder cheerily invited the field team in Terrazas, "but you may choke!" The comment pointed to the respiratory challenges that cooking with firewood entailed (Accinelli et al. 2004; Antrosio 2002).

Although all the towns had electricity, the supply was erratic, and the lights could go out at any moment. The blackout might last a few hours, an entire day, or three or four days on end. Everybody kept candles and flashlights at hand. The town of Terrazas was supplied by a small hydroelectric plant negotiated with the mining company further up the mountain. At the time of the fieldwork, the town was installing nighttime illumination. This might have been long planned, or it might have emerged as part of rebuilding after the earthquake that struck the year before (see chapter 2). With the high school destroyed, the one standing educational facility, the primary school, was being used for morning, afternoon, and evening sessions.

Telephones were a rarity at the time of our 2008 study. Many of the towns had a communal telephone service that operated out of the municipal offices. A long-time resident of Terrazas, Señora Raquel, became the manager of the town's single telephone line when the Telefónica company arrived in the late 1980s and determined that her house would be the best location for the installation. By 2008 Raquel's house had incorporated several computers and one of the town's few internet connections. Meanwhile, in the provincial capital, only the most prominent businesses and public offices had permanent telephone lines. Cell phone service arrived in Yauyos City on July 17, 2008, while fieldwork was underway. The shout went up: "¡Llegó Claro! (Claro, the cell phone provider, has arrived!)" The enthusiasm was palpable.

Politics, Governance, Recognition, and Status

The towns of Yauyos were organized socially, economically, and politically in ways that reflected their origins as *comunidades campesinas* (peasant communities; Puente 2022). The officers and assembly of members of the *comunidad campesina* played an important role in the management of internal affairs.[12] They had legal authority to preserve, protect, and exploit collectively held land, water, and other resources. In Yauyos City and Bellavista, for example, the *comunidad campesina* administered herds of *vicuñas* as part of a conservation project. The *comunidad* could commandeer the labor of community members for activities such as tree planting and repairing roads. *Comités de regantes* (irrigation committees) oversaw the management and distribution of water. Participating in *faenas* (collective work parties) to clean irrigation canals was obligatory for all.[13] Outside of formal political authority, a hierarchy of offices also existed in a ritual and religious realm that took responsibility for organizing festivals such as the annual celebration of each locality's patron saint.

Several new structures contributed to decision-making (Diez 1999; Urrutia and Diez 2016). *Alcaldes* (mayors) and a town council were elected by popular vote, usually with the support of a political party or local movement. They had a broad mandate to act in arenas involving local infrastructure, welfare, and economic and social development. Appointed by the central government, *gobernadores* (governors) served as liaisons with the Ministry of the Interior for purposes of maintaining order and responding to emergencies. In addition, in localities of a certain size, a justice of the peace was appointed by the Ministry of Justice. With so many entities and actors involved in initiatives and decisions, power in the towns was diffuse. Children saw that their fathers—and sometimes mothers, too—could occupy a variety of leadership positions. They could preside over meetings and give speeches, but they could also suffer smear campaigns, lobbying from outsiders, and pressures from neighbors.

Local government projects and investments were financed primarily by transferences from the central government via FONCOMUN (Fondo de Compensación Municipal, or Municipal Compensation Fund). Fines, permits, and rent from municipal properties and enterprises helped with daily operations. Some towns received a percentage of the taxes and royalties paid by extractive industries located within their jurisdiction.[14] Children were the beneficiaries of some investments, such as in playground equipment, sports arenas, and schools. Local leaders could agree on one thing: the need to keep their schools in acceptable shape and to require that children be enrolled, so as not to lose their standing with the Ministry of Education for lack of demand.

Migration and Mobility

Elements of global culture were rapidly being incorporated into the rural Andes as the twenty-first century got underway (Cánepa and Lamas 2020; Huber 2002; Trinidad 2005). The residents of the province of Yauyos (yauyinos) had little control over decisions made by private companies or the Peruvian government as they evaluated the profitability and social benefits of investments in their rural province. The principal strategy of yauyinos for accessing this new world involved moving toward it. It involved leaving the province to go somewhere else, temporarily or permanently. No matter how potholed and dangerous they might be, the roads were at least good for that.

Rural-to-urban migration has been a visible part of rural reality now for nearly a century (Long and Roberts 1984; Pærregaard 1997; Brougère 1988, 1992; Casaverde et al. 1982; Yamada 2010). Until very recently, Peru's poverty was concentrated in the rural Andes.[15] The vast movement of laborers and consumers from that region, building up the cities on the Pacific coast, powered Peruvian development throughout the twentieth century (Amat y León 2012; Aldana and Escobal 2016). To a lesser extent, people sought a better future in the Amazon region. International migration out of Peru intensified in the mid-twentieth century, both educational migration of upper-class youth and labor migration of industrial workers, sheep herders, and domestic servants (Altamirano 2010; Degregori 2003; Berg and Pærregaard

2010; Anderson 2012). The exodus swelled during the political conflict of the 1980s and 1990s. It is estimated that 3.3 million Peruvians—a number equal to 10 percent of the country's population—live abroad (INEI 2022, 5).[16]

Yauyos's location, within a triangle formed by the cities of Cañete, Huancayo in the central Andes, and the national capital, Lima, means there is more than one choice of destination for ambitious migrants. Cañete is a bustling coastal city producing food and light manufactures for the Lima market and increasingly for export. Huancayo, in the Mantaro River valley, is a regional transportation hub, commercial emporium, and supply point for mining activities. Huancayo and neighboring Jauja give access to the eastern slopes of the Andes and the Amazonian area of La Merced and Satipo. Last, metropolitan Lima has been the dream destination for rural Peruvians for decades (Golte and Adams 1990; Matos Mar 2004).[17] Although its location with respect to these urban centers makes Yauyos somewhat unique, more and more rural communities in Peru are being drawn into the orbit of large cities that epitomize the country's insertion in a world system with cultural, political, economic, and spiritual ramifications (Cánepa and Lamas 2020; Golte 2000; de la Cadena 1988).

Over four national census periods between 1981 to 2017, while the population of Yauyos province dropped sharply (from 32,300 to 22,200), the populations of Cañete, Huancayo, and metropolitan Lima swelled. Lima grew from under five million inhabitants to reach its current condition as a megacity, with more than ten million residents. The typical "pull" factors were in play: the offer of work (manufacture, services, small businesses), secondary and tertiary education, the exercise of citizen rights and a sense of participation, entertainment and excitement. There were also the well-known "push" factors: impoverishment of the rural economy, demographic pressures of large families, limited access to health and education, and growing awareness of the possibility of better living conditions elsewhere. And there were facilitating factors: the construction of roads, new technical demands on agriculture, expanding markets for local products, and mass media disseminating models of new and attractive lifestyles. Most rural-to-urban migration in Peru involves a direct leap from the village to the city, bypassing a step-by-step movement through smaller towns.

The six towns that were the focus of our research were affected by migration, some more than others (Brougère 1992). Between the census years of 1993 and 2017, Terrazas, Los Caminos, and the provincial capital Yauyos lost population: almost 20 percent in the case of Yauyos City, 14 percent in the case of Los Caminos, and nearly half—47 percent—in the case of Terrazas. Bellavista and Las Cascadas grew by a few dozen inhabitants each, and Pastizales suffered no significant change. At the time of the research, Bellavista (population 1763) was the largest town, followed closely by Yauyos City and its 1582 inhabitants; Terrazas, Los Caminos, and Las Cascadas were almost tied with around 650 inhabitants; and tiny Pastizales had a population of 332.

FIGURE I.4. A herding child.

Rural-to-urban migration was not the only kind of movement yauyinos saw. The Andes are for walking. Day after day, men and women walked long distances, taking their herds to pasture, tending fields located in different production zones, carrying produce to market, or visiting relatives (Oths 2003). Often they had children in tow, the youngest struggling to keep up, the older ones leading the way. Rural children in the Andes are described in the anthropology of childhood literature as exceptionally mobile (figure I.4; Whiting and Edwards 1988, 56). We see this also in studies of play in Andean rural society, which mark it off as a domain under the broad control of children themselves (for adults to engage in play with children suggested a lack of seriousness; for parents to do so might jeopardize their authority) but, significantly, also as something that typically takes place out of sight of adults: outdoors, in plazas, in parks, on the street, and in the surrounding woods and fields (Panez and Ochoa 2000; Sánchez and Valdivia 1994).

In our study, children in Yauyos saw movement and mobility all around them (Anderson 2013). They bore witness to a constant parade of visitors who came to the province with a wide variety of objectives. The daily provincial bus run marked time in many places. Pickups, vans, and motorcycles came through, bearing police, extension workers, inspectors from the Environmental Protection Agency, and others.[18] Most towns had weekly fair days, when itinerant vendors would set up with pirated CDs and DVDs on the central plaza, alongside vendors of shoes, hats, factory-made clothes, farm implements, household gadgets, personal hygiene items, flashlights, batteries, radios, and DVD players. Less frequently, schools would host sports competitions, or a tournament made up of adult teams would be scheduled, and local teams and fans would suddenly swell the numbers and variety of people circulating on the streets, looking for accommodations, and patronizing local restaurants and bodegas as well as hastily set up food stands. Whether during their school years or as young adults, these kinds of events provided the venue where many couples first got together.

Yauyos City, as an administrative center, had its own kind of movement. Many workers, especially those employed by the regional or national government, left on weekends to go home to their families in Cañete, Lima, or Huacho, the headquarters of the regional jurisdiction of which the province of Yauyos is a part. The exodus included judges and support staff at the courthouse, bank employees, teachers, and workers at the health center. Some restaurants closed due to lack of patrons, and the traffic of cars and buses was reduced to a minimum. By the same token, movement in the city might suddenly increase because of events such as training courses for justices of the peace, police, health workers, teachers, and others that were called to the provincial capital for sessions that might last a few hours or several days.

Even as yauyinos were looking outward and seeking to intensify their connections to urban Peru, many of their compatriots were looking to Yauyos as a weekend vacation spot that offered a return to nature and a glimpse into what rural life used to be. It was advertised as a kind of campesino theme park, complete with Inca terraces. Three of the six towns that were the focus of our fieldwork—Las Cascadas, Pastizales, and Terrazas—are part of the area designated as a *reserva paisajística* (scenic reserve) by the Peruvian government.[19] The natural landscape is a composite of mountain peaks, grass-covered hills, valleys, and patches of open plain, dotted by small lakes, marshes, tiny streams, and cascading waterfalls. The Andean skies are intensely blue, cloudless much of the time, unpolluted, and with the burning midday sun that gestures at the proximity of the equator. Archaeological deposits are common throughout the Andes: burial grounds, signs of pre-Conquest settlements, the footprints of abandoned llama trails and irrigation works. Schoolchildren make expeditions to ancient cemeteries and learn local history from walks and stories heard from their elders. Many towns proudly display in a museo de sitio (archaeological site museum) collections of artifacts pulled out of the ground by local farmers.[20]

While not as scenic as Nor Yauyos, Bellavista, to the south, also had a certain cachet as a tourist destination because of the presence of the upscale resort that we call Aventura Andina. Advertising itself as providing an immersive experience of Andean life, the complex consisted of a hotel, restaurant, and stables, all perched on a scenic outlook at one end of the town. A large pit at the entrance encouraged viewing the sunset from around a campfire, as well as enjoying the typical dish of *pachamanca*, a complete meal cooked in the ground. Several local residents worked at Aventura Andina, although the top manager was an outsider.

Organization of the Book

Although much of its content is far from conventional, our book adopts a conventional style of organization. Having laid out the theoretical guideposts we employed, and having given some background on communities in the Andes and the site of our research, we detail our research methodology in chapter 2, "Knowing Children." The discussion is extensive because of what we believe is a need for greater sharing of approaches to a series of understudied topics: children, their care and caring, and their agency.

The subsequent three chapters explore three entwined arenas, or contexts, of care. In chapter 3, we examine the intimate context of care, considering family formation, the implications of sibling groups and generational order, and everyday household life. In chapter 4, we consider work and the economy: the difference parents' work lives and rhythms make for children and their incorporation in family economies. In chapter 5, we look at the health and well-being of the children in the context of the environment they inhabit. Not only do the children of Yauyos eat what the land produces, but they are a vital part of that production.

In the following three chapters, we focus directly on the practices of care in Yauyos. Chapter 6 analyzes moments of caretaking that children participate in as caregivers, care recipients, observers, and commentators. Yauyinos, young and old, have their own thoughts about what caring means, and they have a large repertory of caring practices that are drawn on in situations involving children. From there we delve into the moral worlds of childhood and adulthood in Yauyos. In chapter 7 we sketch out the limits and failures of care and what seem to be their consequences for children. Chapter 8 offers a more positive note as we address Yauyos children's happiness, aspirations, and hopes. For many, a bright future entailed becoming an educated person, a rather ambiguous goal, as we shall see.

We end by proposing answers to our initial research questions and suggesting, as the twenty-first century advances, what the Andean community—and Peru more broadly—look like through the eyes of children.

2

Knowing Children

This was the exchange at the end of a child's interview, just before the recording ended. Gaby was the vivacious, charismatic field-worker, hardly taller than many of the children, and Dionisia the twelve-year-old girl she spoke with.

GABY: How do you feel now? (¿Cómo te sientes ahora?)

DIONISIA: Happy, because you want to know about my childhood. (Feliz, porque quieres saber de mi infancia.)

GABY: I'll say goodbye. Do you want to say goodbye? (Yo me despido. ¿Tú quieres despedirte?)

DIONISIA: Yes. You go first. (Sí. Tú primero.)

GABY: Bye, Dionisia. Thank you for talking with me. (Chao, Dionisia. Gracias por conversar conmigo.)

DIONISIA: Thank you, Gaby, for knowing about my childhood. (Gracias, Gaby, por saber de mi infancia.)

The research for the present book, conducted in 2008–2009, was supported by the Wenner-Gren Foundation for Anthropological Research via a granting mechanism, since discontinued, that promoted international collaborative research, as well as a CIES[1] fund which made possible the participation of two Canadian graduate students. The study was run by the two co-authors, who trained—with the support of three South American experts—thirteen field-workers (graduate and undergraduate students, Peruvian and Canadian). Largely in male-female pairs (with two exceptions: one with two women and another with two women and a man), the field-workers lived in the six communities over six weeks between July and August 2008. All the fieldwork was conducted in Spanish. The project resulted in a massive database that has taken years to organize and interpret. It produced hundreds of observations of daily activities and of the many festive events that took place over the Independence Day holidays (July 28–29), anniversaries and patron saints' days, and cattle-branding parties held in August before the drive of the herds to high-altitude pastures.

In choosing where to pursue our inquiry into childhood in the rural Andes, we applied two of the time-honored strategies of ethnographic work, also common in Andean studies: controlled comparison (Eggan 1954) and the revisit. We revisited the province of Yauyos a decade after it was the site of the Yauyos Values Study, where social scientists affiliated with the Pontifical Catholic University of Peru were asked by the Peruvian Ministry of Education to produce a comprehensive review of education in the province in 1998–1999 (Anderson et al. 2001). The Yauyos Values Study is used as a baseline and reference in this book. Generations of students at the Pontifical Catholic University of Peru have had their first field experiences in localities of Yauyos, which are relatively accessible from Lima, whether as part of one of these larger projects or conducting independent thesis projects (for example, de la Cadena 1980; Alzamora, Nué, and Pastor 1998).[2] More recently, Yauyos was the setting for a study of rural supply routes for child domestic labor (Anderson 2007).

In commissioning the Yauyos Values Study, the Ministry of Education sought insight into how the education being offered in rural areas responded to the beliefs, lifeways, and aspirations of the population. The entire educational system was up for consideration, from preschools to technical institutes, various modalities of nonformal education, and the opportunities that children and adults sought outside the province. Given this mandate, the research group, loosely coordinated by Anderson, deployed a wide range of methods and techniques. They held interviews and group conversations with teachers and administrators, current and former students, and migrants who had left to study or work elsewhere. Family histories, based on ninety biographical interviews, allowed for tracing changes over three generations. Through ethnography and narrative, key sources of local identity were explored: fiestas, monuments, landmarks, and historical references. Researchers documented the politics and agendas of multiple migrants' associations in Cañete, Huancayo, and Lima. Meanwhile, the education specialists in the group analyzed official statistics to identify patterns of student enrollment, attrition, and achievement, and teachers' qualifications and performance.

The Ministry of Education also wanted quantified evidence of the situation in the province, and the research team designed a household survey to explore living conditions, social connections, and value orientations. The respondents were a representative sample of 383 adults distributed over ten localities that were selected to reflect regional variation within the province.[3] We use an extract of the survey in our discussion of social exclusion (chapter 7). A questionnaire inquiring about the plans and aspirations of advanced high school students was administered to 162 fourth- and fifth-year students from secondary schools in seven localities. Based on an opportunistic sample of cooperating institutions, it overrepresented the larger schools of the provincial capital. Nonetheless, the results helped set the stage for our discussion of what happiness and flourishing meant to children and youth (chapter 8).

The backbone of the Yauyos Values Study was forty-five days of ethnographic fieldwork in nine of the province's thirty-three districts, distributed over the length and breadth of the province, though weighted toward more populous settlements. During our research in 2008, we revisited four of the original nine localities and added two new ones. We aimed to balance towns in the northeastern sector (oriented to stock raising and densely connected to the central Andes) with those in the southwest (oriented to agriculture and the cities on the Pacific coast). With this in mind, we included the towns we call Pastizales, Las Cascadas, and Terrazas in Nor Yauyos, and, in the region locally known as Sur Grande, the towns we call Los Caminos and Bellavista. The provincial capital, Yauyos City, lies in the middle. The two new additions deepened the contrasts within the group. One (Pastizales), populated by some 150 families, was especially small. The other (Terrazas) was relatively privileged due to the royalties it received from mining activities in the area. All six localities are strung out along or near the main road through Yauyos, following the course of the Cañete River, or along one of its tributaries. Although a few families participated in both the 1998 and the 2008 studies, the turnover of population was considerable in the decade between them, and there were many other notable changes.

The Research Design

Inspired by the productive combination of ethnography, interviews, group discussions, and document reviews in the Yauyos Values Study, we chose a similar approach a decade later for our research on children in the rural Andes. The bulk of our data consist of field notes that capture the field-workers' daily observations as they participated in community life. What they saw, heard, and registered depended on the openings they were given by the population and the opportunities they seized or created to observe a wide range of children's experiences in natural context. From these experiences and subsequent discussions, they would gradually be able to first infer and ultimately recognize elements of caregiving, a local community ethos surrounding care and contextualizing its practice, and shared conceptualizations of young people's agency.

To gain focus and comparability among the research subjects, we added the construction of biographies of a select group of children. As the fieldwork progressed, the teams identified the children they would feature. The route of entry began as the field-workers found ways of engaging with children—any and all that crossed their path and might be persuaded to engage in a ball game, drawing and coloring session, or chat. Having identified a child that might be of interest for a biography, the teams presented themselves to the parent or parents (or unrelated informal guardian, in one case of an adolescent boy) to ask permission to spend time with the child and talk with the caretakers and members of the child's social network as opportunities arose. We constructed the biographies from observations; interviews with parents, siblings, other relatives; and informal comments by teachers and community members. A few of the children belonged to families that the field-workers boarded with (siblings Lenin and Betty, Elisa) or arranged to receive meals from (Yeny). This process yielded thirty-six biographies, an intentional sample that was stratified by age (ranging from three to fifteen years) and evenly divided by gender. The field-workers were able to trail several of the children through an entire day to produce a record of "a day in the life." All the biographies incorporated a kinship diagram, and in most cases it was possible to sketch the children's houses and comment on their living conditions from direct observation. The child biographies pay special attention to key inflection points in the children's lives ("vital conjunctures," as discussed by Johnson-Hanks 2002).

The subjects of biographies were also chosen to reflect the variation within the towns according to rough indicators of socioeconomic status. Differences in wealth, social status, and political power are significant in rural localities of Peru, but they do not create separate social spheres with fixed barriers. In the six communities under study, with their small populations, people met up with each other and inhabited collective spaces with relative fluidity. This made it possible to spend time and grow close to large stockholders and the day laborers that did their herding as well as with the manager of the Yauyos municipal hotel and the woman she hired to clean, make up the rooms, and assist her in attending to her child.

The field teams arrived in town with supplies of notebooks, colored pencils, felt-tip pens, drawing paper, and large sheets of butcher paper. They could use the materials as they saw fit and as occasions arose. Some organized parties for several children, who worked at drawings on benches or on the floor of the bodega of an owner willing to host them. Others simply invited one or two children to scribble on a page as they waited for the action to begin with the play group on the plaza. We had no illusions about our ability to make sophisticated interpretations of the children's artwork and, indeed, our impression was that it was far too influenced by school-based norms of good and bad picture-making for it to reflect the children's innermost feelings (compare Isbell 1976). The children—even some of the adolescents—seemed to like drawing and coloring, however, and it was an effective path to interacting with many of them.

We asked the field teams to seek interviews and informal conversations with representatives of the principal organizations and institutions in the towns to build a description of the collective environment. These included governing authorities (mayors, municipal council members, presidents of *comunidades campesinas*, governors), school principals, teachers, officers of the parents' associations, health center personnel, and representatives of community organizations such as church groups and political parties. All the teams met the goal of constructing a picture of local power and institutional projects in the towns.[4] All of these interviews and conversations were guided by the interests and agendas of the interviewees. In that sense they were very loosely structured, if at all, by the field-workers. Some were recorded and transcribed; others are summarized in the field notes. Some of the conversations are quite long and detailed; others are perfunctory. We realized only in the process of analyzing the information at the community level that we had not paid sufficient attention to the business sector in each locality. We did not learn as much as we would have wanted about business enterprises and associations: transportation, meat, fish farming, agricultural associations promoting innovation in new crops, markets, and technologies.

The field-workers carried letters of introduction from the Pontifical Catholic University of Peru (PUCP) as the sponsoring institution. The PUCP had no ethics review board or even rules at the time, a situation that has since been remedied. To evidence consent at the community level, we applied the "Smith rule" (Smith 2006). This recognizes as legitimate various methods of ascertaining whether a community accedes to the presence of outside researchers. The central idea is that people manifest their willingness for the collectivity to be involved in a project through simple, quotidian expressions of engagement and tolerance. At the same time, both community members and researchers understand that individual actors are free to participate or not, as they see fit, and each relationship must be negotiated personally. We did not use written and signed statements of informed consent, which are a jarring transgression of understandings about how relationships evolve in rural Peru. Almost all of the parents and other adult interviewees were recorded, however, in conversations that make explicit their voluntary acceptance of the interaction.

All the communities were made aware and reminded continuously that the young professionals among them had a research agenda that involved children. We could have done a better job of preparing the local authorities, who were not given advance notice. Still, many of them found a study of children to be of negligible interest, and none found it threatening. As Berman (2011, 275) has written of the children she studied, they are "in the ironic situation of having influence on the adult social world precisely because adults do not view children as influential."

The Team

A large cast of characters contributed to conceiving the study, preparing the field-workers, completing the biographies, and analyzing the corpus of materials that emerged. Anderson and Leinaweaver, as co-directors, developed the basic design, but anthropologists Claudia Fonseca (Brazil) and Maritza Díaz (Colombia) and psychologist Beatriz Oré (Peru) participated in the students' prefield training and were wise consultants at many points during the implementation. Julio Portocarrero, who also worked on the Yauyos Values Study and is a specialist in research methodology, was an active advisor throughout, and Helen Palma was the project assistant. This entire group coalesced in Lima for the training and induction of the field teams in June 2008. Once the data were in, Margarita Velasco, trained in philosophy and political science, took on a major role in the analysis.

FIGURE 2.1. Many members of the research team. Back row, left to right: C. Chirinos, I. Vargas, S. Torrejón, C. Little, a visiting exchange student, L. Minaya, D. Geng, G. Agüero, a visiting faculty member, R. Ocaña. Front row, left to right: J. Leinaweaver, a driver of research vehicle, G. Medina, V. Navarrete, C. Astudillo, N. Padilla, a driver of research vehicle. Not pictured: J. Anderson, J. Sifuentes.

We use real names for the young anthropologists and sociologists who took up residence in the towns for six weeks of observations, conversations, note-taking, and efforts at understanding (pictured in figure 2.1). For several of them, this was their first experience using ethnographic tools in their professional careers. Yet, when consulted about being identified as those ultimately responsible for what we came to know about childhood in Yauyos, they agreed. Gabriela Agüero and Ignacio Vargas worked in Los Caminos; Sandra Torrejón, Roxana Ocaña, and Christopher Little went to Bellavista; Nadya Padilla and Jhon Sifuentes traveled to Yauyos City; Gabriela Medina and Carlos Chirinos carried out their research in Terrazas; Cynthia Astudillo and Diego Geng were the investigators assigned to Las Cascadas; and finally, Li Minaya and Violeta Navarrete took up residence in Pastizales.

Pairing a male with a female field-worker in each of the communities was an important decision with notable precedents in the region (Escalante and Valderrama 2016). Recruiting men for a study of children was not as easy as we expected, however. In fact, we fell one man short, and in Pastizales the field team consisted of two women. One of them, Violeta, was a student at the National University of San Cristóbal de Huamanga in the Andean city of Ayacucho, on an exchange program at the PUCP. Her insights were often unique. On more than one occasion she remarked in her field notes how she had had some of the experiences that she was observing in the children of Yauyos.

Deploying a mixed pair provided the well-known advantage of allowing the team to organize the work according to who would be the best person to approach various situations and individuals. Many observations were done in tandem, but often the pairs separated.[5] As anticipated, the women tended to have better luck exchanging confidences with girls and women in the communities; the men, with boys and men. And, as is always the case in ethnographic work, some of our interlocutors, whether adults or children, were more willing than others to open up about their feelings and experiences. They highlighted different matters, often complementing each other. Friendships were established, and requests were made and a few ceremoniously accepted for the field-workers to become *padrinos* and *madrinas* (godparents; see Leinaweaver 2008, 5–8). The field teams became valued customers at bodegas and restaurants. Many children sought them out as companions and enjoyed teaching them about their lives. Children delighted in seeing their photos and borrowing the field-workers' cameras.

The focus on children was mystifying to many community members and authorities. It was not habitual for adults to spend much time conversing or hanging out with children, certainly not unrelated children. Showing interest and associating with the town's children caused some suspicion initially and, for some people, to the very end. Individual community members could and did reject, ignore, and exploit the visitors. They sometimes behaved aggressively, as occurred with Gabriela as she was photographing children on the plaza at nightfall. Standing nearby was the husband of a prominent shop owner, a man of dubious reputation in the town. He abruptly demanded that she erase the photographs, which she did, even as she explained what her purpose was. Not content with that, he grabbed her arm and only let her go when another community member happened by.

The field-workers were instructed to believe the children yet seek confirmation of things they said from other family members or other observers or by going back over the same topics time and again with the child in question. This aligns with best practices in the field of childhood studies (Moran-Ellis and Tisdall 2019; Hammersley 2017). Greene and Hill (2005, 7) insist that "children are not exempt" from any of the foibles that occur in researching adults: forgetting, presenting oneself in the best light, outright lying, or having the intent to deceive.

Biographies and Analysis

Back from the field, the team held multiple discussion sessions, out of which emerged a format for systematizing the biographies. Simultaneously, the field-workers were finishing up the digitization of their field notes. Everybody (except Jhon Sifuentes and the two Canadian field-workers, who were no longer in Peru) then fit the information they had collected about the young biography subjects into the format, including their own judgments about states of mind and quality of care that the children were receiving. Anderson pieced together three boys' biographies for Yauyos based on Jhon's field notes. She also contributed to biography construction for several children in Los Caminos, because Ignacio and Gabriela collected extensive information about many children and ran out of time to complete the systematizations.

A subset of thirty-six children makes up what we call the "biographies sample." These were children chosen for special attention in each town. They are not a representative sample of children in their communities in a statistical sense. They constitute a sample of a type frequently used in qualitative studies: a stratified intentional sample. The sample contains six children from each community, with two minor exceptions: seven for Terrazas and five in Los Caminos. The biographies sample includes three pairs of siblings (Betty and Lenin, Nieves and Moisés, Pamela and Carlos) and one pair of co-resident half-siblings (Gladis and Pascual), so the sample includes a total of thirty-two households.

Table 2.1 shows the age and sex of the children in the biographies sample. All of their names are pseudonyms, as are the names of siblings, parents, and all other individuals connected to these protagonists wherever they are mentioned in the text. Those with no more than a mention or two are identified by their status and roles. Because age is undeniably important to the way we interpret children's words and actions, and because our study defined "children" as anyone under eighteen years of age, when referring to these participants, we add ages in parentheses after their pseudonyms. We have done our best to make these actors easy to trace and their situations comprehensible.

The field-workers in each town selected the children for biographies independently of the selection made in the others. The sample manages to suggest tendencies and proportions because of what we believe to be the absence of any clear bias in the choices. In the end, the biographies were only part of what we learned about children in the communities. Older adults talked about their childhoods. Children and adolescents were observed and engaged in many conversations with the field-workers outside of the focus on the thirty-six biography protagonists. Most of them were part of a sibling group, and often we came to know as much about others in the group as about the protagonist. One outstanding example is bold, skillful, and athletic Dionisia, sister of Renzo. The information we collected is not the same for all the children, even among those for whom a biography was constructed.

The field-workers were asked to keep a separate diary, or footnotes in their field notes, to note their methodological observations. They registered action around cameras and videos, made sometimes frustrated comments about kids asking repeatedly for candy and food, and wrote about the difficulty of finding ways to converse with people about abstract concepts such as "care." One of the most interesting things to emerge from this exercise in reflexivity was the difference in styles and priorities of the various field-workers (figures 2.2, 2.3, 2.4; see Anderson 2018). They saw and heard different things, according to their own interests. Jhon drew the children out on their knowledge of supernatural beings and beliefs, topics he was particularly curious about. Sandra, grounded in medical anthropology, took special notice of indicators of the children's states of health and

TABLE 2.1
The child research participants

Age group (years)	Girls	Boys	Total number of children
3	Consuelo	Erick Pascual	3
5	Yovana Lizbeth	Lenin Samuel	4
6	Elisa Haydee Dalila	Jhony Carlos	5
7	—	Guille	1
8	Camila	Junior	2
9	Dina Pamela	—	2
10	—	Oscar Jeferson Renzo	3
11	Estela Yeny	Leoncio Tomás Moisés	5
12	Maruja	Nilton Isaac	3
13	Aurora	—	1
14	Betty Gladis Silvia Nieves	Hilario	5
15	Rufina	Braulio	2
Total	18	18	36

nutrition. Gabriela, with a background in mental health and sensitive to issues of child abuse (more openly discussed in her Canadian city than in Peru), zeroed in on manifestations of those phenomena. Ignacio achieved instant acceptance as a volleyball coach and used his willingness to rise up to any physical challenge as a tool of entry, whether to work gangs or extenuating fiestas. Cynthia became indispensable as a tutor for English, an obligatory subject that inspires fear in many secondary school students. Diego, a sociologist deeply involved in studies of

FIGURE 2.2. Ignacio Vargas in conversation with a small research participant.

the power relations underlying water management in the Andes, deftly managed political discussions that revealed the extent of the manipulations of power in ostensibly egalitarian communities. Roxana struck up a friendship with the Diaconía team (from a Lutheran international aid agency) that was working in postearthquake reconstruction projects in the town and who, as psychologists, had many insights into the undercurrents of people's desires and frustrations.

The analysis revolved around the identification of themes and creation of various formats for visualization of tendencies and patterns in the data. For this, Anderson read and reread the field notes: by author, by community, and all together. Gradually a set of themes and subthemes emerged that could be grouped into the various chapters of the book. As far as possible we chose "emic" themes, that is, concepts that were salient for the population itself and that could be described using their own words, concepts, and examples. Some additional themes were suggested by words and concepts found in the literature on children and Andean communities. Had our corpus leaned more heavily on interviews and discourse, as opposed to observation, we might have had a larger selection of local terms ("codes") to start with. Still, nobody in Yauyos talked about *reciprocidad* (reciprocity); they just enacted it. People did not talk about "disciplining" children; they just did it.

Once tentative categories were defined, we copied tranches of field notes into long lists of relevant quotes, incidents, ideas, and conversations. There were over a hundred observations for each community. Some are a few minutes long, others

FIGURE 2.3. Gabriela Agüero on a hike with a young research participant.

lasted several hours (parades, parties, cattle brandings, Independence Day events). We sought to give full berth to divergence in the data and to revealing the range of variation within themes and subthemes, as opposed to analytical strategies more attuned to convergence (Richards 2005, 124–145; Puddephatt et al. 2009).

The approach through themes has deep roots in the classical tradition of ethnography, though it has not always been explicitly discussed.[6] Grounded theory,

FIGURE 2.4. Carlos Chirinos and a young research participant.

although strongly associated with formal coding systems, recognizes codes as the building blocks of themes (Strauss and Corbin 1990; Saldaña 2009). Much of the reasoning behind these approaches has recently resurfaced in reflective thematic analysis (Braun and Clarke 2021). We found writings on reflective thematic analysis to be useful, particularly in their discussion of how themes grow and wane in importance, how they may split into subthemes, and how they transform during the process of analysis.

Our first step toward analysis was classic: felt-tip pens in hand, we color-coded a sample of field notes (marking children's emotional states, expressed and inferred; services; community organization and governance, among others). That led to identifying domains (play, work, education, health, household functioning) and those—as predicted by Braun and Clarke—shape-shifted into concepts: intimate relationships, economies and ecologies of care, nonfamily care, and moral worlds. Many of the transformations and changes in the salience of themes (for example, children's autonomous relations with nonfamily care providers) happened only in the course of writing, for which Richardson has made a strong case as a methodological bolster (1998).

Building from the information from the biographies, we constructed matrices that synthesized the evidence around particular topics and facilitated a rapid visualization of associated patterns. The topics included household composition, occupations of parents and other family provisioners, parents' and children's education, experiences of travel and migration of children and their caretakers, children's work and play activities, parents' and children's aspirations for the future, and children's health status. We quantified all the information that lent itself to counting: for example, the members of households, the size of sibling groups, the ages of mothers at the birth of their first child. The biographies invited and facilitated comparisons: among children, among households, among family groups, and among communities, and between age groups and genders. Children could be compared not only as individuals but as parts of kinship networks, economic enterprises, and affective communities. The biographies extended the timelines for the cases and encouraged cross-checking.

The analysis was a lengthy process, probably made possible only by Anderson's retirement from full-time university teaching and ultimately by the lockdowns of COVID-19. Anderson and Margarita Velasco, her adult daughter, co-resident during the restrictions imposed by the Peruvian government, talked throughout the process of analysis. Despite the high investment of time, we are convinced that the process we adopted was our best choice because it allowed for preserving the context in which things were said and events occurred. It made it possible to follow the same actors through many situations, relationships, and interactions, cross-checking the evidence of their attitudes and references, often comparing what two different observers captured from a scene or story. We put our best energies into ensuring the quality and consistency of the data and keeping the resultant text as close as possible to the observations in the field.

A major dilemma in reporting on ethnographic work, one that assumes special force in studies of face-to-face communities, is how to protect the confidentiality and disguise the identity of the participants. The necessary precautions are even more stringent in the case of children. Changing the names of participants is a minimum requirement, but it is far from enough. In small towns such as those involved in this study, the possibility of identifying who said and did what remains despite the pseudonyms. We have not tampered with facts such as the composition of family groups, for example, or the occupations of parents and other possibly distinguishing factors. The solution we found was to address the corpus as if it referred to a single composite community, wherever possible and wherever the risk of identifying individuals was high. Thus, the children are identified by age but not always associated with the town where they lived, except when that association was essential to understand the incident or situation in question. The fact that more than a decade has passed since this research was conducted also helps obscure individuals' identities, as the daily events have faded in memory and the children have grown into adults.

The comparisons that we initially proposed among the six localities shrunk in importance as the identities issue increased in gravity in our minds and as we realized how much information would have to be supplemented to do this credibly. Some obvious differences make their way into the text, especially the contrasts between Nor Yauyos (Pastizales, Las Cascadas, Terrazas) and Sur Grande

(Los Caminos, Bellavista), and between the communities heavily dependent on stock raising and those more reliant on mixed cropping and labor migration. We were able to make some arguments about the benefits for children of better local government and better-endowed municipal budgets, but here more research is needed to establish clear trends. One line of comparison that we had to abandon for lack of sufficient information concerns the levels of internal inequality in the towns. Andean communities are not the homogeneous, leveling societies they were once reputed to be, and we found large differences in the material conditions of life of different children. Yet we can only speculate just what were the consequences of such differences and what were the possible harms of growing up in a tightly knit society where different members seemed on track to occupy very different positions in their adult lives.

Conditioning Circumstances

Three key events that took place in the weeks, months, and years before our fieldwork influenced the way people were living, the things they had on their minds, and the way children were feeling. One was a seismic event, another was a social and political cataclysm that affected all of Peru, and the third was a recent tragedy on the treacherous roads of the province.

On August 15, 2007, the coast of Peru was shaken by a major earthquake. The epicenter was in Nasca, to the southwest of Yauyos, but the province, especially the part closest to the Pacific Ocean, was greatly affected. People could not run because objects were falling down all around them in clouds of dust. Many houses collapsed, the adobe reduced to rubble, and others were left with open cracks in the walls. Parents tried to reach children that had been left at home, fearful they might have been crushed by falling roofs. As Jeferson's mother recalled, "At the moment of the earthquake, my children started to cry. We were all crying. At that moment we were remembering God. At other times you may forget. You're thinking only of material things, not spiritual ones. But that's when you remember Our Lord. At that moment all of us neighbors got down on our knees to pray."

Earth tremors are frequent in Peru, but they never cease to be fearsome events. In settlements located in mountain valleys, they send down cascades of boulders amid an overpowering rumbling. Lakes above the towns may release flood waters and mud slides. In much of Yauyos province, the electrical grid went down. Telephone communications were cut off. Children refused to be left alone. In the areas most affected, for fear of aftershocks, people preferred to sleep outside, in makeshift shelters, improvised tents, on mattresses in the open air of the town square, or even on their doorsteps.

The earthquake had social aftershocks as well. All too slowly, staff from the national government's disaster relief agency arrived with tents, blankets, food, and warm clothing.[7] Some children got their first taste of brand-name clothing, as fashionable department stores in Lima sent donations. Later there were tents, mattresses, and eventually prefabricated houses donated by the European Union and USAID.[8] People were promised cash stipends to rebuild and repair houses that had been left with rooms roped off and posts propping up walls. Some stipends came through; many did not. Public buildings, including some schools, were damaged or destroyed. In the wake of the disaster, some families moved to other houses while others simply left town. After seeing images of the destruction when looking at his mobile phone in Lima, the new doctor that Terrazas had just hired decided not to come to work there after all.

The earthquake of 2007 tested the capacity of Yauyos communities to come together to provide immediate help to their neighbors and then to carry forward the reconstruction efforts. Many observers and community members complained about the dissension and backbiting that were on full display in the attempts to restore safety and livability to the towns after the trauma. Diaconía sent a team of psychologists to assist with mental health issues. They counseled individuals and families and worked with community authorities in activities such as seminars on violence prevention. One year after the earthquake, in Bellavista, they had turned their attention to creating a community dining hall in the hope that sharing in a new endeavor might rekindle the bonds of solidarity.

Two decades earlier, Yauyos had suffered another major trauma and displacement of population. This was during the violence and civil conflict instigated by Sendero Luminoso (Shining Path) (CVR 2004; Starn and La Serna 2019; Degregori 1990, 2015; Gorriti 1999). Yauyos province was a corridor between Ayacucho, the region where violence first broke out and where it was most intense, and the cities of the coast, especially the capital, Lima. In the early 1990s the movement's strategy shifted from a Maoist insurgency in rural villages toward one of choking off the cities and provoking uprisings there. Residents remembered the way many of the towns of Yauyos were occupied repeatedly by columns of Senderista combatants. They might stay for a few hours, haranguing the students and teachers at the school, summoning the town's population to the plaza, and preaching their vision of revolution in Peru. People were forced to witness the execution of authorities and prominent business owners branded as collaborators and capitalist exploiters. The Senderistas requisitioned food and supplies and attempted to recruit followers to join them. Parents were afraid that their sons and daughters might be kidnapped, as had happened in other parts of the country.

During this period, not unlike during the earthquake's aftermath, movement and migration were a rational response to disruption. When Senderistas descended on the August anniversary fiesta in Pastizales, the townspeople were terrified. Many left their homes and slept by the river, hiding in caves or in the hills. Some escaped to the city. A young man, just starting out on a teaching career in an annex of the town, gave it all up for a job in an asparagus cannery in Cañete. One woman and her family left their home in Las Cascadas after the Senderistas forced randomly chosen residents to support their group by knitting caps and sweaters. A week later the police showed up with a list of names, accusing those who had been co-opted of being terrorist sympathizers.[9] Señora Elva abandoned her store and ample herds in Bellavista and went to Lima after two close family members were killed by Shining Path. When people left, their houses, fields, and herds were at risk of being appropriated by strangers or even neighbors, and some families adopted a strategy of leaving women and children behind to protect their belongings.

The violence enacted by the insurgents was accompanied by other forms of violence perpetrated by state actors charged with ending the rebellion. By 1990 half the country had been declared in a state of emergency and was, in effect, under martial law. The Peruvian military had taken over the war against Shining Path from the police, and denunciations of torture, extrajudicial killings, and even massacres of entire communities were growing (CVR 2004; Starn and La Serna 2019). The Truth and Reconciliation Commission found that the majority of the victims of violence were rural peasants and small-town poor (Henríquez and Ewig 2013). Bellavista and Los Caminos were part of a "red zone" under special vigilance by the police and military forces because of what they believed was a high level of infiltration by Shining Path. A detachment of police was installed in Bellavista. A column of Senderistas arrived and attacked the post at a moment when a single policeman was on duty. From the amount of ammunition exchanged, and the duration of the attack, the population was convinced there was a large contingent inside. The post was overrun and ransacked. The Senderistas looked everywhere for survivors, even invading neighboring houses. The sole policeman defending the post had hidden in the latrine.

Under pressure from all sides, the local system of governance was weakened. Competent officials were driven out by threats. Some that stayed could not shake off suspicion. One leader in Bellavista had been in prison in Cañete, condemned as a collaborator. He let some Shining Path fighters stay briefly in his home; it was impossible to refuse, he said. He served his term and was released but had to report to Cañete every month. When he could not afford to make the trip, he was incarcerated again.

Among ordinary citizens, the social contract was deeply wounded as well. Neighbors often had reason to question the actions of neighbors during the conflict (Theidon 2004). Denouncing someone for having been a terrorist could be a means of settling old disputes or laying claim to rivals' properties. Cattle rustlers pretended to be Senderistas to discourage pursuit. The trauma of this time is rarely discussed, but it is never far away. Its echoes shape present-day Yauyos politics, society, and economy.

Meanwhile, even quotidian activities took forms that reflected the precariousness of rural life exacerbated by decades of underinvestment in infrastructure. The mountain roads of Yauyos were treacherous whether in rainy or dry season. Many of the children's school excursions involved piling into the backs of trucks, which lurched and careened over narrow, poorly maintained access roads. The chaperones, parents and teachers, would have the children huddle on the floor while they banged on the railings and shouted to the driver to slow down.

Almost any means of transportation, and any transportation route around the province, could bring tragedy. Accidents involving trucks, buses, and vans were a source of generalized concern because everyone needed to travel. Mechanical failures or any miscalculation by drivers could cause them to plunge over a cliff. At the time of fieldwork, both Yauyos City and Pastizales had been affected by recent accidents that involved the vehicles that plied the main route between Cañete on the coast and the high-altitude communities. Just weeks before the fieldwork began, the San Juan bus, on its daily route up and down the valley, went off the edge at a curve. Several passengers died.

While still fresh in memory, such events were a constant topic of conversation. The preschool teachers in Yauyos City felt they needed to help their pupils understand what had happened and manage their fear. One of them described the result:

> Everything with an impact that happens here is something that the children express in due time. For example, when the San Juan bus crashed. We have here a little boy, 5 years old. He doesn't talk well. It's a delay in his development. Little by little he'll catch up. All the bodies that were brought up from the crash were taken to Yauyos City. The townspeople, elders and children, crowded around to see the huge numbers of coffins. So this little boy who doesn't communicate very easily, doesn't pronounce the words well, he was with his teacher in the patio and maybe four days had already gone by. Out of the blue he said, with perfect clarity: "Teacher, in the health center there are many dead people (Profesora, en el centro de salud hay muchos muertos)." We were all open-mouthed because he just doesn't talk that way. Sometime later we celebrated Early Childhood Education Day with prizes for best drawing and best painting. Many of the children made pictures of the coffins. "Who is that?" we asked them. "It's the dead people of San Juan," they said. Many of them even drew the coffins on top of the tables where the dead were laid out for the wake. (Interview, preschool director)

Through the Eyes of Children

If children as actors have been largely absent in classic treatments of Andean village society, their perspectives on their lives and surroundings have merited even less consideration. They have too often been portrayed as shy, tongue-tied, and unwilling to engage with outsiders. Children are not always considered reliable and capable informants about their own lives. Yet serious ethnographic work with children has found that—like other research collaborators—children must be approached in terms that they can understand.

Feminist standpoint theory (Smith 1987; Harding 2004) offers a justification for learning from subordinated social actors, and privileging their version when competing accounts differ (Borneman and Hammoudi 2009). Graeber (2015, 58–60) goes further, noting that subordinate actors are quite often experts on the behavior and thoughts of dominant actors, which they have studied in detail since their very survival may depend on it. This perspective helped us to hear the children as they reflected on the violence of some of their intimate relations, the value of their own labor, and more. Children interpret what they see in ways different from adults, but children also see different things (just as adults see different things from children). Anthropologists and others who study children undoubtedly see yet other things.

One illustration of this principle emerges from an important event in the herding communities of Yauyos. Andean towns have many festivals, but some of the most important are *herranzas*, cattle-branding parties (figure 2.5). Everyone participates, from infants on their mothers' backs to *abuelitos* (oldsters). The herd owners and invited guests begin the evening by sharing a meal, lubricated by abundant draughts of *chamis*, the local liquor.[10] People are seated on stools, rocks, or on the ground. The women of the family, with their close friends and allies, are preparing the food and serving laden plates. Musicians and clowns weave among them, animating the party. Meantime, cattle are being moved to a corral, where the marking is done. This may involve branding irons or may only entail piercing

FIGURE 2.5. An *herranza* (cattle-branding party).

KNOWING CHILDREN   39

the animals' ears to attach unique combinations of colorful ribbons and tassels. Once marked, the livestock are let loose as a shower of candies rains down on their backs. The herd owners are admonished that a successful calving season depends on their generosity in providing the sweets. The children struggle to rescue the candy from the hooves and the churning mud. A preponderance of round candies means there will be many females among the year's progeny, an auspicious outcome.

We cite, in turn, a patriarch of an important stock-owning family describing this event; a child that participates on the edges; and an anthropologist who offers an interpretation.

The patriarch[11]:

(Do you have family get-togethers?) Yes, we do. Based on family tradition. Every August the entire family gets together. It's to put their adornments on all the animals. To mark them. I bring a book where I've registered the births of all my animals. Those of all my children. Elías (his oldest son): so many cows, mothers, heifers, bulls, sheep. (He names his many sons and daughters and the numbers and class of animals assigned to each.) All of them have their animals. Everyone has to prepare the ribbons, the medicine they will get. We have the custom of staying up all night with our animals. We prepare a pachamanca or tripe stew. We pass the night there and give all the animals new names. Every one of them has a name. It's a beautiful tradition. Still, many others don't do it. They ask me: where do you get the patience to give each animal a birth certificate? But it is necessary. That's how you know the ages of your herd, and the production of every cow. What if you should forget? You could sell a cow that's still capable of producing three or four calves. With the birth certificate, you can't make a mistake.

The child:

It's when they throw out candy and you have to scramble to get it. See, it's when you have the pleasure of candy. (Cuando avienten caramelos y tú te tienes que lanzarte para atrapar. Cuando gozas de caramelos, pues.) (Elisa, 6)

The anthropologist, in full-throated interpretive mode:

... In the final scenes of the ritual ..., the cattle, in order to be "domesticated," are treated almost as human beings. In this context, it is not difficult to understand what moves people so much: the painful paradox of a love that is shown so vividly, accompanied by a violence that cannot be hidden anymore. This paradox has its climax when ... the owners give their cattle human names, dress them with necklaces and earrings, and even arrange weddings between their calves and young people ... At the same time, they sell their herds for slaughter to the businessmen who come from the city. It is during this climax when peasants (through the collective songs everybody knows) make their cattle ask why they are selling . . . what they consider to be almost like themselves. (Rivera 2005, 148)

These contrasting narratives highlight one of our framing questions: how do children and adolescents perceive the Andean communities they are part of, as opposed to their adult co-residents? How do they view their alternative worlds, the one they inherit and those they are in the process of building?

Conclusions

This chapter has described the research process in Yauyos, which ended with the writing of this book. We have gone into more detail than is customary in many anthropological works because of the need to explain the many actors and their roles in the study, as well as to reveal the many sources of our knowledge about, and interpretations of, the lives of children and their care providers in this rural region of Peru. We also recognize that the nature of this study is unusual. Most cultural anthropological work is done by a single ethnographer. This research was done by a team of thirteen students, learning and, at times, forging new paths in how to do ethnography with young people in a respectful and careful way that best reflected their experiences. In this chapter, we have shown both how those field-workers produced their data and how we used it to innovatively build a database from which we make our arguments. Our hope is that the following chapters will be more accessible because of the information provided, and even that some readers may imagine themselves in the shoes (and sandals) of the field-workers and their interlocutors.

3

Intimate Contexts of Care

One fine day in July, as the sun burned off the morning chill, field-worker Chiri recorded the following scene. He had arranged to have a chat with Camila's father by way of constructing her biography. They were seated on the patio at the entrance to the house.

The house lies at a lower level than the sidewalk and street so you go down a packed dirt incline to enter. This bifurcates at a certain point. One path leads to Camila's house and the other to her cousin's. You walk a further two stairsteps down to reach the patio. Camila (8) and her mother are washing clothes today. On the right side is a stone wall that separates the patio from the workshop of father Teodoro: it is strewn with wrought iron, electrical components, soldering tools. On the left is the entrance to the house proper. The original adobe walls have been replaced by prefabricated panels that were distributed after the earthquake; the roof is sheets of corrugated tin. The sound of music from a radio comes from inside. Heaped up against the wall is a large pile of stones. A bucket with a spigot stands atop a steel barrel, the source of clean water. Camila uses it to fill a large plastic tub where she submerges a pair of tennis shoes, shoelaces, school uniforms and sundry other items of clothing. She's been washing her school uniform since she was in first grade, she says. She tosses the used water over the stones and places the shoes and clothes there for draining as she finishes wringing them out.

Meantime, sister Sonia (6) and a cousin from next door are playing on the patio. The cousin, says Camila, comes every day "to visit my mother." Sonia appears in the doorway leading to the house. She has put a pair of her mother's high-heeled shoes on and is dancing to the music. Camila and the cousin laugh. The mother calls her name, sternly, and Sonia rapidly returns inside. The cousin is playing with chipitaps[1] at Camila's feet.

Camila now places the clothes she has washed by hand in another bucket and proceeds towards a clothesline which is strung between two poles at the back of the patio. The line has been set up on a raised heap of earth that almost reaches the height of the roof of the house and father's workshop. "Bring in the dry clothes," calls her mother from inside. Camila collects them in a pile on the roof of the house. Balancing herself on a board extended between the earth heap and the roof of the workshop, she carefully lays out the wet clothes on the line.

Her mother comes out of the house where she has been starting the lunch. She also has some washing to do, using the same procedures with buckets and tub. At one point she laughs when she realizes that she has rinsed some clothes that Camila already washed. The two of them, mother and daughter, clamber up the heap again to hang the new load of washing on the clothesline. A pole from the neighboring house has fallen against the clothesline. Camila's mother tells her to push it back so it is resting on the roof instead. Camila hands her mother the pieces and her mother places them on the line. She inspects a blouse that Camila washed and hung to dry. She calls her daughter over. "You didn't do that well," she admonishes, as she rubs a spot between her hands.

The daily washing over, Camila's mother puts the tubs away and then wipes off a couple of chairs that have been sitting on the patio. She takes them into the house. Camila, who is wearing shorts and some old tennis shoes with the heels broken down so they look more like sandals, rinses off some dirt that has clung to her legs. She also goes inside, taking a pencil and scissors that Sonia has left strewn on the patio. "What a pain, she leaves everything lying around," she mutters. Camila's older brother had also washed his uniform and other items earlier in the morning. He now moves from the kitchen to the workshop. The two spaces are divided by a large blue sheet of plastic as an extension of the wall. He could be heard moving some pieces of metal around for several minutes. "Ya, papá, you'd better do it," he calls out. His dad answers: "No, it's time you learned."

This chapter is about emplacement (Olwig and Gulløv 2003): placing the children of Yauyos in the intimate settings of their daily lives, both physical and social, on one hand, and, on the other, disentangling the processes by which children become meaningfully connected to those places (Bodenhorn and Lee 2019; Remorini 2013). Some of the most widely used tools for understanding child development foreground their location in space and time; for example, Bronfenbrenner's (1979) concept of "ecological contexts" or Harkness and Super's (1994) notion of "developmental niches." Adults place children spatially in relation to people, activities, and material objects that they believe will ensure for them "proper childhoods" (Boyden 1997, 197–202). They monitor and limit children's access to inappropriate places, including both ideational and ideological ones

(Low and Lawrence-Zúñiga 2003). Somewhat ironically, then, having argued forcefully for children's agency, we add a nuance to our argument in this chapter with our full recognition that adults have overdetermined power to create the places that children occupy and to prohibit others.

We begin with the houses—like Camila's—and the streets they lined. We then show how households came into being as social groups through the encounter of two partners and the incorporation of children, and how they shifted under various stresses over the long cycle of domestic groups. The discussion resembles accounts centered on the "life course" (Shanahan 2000) and its transitions (Ames and Rojas 2010), but it heeds Jennifer Johnson-Hanks's (2002, 866) call to recognize the "uncertainty, innovation, and ambivalence" that mark real life histories. While we focus on the children in the biographies sample and their families, we often bring in other community members and even stray into the annals of kinship studies in Andean communities. In fact, many of the concepts that have described Andean systems of kinship and marriage historically proved useful in Yauyos, albeit in novel ways.

Houses: Local Design and Construction

Houses in the rural towns of Yauyos were relatively small, highly functional, and intensively used. They were adapted to the agrarian economy and the ecological setting. Some were built on different levels created by a mountain slope. They were living spaces for people and closely associated animals. Nonfamily members who came through were customers—bringing repair jobs to a workshop, making purchases at a store fronting on the street—or they were neighbors dropping by for a brief chat at the entrance.

The first floor comprised the daily living and workspace. Typically, it included a kitchen, whether a partially covered stone hearth attached to an outer wall or a stove, sink, and spigot in a dining area with a large table (see figure 3.1). Wealthier families, many of whom had held positions as community authorities, sometimes had a separate room for receiving visitors. Invariably there was a large patio, an open-air enclosure, in the center, at the back, or off the side. Many houses had two such patios. There, firewood and tools were stored, protected by sheets of plastic or corrugated tin. Old furniture and tools were sometimes strewn about. Sacks of produce were sometimes temporarily stored there while others were being processed: large quantities of potatoes being peeled for freeze-drying and converting to *chuño*, for example. Guinea pigs scurried underfoot, busily eliminating scraps. Other animals shared space with the humans as well: a dog or cat or two on the patio, and occasionally a sheep or goat in transit. Nearby, a corral enclosed chickens and ducks. Bathing and clothes-washing in tubs placed in the patio (as we saw Camila doing) took place in sunshine and under open skies. Sometimes there was a shed at the back for a latrine, or in other instances simply a designated space.

FIGURE 3.1. Inside an adobe kitchen. The hearth is visible as a health worker visits the family.

Nights were cold in the high Andes. No houses were heated, except at the moments when firewood was lit in stoves and food was on the cooker. The heat given off by human bodies, added to blankets and sheepskins, got children through the night. The architecture of houses in Yauyos respected the logic of heat conservation, and spaces for sleeping were almost always on the second floor.

The architecture also respected the properties of the predominant building material—adobe bricks—and the risks of earthquakes. Two stories was the practical limit for an adobe construction to be able to withstand tremors (see figure 3.2). Houses were built by relatives and neighbors and thus stayed within the limits of local knowledge of construction as well (Gose 1991). Some had concrete walls or floors, but cement was expensive, in part because it had to be trucked in. A very few of the wealthiest families (especially in Las Cascadas, where the tourist trade meant extra rooms could generate income) were adding third stories and replacing adobe with bricks and mortar. Many neighbors considered this shift away from adobe and tile roofs to be a regrettable loss of community and aesthetic values (see Leinaweaver 2009).

Children were entirely integrated into all household spaces (Haboud de Ortega 1980; Bolin 2006). No house had a special room for schoolwork or a library, though some had a collection of books and papers on shelves or in an enclosed bookcase, possibly shared with glassware, trophies, photographs, and other family

FIGURE 3.2. Adobe houses, with adobe bricks drying in the sun.

mementos. Many did have a table designated for children's homework. It was likely to be set directly amid the conversations and activities that carried on throughout the house and throughout the day. Given the rural logic of early to bed and early to rise, there was not much shared family entertainment. Though some had television sets, families did not regularly sit down in the evenings to watch a program. Most of the activities that implied games, laughs, and good times were community events.

The idea of a child having a room of their own was almost unheard of in Yauyos. It would have seemed repugnant (lonely and sad, rather than selfish). Most children could not even imagine having a bed of their own.[2] For families, a typical sleeping arrangement would be for male children to share a bed and female children to share another, possibly with a wall or curtain separating the two. Fathers might room with their sons or could occupy a room or curtained-off space with their wives. The youngest children slept alongside their mothers.

Creating the Households

Emplacement also entails locating children in the intimate social spheres of home, family, and neighborhood. That will be our task in the remainder of the chapter.

Two basic principles governed marriage and family formation in the Andes. It was felt that all adults should be united in pairs—in fact, establishing such a union is tantamount to entering into adulthood—and these pairs were complementary. In a stable and harmonious union, a man and woman would work hard in separate spheres of activity, supported by a network of kin to provide material help and moral support. Romantic love and sexual attraction were not absent—witness the lyrics of *huaynos* and other Andean song forms (Tucker 2019)—but a shared project of progressing as a family enterprise grounded these unions in principle.

The second principle recognized that establishing a union, a new household, and a family was a process (Bolton 1977; Carter 1977). It involved gradual consideration of potential partners, learning about their character and compatibility, and figuring out what worked. Women carefully assessed men's propensity to isolate, control, and use violence against them. Traditionally the marriage process was marked by a succession of rituals, one being the formal *pedido de mano*, in which the groom's family, bearing gifts of food and liquor, visited the young woman's parents to request her hand. Some in Yauyos remembered this practice. Another related tradition, also now largely abandoned, was that a young couple could initiate a "trial marriage" (Carter 1977) in the knowledge that, if a pregnancy occurred, mother and child would have the support of her parents, whether or not the young couple decided to make their union permanent. This tradition makes clear how children were desired under almost any circumstances. While in daily life no distinction seemed to be made between formal and common-law marriages, some sought a marriage license from the civil authority, which could turn out to be important in disputes over child support. It was vanishingly rare to consecrate a union in a religious ceremony, due in no small part to the high costs and logistical challenges of a church wedding in towns without a resident priest or Protestant minister.

Traditionally, the ideal of an enduring union was supported by a preference for endogamy, or marrying within the community. This kept property from dispersing and prevented the dilution of communal rights. It also meant that each spouse's family knew a great deal about the other spouse's family, and in-laws and *padrinos* would be nearby to counsel and discipline the couple in case of problems. For women, having close relatives at hand could provide some insurance against domestic violence (Harris 1978). But more recently, in Yauyos, and increasingly throughout the Andes, limiting marital choices to the community one grew up in, and accepting parents' decisions over who would make a good partner, was becoming the exception. Our data from Yauyos indicate a preference that spouses come from the same general area but not necessarily the same community. Of the thirty-two households in the biographies sample, twenty-four included enduring unions.[3] Five of those were unions of a man and a woman from the same town, while over half (fourteen) involved persons from the same district (typically, a town and one of its annexes) or neighboring districts. Of the eight unions that did not endure, two were interrupted by death, and six ended in separation. As four out of these six involved partners from the same or neighboring districts, proximity was no guarantee of success.

Even where couples had grown up together, they were likely to have spent a few years apart during adolescence or early adulthood. Each went their own way, and they got back together after a time of working or studying elsewhere. Those who eventually married outside the community had to find ways of making the acquaintance of potential partners. They had to meet enough times in enough venues to be reasonably well acquainted before they decided to move in together (or a pregnancy occurred). Several partners had met at school competitions, sporting events, or fiestas in one or another of the neighboring towns. Often there would be cousins and other relatives there that could make introductions and create the pretext for visits. But these meetings could be difficult when parents were hostile to strangers who might threaten the future of their son or daughter. Pilar, owner of El Puente restaurant, worked selling trinkets at traveling fairs when her children were young. She came home from one trip to find a strange man at the kitchen table with her daughter Yelitza (sixteen at the time). He was a student teacher from Lima that had been assigned to a school in Terrazas. The two met there at an interdistrict school event. Yelitza's brother, who had been put in charge of safeguarding the household, justified the stranger's presence and his own lack of zeal in defending his sister's honor: the interloper was helping Yelitza with her math homework. Pilar scoffed. The young man declared his desire to form a family with Yelitza. Pilar threw him out of the house, but Yelitza ran away to join him in Terrazas some days later. As a couple, several years and several children later, they were an indisputable success. Pilar eventually reconciled with her daughter, and Yelitza became her essential assistant with booking and billing for El Puente.

Many men and women looked back on the moment of choosing their partner—often with a baby on the way—as a sort of "vital conjuncture" (Johnson-Hanks 2002), a cutting-off point for some of their more ambitious plans, especially aspirations that hinged on higher education. A few couples had met during periods in which one or both were pursuing a college education, and starting a family frequently became a reason for truncated college plans. A stint in the capital, Lima, or in another city figured in the histories of many of the couples. Many yauyinos allowed themselves a period of exploring the possibilities (Ortiz 1989; Anderson et al. 2001, 63–89) before finally deciding to settle in the countryside.

Jeferson's parents are an apt example. They met at a party sponsored by the Lima association of migrants (*residentes*) from Terrazas. He left to enroll in a pedagogical institute with the idea of becoming a physical education teacher. She came from an annex slightly north of Terrazas and was trying her luck as a street vendor. They had their first two children while living as a couple in Lima. Apparently driven by health and economic problems, they returned to their base and have lived in Terrazas or nearby towns ever since. Jeferson's father never finished his teacher training.

Jeferson's parents illustrate another traditional preference in Andean kinship: virilocality, or the residence of the young couple with or near the husband's household of origin. Couples met and joined their fortunes in a wide range of places, but those that came back to live in Yauyos tended to return to the husband's hometown. Like the preference for endogamy, this too could keep property and communal rights together, while privileging the husband's possibility of sharing and eventually inheriting resources, in a context where custom—contradicting Peruvian law—greatly favored the transmission of property in the male line. Yet the preference for virilocality was not a hard and fast rule. Of the twenty-four long-standing couples in the biographies sample, fewer than half (eleven) were living in a town where the husband (not the wife) had family. Four were living in a town where the wife (not the husband) had relatives; two were living in a place where both had relatives; and seven couples were living in a place where neither had grown up and neither had family ("neolocality").

First Child

The birth of a first child was a critical moment, with far more significant implications for women than for men (Oliart 2005). Having a child, like entering into marriage, could transform a girl into an adult, with some of the corresponding rights and privileges (Olthoff 2006; Van Vleet 2008, 2019). If the pregnancy occurred absent a recognized conjugal union, the implications were profound and, at the same time, ambiguous. In the past, in a context of village endogamy, men might be held to account for impregnating a woman, and parents on both sides might provide support. That was no longer the case in Yauyos. Still, "unwed mother (madre soltera)" was not locally considered to be a permanent identity or status. It was understood that this was, for some women, just one more phase in the progressive construction of a permanent union and family (Yon 2014).

As things stood, most young unmarried mothers simply had to deal with the situation as best they could: to raise the child with the help of their parents and siblings, to leave the child to be raised by the grandparents and go away, to find a relative willing to take them in, or to get a job that allowed for childcare. In the opinion of some yauyinos, having the child was a well-merited punishment for irresponsible sexual behavior. But single motherhood could also be regarded as an opportunity to learn. A young woman might redeem herself if she emerged from an early pregnancy as a responsible mother and family member (Van Vleet 2019).

In Yauyos, more than a quarter of the mothers in the biographies sample (nine out of thirty-two) had had a first child without having established residence with the father, an enduring partnership, or the promise to form one. As well, two of the older sisters of biographies children had become mothers, and their children were absorbed into the maternal grandparents' homes. Another case we learned about was Dalila's (6) older sister, who had been sent away to the city after becoming pregnant in high school; her child stayed behind to be raised by the grandparents. Most of these mothers were not teenagers at the time of their first pregnancy.[4] Single mothers in Yauyos were most commonly young adults. Some had already left home; for example, to work as domestics in Cañete or Lima. One man described the stepdaughter he was raising as "una hija de su soledad" (a daughter born from his wife's loneliness).

We will have more to say about the stepfathers and the care of these first-born children in chapter 6. Here, we want to emphasize the strong relationship that the first-borns had with their mothers. Estela (11) had almost a sisterly relationship with her twenty-six-year-old mother. We also learned how important their eventual contribution to their household and family would become. Lizbeth's (5) beloved older half-brother had recently struck out on his own, but he continued to be a firm support for his mother. Similarly, a steadying influence for Katherine and Isaac's beleaguered mother (we will meet her repeatedly in the chapters to follow) was the son she had borne when she was sixteen years old. Although he had his own work and family in Cañete, he was there with advice and material assistance when it was needed.

Juana and Helme's experience illustrates many of the complications of unexpected pregnancies. Helme and Juana conceived a child while she was still in high school, causing a scandal and creating resentments that were intense even a decade later. They both spoke openly about all they could have done in life if that pregnancy and early union had not occurred. When Juana gave birth to Pamela, her mother told her that "una hija no es nada (one child is no big deal)." She meant that there was still hope for Juana to make her own life, free of Helme. She encouraged Juana to leave town, to break off definitively from the man who had already fathered at least one other child by another woman in the same town. When Juana decided instead to try setting up house with Helme and a second child, Carlos, was born, the die was cast, the "vital conjuncture" (Johnson-Hanks 2002) completed its arc, and other possibilities were lost. Though fraught with jealousy and conflict, the partnership endured.

While a first child outside of marriage could become a cherished companion and important support, most parents in Yauyos were inclined to fear the potentially dire consequences of their daughters making a bad choice of partner or making the choice too early (Harvey 1998; Van Vleet 2019). Still, all but one of the fourteen- and fifteen-year-old girls in the biographies sample had boyfriends. They had to hide their romantic interest from their parents and content themselves with brief, surreptitious meetings at school or on the street as they went about their errands.

Having a first child had a radically different meaning for men. We came to know of several men who had been teen fathers, whether as momentary partners or after a brief cohabitation. In these cases, the father, his parents, and other family members generally disavowed responsibility and quickly disappeared. Once gone, fathers tended to have little presence in their children's lives, and the children had a precarious connection, if any, to the family and household that their fathers eventually established as "official." Guille remembered seeing his father twice in all his seven years of life; on one occasion the man gave him a toy. Aurora (13) knew she had a half-brother on her father's side who lived in the same town, but they did not greet each other on the street. Still, her father had gotten his son a job at his workplace, the Aventura Andina resort.

Under duress, a few men were making at least sporadic payments of child support. Relatives of Guille's dad had chipped in to meet his mother's demand for a long-delayed down payment. (It financed a refrigerator for the restaurant she ran.) Leoncio's father only recognized him formally when he was ten years old, after legal actions by the grandparents who were raising him.

Other fathers had initial relationships with their children, while they navigated complicated circumstances. Some couples separated by mutual agreement, like Lizbeth's mother and father, who parted ways shortly after her birth. Both of them were teachers subject to annual reassignment anywhere in the school district (Díaz and Ñopo 2016) and maintaining a shared family life seemed impossible. When Consuelo's (3) parents decided they had incompatible life projects, they divided their two children between them, her five-year-old brother staying with their father in Cañete while she came with her mother to Yauyos City. A potential stepfather visited from Lima every two weeks. Hilario's (14) father only began distancing himself as it became clear that the boy had major developmental problems. Another complicated circumstance was extramarital children; the most notable in the biographies sample was Pascual (3), the circumstances of whose birth we shall explore further in chapter 7. Here, too, legal action was necessary to get child support, and it required Pascual's mother to travel every month to Huancayo to receive the payments.

We had ample reason to believe that many of the adolescent males in the towns were sexually active. Several of them boasted about sexual encounters they had in neighboring towns and on school outings. They sometimes admitted to stealing a kiss or more as darkness closed in at *herranzas* and elders were distracted or drunk. Yet they did not own up to having girls they particularly liked, much less steady girlfriends. Clearly informed about the biology of conception and pregnancy, adolescent boys and young men were avid consumers of the free condoms that the health centers distributed. The nurse in Pastizales said she was bombarded with requests in the days before she left for vacation.

Growing Up with Siblings

For most couples in Yauyos, having children together solidified their union and were an expected and welcomed part of adult life. Most of the children in the six towns lived with two parents (or surrogates) and had a small to middling number of brothers and sisters (see figure 3.3). A full two-thirds of the children in the biographies sample had one, two, or three siblings. One-child households often reflected a transitional state; for instance, Samuel (5) lived alone with his biological parents, but a sibling was on the way. A one-child household could also reflect an exceptional circumstance. The other two singletons, Leoncio and Tomás, both eleven years old, were being raised by grandparents, having been rejected by their

FIGURE 3.3. An older child tends to a younger child's hair.

mothers and never acknowledged by their fathers. Large families were increasingly unusual, as is seen more widely following both Peru's demographic transition (Aramburú and Bustinza 2007) and draconian family planning policies during the 1990s (Ewig 2006; Molina 2017).[5] Contraceptives were readily available in health centers throughout the country, and in Yauyos, there seemed to be no stigma attached to their use.[6] Among the children in the biographies sample, nine had five or six siblings and one had seven.[7] Only in one case—that of Moisés and Nieves—were those siblings all housed and growing up together. This too was a transitional state, as in the rest, the older children had left the household to work or study elsewhere by the time the younger children were starting school.

Children do not have much power of decision over the number of their siblings, yet the number, ages, gender, and personalities of the children they share parents and household with is certainly important for their lives. A simple count of siblings hides many nuances of children's relations with other members of the same household. Lizbeth's (5) nineteen-year-old half-brother was more like a father than a brother to her. Yovana (5) and Dalila (6) were the indulged youngest child in their families, but they had to share that status with a niece (4) and nephew (1), respectively, children born to their unmarried older sisters. Even school-aged siblings were not necessarily a permanent part of the household. Several lived with relatives or spent a large part of each day or night at a relative's home. Dionisia, Renzo's twelve-year-old sister, spent much of her time, and slept nights, at the home of their maternal grandmother. Dionisia had been given to her maternal grand-mother as an infant, and she met her birth parents at an *herranza* when she was five years old, moving in with them when she was eight.

Two of the older boys of the biographies sample had more unusual households. Nilton (12), youngest in a sibling set of eight, participated in a living arrangement that is not uncommon for rural areas of Peru, where secondary schools exist only in the towns, not in sparsely populated annexes. He shared a house with two of his sisters (ages 18 and 15) as well as five nieces and nephews, children of older siblings. His parents regularly visited on weekends to bring food products from the farm. Braulio, nearly sixteen and the oldest of all the children in the biographies sample, was a live-in worker for an unrelated person who, through an agreement with Braulio's parents, took him under her protection and authority. This was Señora Pilar, whom we have already met in her role as worried mother of Yelitza and owner of El Puente restaurant and hostel. Braulio worked for her in exchange for room and board and the occasional "tip." His duties included waiting on customers in the restaurant, helping with the cooking and dishwashing, cleaning, running errands, taking care of animals and odd jobs as needed. This was his parents' second attempt to find a place in town where Braulio could live and finish his high-school education. A year earlier he had been placed with another family, but the arrangement collapsed. Under Señora Pilar's vigilant eye, he was walking a careful path.

Children growing up with brothers and sisters had to be looking to the adult world—their maternal and paternal aunts and uncles; siblings of their parents—in thinking about what these sometime accomplices, sometime competitors meant to them. Same-generation relatives connected by horizontal ties are tremendously important in the Andean context, even exceeding the significance of vertical ties between the generations (Lambert 1977, 11–15). These siblings, cousins, and sisters-and brothers-in-law, were within the realm of generalized reciprocity (Sahlins 1972), of helping each other without being asked (Orlove 1974). Although most Yauyos households operated as independent economies, we did find examples of brothers who were business partners (Elisa's father and uncle, for example, in a highly successful cattle business).

Yet conflicts could also erupt over the distribution of family resources and the obligations that siblings had to each other (Bolton and Bolton 1975; Van Vleet 2008, 69–74). With the commonality of early unions and long reproductive cycles, some older and younger siblings could be separated by twenty or more years, neither co-residing within the household nor developing a sense of closeness and attachment. Bellavista restaurant owner Jesusa said, with a sense of guilt: "I ought to share everything with my oldest sister, as if she were a mother, but I can't. I don't trust her. She gets angry. You can't talk to her." Amid a wide range of available kin, people in Andean communities made strategic choices and formed alliances selectively among their siblings, aunts, uncles, grandparents, and other relatives (Bolton and

Bolton 1975; de la Cadena 1980; Golte and Adams 1990; Leinaweaver 2007b, 2008, 2018).

Shifting Household Membership

Some of this selectivity and choice took the form of lending a child to another household, also called the "circulation of children" (Leinaweaver 2008; Van Vleet 2008). In a setting where daily tasks were roughly geared to match the strength, stamina, knowledge, and ability of all the participants, one common aim of this practice was achieving an age and gender balance in the household so as to ensure that the workload was evenly and viably distributed. If men and boys outnumbered women and girls, the female-marked tasks—small animal care, herding, gardening, spinning, weaving and care of clothing, food processing and preparation, childbearing and childcare—became overwhelming. In a pioneering study in the north central Andes, Oths (1999) documented how the malady known as "debilidad" (weakness) was especially likely to occur in women under these conditions (see also Larme and Leatherman 2003). Rather than adjust the division of labor, perhaps by shifting men's efforts into the women's column, households tended to adapt through temporary fostering or changes in their adult membership. They drew on a pool of relatives and ritual kin from which to choose: parents and parents-in-law, sisters and brothers, nieces and nephews, godchildren, or orphaned and supernumerary children.

Giving children away could also be a kindness to someone who lacked children altogether, in a context where children are valued and needed. Erick's (3) twin sister was sloughed off to a niece of his mother in Huancayo immediately after birth. The niece was childless after ten years of marriage. At the time of the twins' birth, their mother was thirty-five and was not living with their father. The household she presided over contained her two older children and two adult residents: her elderly mother and an uncle who were both still self-sufficient but might not be much longer. She did not feel capable to take on two infants. The solution she found ensured the baby's care, eased the birth mother's load, and gave the foster mother a new and desired role. Erick had been taken to visit his twin sister, and the plan was that someday they would be told the truth about their relationship.

At other times, lending a child to another household occurred when a caregiver felt incapable of properly fulfilling the responsibilities. Lorenza, an older mother, raised her son until he was eight years old. He was a passionate fisherman and would go almost every day to the river, sometimes staying very late, and sometimes taking a friend or two along. Lorenza began to worry that there could be an accident, maybe even a drowning, and that she would feel responsible. "It was impossible for me to go looking for him down by the river at midnight," she said. She began to take him on visits to a paternal uncle in a neighboring town.

The visits became longer and longer until it was finally agreed that the boy should live with the uncle. He adapted well (*acostumbrarse* is the concept Leinaweaver deploys, 2008) and became an apprentice in the uncle's hardware store. Lorenza also sent her oldest daughter, Anita (19), to Lima to work in domestic service. Anita had been hanging out with undesirable friends (*mala compañía*), and the mother's fear was that she would run away with them to the city. By placing her with an employer, someone known to Lorenza, she preempted that eventuality. Under the señora's custody, Anita finished secondary school and was on a path to a technical career. At Christmas and for the July–August holidays, both son and daughter returned to be with the family.

How much of a say do the children themselves have over whom they will live with (Leinaweaver 2007a)? Betty (14) spent the days in her parents' household, where she was an essential assistant to her mother, and spent her nights looking after her paternal grandmother, recently widowed, at the grandmother's house down the road. Removed for part of the day from her mother's incessant requests, she seemed quite happy with the arrangement. Dionisia (12) chose to do homework and sleep at her grandmother's house because her own was "too crowded." For younger children, being able to choose an alternative to their parents' roof depended upon finding another household willing to take them in. For adolescents, particularly adolescent girls, given their capacity to work and contribute, that was not difficult.

Long Cycles of Reciprocity

Part of the logic behind the circulation of children—and even behind having children in the first place—had to do with ensuring support in old age and having the assurance that the fruits of one's earthly labors will be passed on to heirs to whom there is an emotional connection and who have somehow earned the right to that inheritance. Children were old-age insurance where social security was essentially nonexistent for rural farming families (Vincent 2021). They were the continuation of family projects, valued not only as heirs but as companions. The children of old age were a recognized phenomenon. While some arrived as a surprise, like Yovana, born sixteen years after her closest sibling, others were part of a conscious strategy. Celso and his wife had children aged twenty-six, twenty-four, twenty-three, and fifteen. Their youngest child, Virginia, was five. Celso said: "We wanted to have her so we wouldn't be left alone (queríamos tenerla para no quedarnos solos)."

Children, in the eyes of yauyinos, affirmed the lives of their progenitors and caretakers and ideally reciprocated their care and company. Several of the adults in the biographies sample had returned to their rural origins because of the illness of parents or to help out with their farms and animals in parents' years of declining physical capacity. Most children in Yauyos grew up with grandparents, often granduncles and grandaunts as well, as part of their intimate social world, even if they did not live in the same house. Congruent with the patterns of mate selection and marriage that we have identified, parents-of-parents were nearby, possibly even next door. A frequent pattern was for the elderly grandparents to live in an annex while the adult children and grandchildren occupied a house in town. The youngsters might spend part of their school vacation on the farm with their grandparents, helping out and learning. Forging close ties between grandparents and grandchildren had the value of inuring them to the challenges of rural life, teaching them the skills they would need to make a success of it, and persuading them emotionally of the rewards of staying close by. The specter that haunted the rural towns of Peru was the possibility that all the young people would go off to the city and the assets accumulated through enormous effort by parents, grandparents, and earlier generations would end up unwanted and unused (Nué 2000).

Members of the older generation recalled how often parents would tie children to them through a mix of economic blackmail and moral coercion. Señora Raquel, telephone and internet magnate of Terrazas, was the youngest of nine. When she finished school, she had siblings and cousins living in Cañete and Lima that were willing and able to help her further her education in the city. But her mother "didn't want to let go of her (no la quería soltar)." She cared for her mother throughout her entire life.

> "You are the youngest daughter, who else can I be with?" my mother insisted. And I stayed. Sometimes I get really angry with my mother. I give her a bath and she looks beautiful. Then she goes to the bathroom and doesn't remember to lift up her skirt. Everything's dirty. I have to change her again. Sometimes she gets sick, she overeats, or she wanders away and dirties her clothes. I have to wash them. It's uncomfortable. But I say to myself: who else is going to take care of her? A stranger isn't going to show up and do it. So I just have to deal with it. And I have to put myself in her place. In the same way my children will care for me. They will do it if I have a long life, or at least that's what I think.

The parents we met tended to resign themselves to the new order as it affected their plans for the future and their thinking about how and where they would live out their final years. Aracely, administrator of the municipal restaurant in Terrazas, quoted her husband as saying, "If the kids want to take care of us in old age, that will be because they chose it. Meantime we two should be preparing ourselves for growing old." The theme was that children could not be forced to do what did not come from them voluntarily.

We end the chapter as we began, in a chat with Camila's father. Here, he imagined getting old:

> My only hope, they (his three children) are my bank account. That's why I'm betting on them. (Laughs) They'll pass me at least a sol. (Who will care

for you?) My family is the only possibility. In whatever way. Like we're caring for them now. When we're old it will be the two of us, God willing. I'll be a grandfather and I'll look after my wife. I'll look after her and she'll look after me. That's just the cycle of life, my brother. Now, if one of us should go prematurely, well, maybe I'll be the one that's left. I'll have to carry on for my children's sake. At least one out of the three will remember me. (Laughs again) Because I don't think I'll be so unlucky ("tan piña") that all three will forget and leave me on my own. One will take care of me. They'll provide me with something. Just like I always remember my own dad.

Conclusions

The rooms, patios, doorsteps, and neighboring walls in the rural towns of Yauyos were the spaces that contained and shaped the daily activities of children and adults. We saw in this chapter how houses were simple, practical, crowded with implements, lacking in luxuries, short on privacy. They were permeable to the larger environment: cold, heat, wind, rain, dust, morning light, enveloping nighttime darkness. The houses, sidewalks, streets, schoolgrounds, and plazas provided a framework for a first level of emplacement of the actors in Yauyos for the purposes of analyzing manifestations of care and agency that are associated with intimate, quotidian, and familial spaces. Confidently, the children themselves gave use and meaning to the places they occupied and often refashioned to their purposes.

Households everywhere are processes over time (Fortes 1958). In the Andes, and in Yauyos, this principle takes on a special meaning. Adults in Yauyos had both freedom and constraints as they worked through the progressive formation of families, their consolidation, and, in some cases, their dissolution. Several principles associated with classical kinship studies in Andean communities underlay their thinking and actions, yet some consecrated practices, such as liaisons involving pregnancies that in earlier times would have resulted in marriage, were being redefined. Connections with elderly parents, including relations between grandparents and grandchildren, were increasingly unpredictable. Observing how adults treated the rules with flexibility, children too experimented with living arrangements, some more than others. Those with numerous relatives in the hometown had the most freedom. Many children's core care providers were displaced or replaced during their childhood. Such movements appeared less traumatic than might be expected because most of the actors remained on the scene.

Children could visit, remember, and even go back and forth between one context and another. The movement of children between households through daily visits, prolonged stays, or informal adoptions was an expression of child agency as much as adult decision-making (Leinaweaver 2007a). Almost all the children had, or soon would have, siblings, yet the place they occupied in individual children's lives was wildly variable. As children moved about in familiar surroundings, their actions and engagements suggested many of the topics we will develop in the coming chapters: the heavy workloads and economic insecurity that created strains in family relations, the range of situations in which care was offered or denied, and the search for emotional satisfaction and closeness in valued relationships.

4

Economies of Care

What sustained the households, family groups, and individuals we have just met? We have shown how the houses and their surroundings were material spaces, endowed with meaning and social significance by their inhabitants. Their functioning obviously had a material base as well, one that was similarly overlaid with multiple layers of meaning. What livelihood strategies unspooled in the study sites? What implications did they have for children's care and agency? What was the meaning of work for the children of Yauyos, and what were they learning about the place of work in human life? This chapter addresses these questions.

In point of fact, everybody in Yauyos worked. Everyone was understood to be a contributor to the household they belonged to and to the community as a whole, channeled in various ways by gender roles, physical capacity, age, and personal inclination. In what follows, we describe the kinds of work done by the adults with whom children lived before exploring the economics of childhood in detail: both the costs of having children and the diverse ways that children recognized and reciprocated the investment being made in them.

In Yauyos, children were ubiquitous in activities within the household and beyond that had obvious implications for people's material conditions of life. What some might call "work" took just as much time as other activities such as school, play, exploration, idling, and simply "hanging out." Child development experts presume that children are naturally inclined to play and to resist the "chore curriculum" (Lancy 2008, 235) that adults seek to impose on them. Parents and grandparents in Yauyos held that children's contribution to the household economy was a long-term investment in their own futures. Some stood to inherit the house, farm, herds, and status of community members in good standing. Others were learning a trade or were part of a family business that they could perpetuate and grow. All, in principle, were learning a work ethic and the much-touted Andean value of industriousness. At the same time, the family's immediate survival often depended on children's contributions, a labor force that was unpaid and involuntary. Some of the most complicated questions raised by the field data concern children's interests: to what extent they coincided with the interests of adult caregivers, and when and how their own interests were being served.

The Economic Context

Our field data reveal a wide range of livelihoods in the towns of Yauyos, in line with contemporary rural Andean communities in general (Asensio 2023; Diez 2022; Mayer 2003). While agriculture and stock raising dominated the economy, twelve of the thirty-two households in the biographies sample took no direct part in it. These included men with technical skills that allowed them to operate workshops—soldering, electronics repair, carpentry, mechanics—or more advanced training that gave them access to local government contracts on projects involving infrastructure, such as installing electrical cables. A couple of men were teachers and another pair worked as miners. The women in nonfarming households worked as municipal secretaries, teachers, or ran small businesses, such as a hair salon, a restaurant, or lodgings for tourists. Several of these households were new arrivals in town who aspired eventually to be granted access to land and pastures by being admitted to membership in the *comunidad campesina*. On the flip side, seventeen of the men (fathers, stepfathers, grandfathers) and fifteen of the women (mothers, grandmothers) in the biographies households had farming and stock raising as their principal occupations. In varying amounts and proportions, they produced and marketed cheese, honey, meat, and live cattle along with agricultural produce. A few—three women and two men in the biographies households—worked as day laborers and herders.

Even this complicated picture underrepresents the true diversity and complexity of the households' income streams. Both men and women had many ways of complementing the earnings from their main occupation. Many households combined farming with running a bodega in town. Jeferson's mother, for example, staked her tiny herd of sheep out on the hillside each morning and, from her shop, kept track of them through the day with a pair of binoculars. Women earned money selling snacks, taking in laundry, or weaving and embroidering items of traditional clothing. Men might take temporary construction jobs in town, in a neighboring district, or in the city. Households might be pooling the earnings of resident adults beyond the main couple, and they might receive contributions from persons not living there: children that had grown and moved away, for example, or absent fathers that were paying child support. Some activities were one-offs; for example, participating as an extra in a telenovela filmed on communal lands. Some of them were hardly even nameable; for example, clowning around for tips during the preambles to a cattle branding. Some were illegal (cattle poaching, stealing standing crops in the fields, fishing out of season) or of questionable legality (guiding high-rolling European hunters on expeditions for trophies of protected Andean species).[1] Men employed in the mines were suspected of smuggling minerals out when opportunities arose. Workers and authorities in local government offices might be taking bribes for contracts for public works or access to decision-makers.[2]

One factor that contributed to this notable diversification of income sources was the seasonality of the agricultural economy. Most crops were planted in the weeks leading up to the rainy season—November to March, most years—and would be harvested and sold in the months after. Seasonality was also an issue for the households that had restaurants or rented rooms to visitors. The rainy season was a metaphorical dry season for tourism-related businesses. Roads became clogged with mud, and landslides threatened. Tourists came to Yauyos in Semana Santa (Easter week) and for Independence holidays and the *fiestas patronales* (town saint's days) that were concentrated in late July and early August. Fiesta season was a time when a number of men picked up extra income as part of the musical groups that provided live entertainment in far-flung towns. For women, it offered opportunities to sell their handicrafts, set up food vending stands, or send the children out with snacks for sale.

Although men's and women's occupations tended to be gender marked (Harris 1978; Isbell 1985, 99; Allen 2002), and although they operated to a large extent in separate, parallel economies, it was often difficult to distinguish between the mother's and the father's economic contributions to the same household. Haydee's family was prosperous. They operated the largest bodega in town, with the mother in charge. They had a pickup truck that was used for restocking the store in their closest big city, Huancayo, and to offer a letter and package delivery service along the route. Haydee's father made the weekly drive. (We did not observe any women driving vehicles in Yauyos in 2008.) In addition, the couple owned a bus that provided a regular passenger service to Huancayo. They were members of the *comunidad campesina* and had farmland and herds. The source of much of their property seemed to have been her family.

Insofar as the biographies sample reflects a more general situation, about half of parents, men and women alike, were routinely out of the house for most of the day and for most of what they did to provide for the household. These were the farmers, those caring for dairy herds who often did their milking and cheese-making in the field, and the day laborers, together with salaried employees subject to a time clock in local governments and businesses such as the Aventura Andina resort. But many mothers and fathers worked at home, in a room or two dedicated as a store, storeroom, or workshop. They interacted with their children throughout the day, limited only by the children's attendance at school.

The evidence does not suggest a direct relation between household income and the care that children were receiving. Too many other factors intervened; for example, the one just mentioned, how present the parents were in the home. All rural Peruvians were vulnerable to natural disasters, and to human-made disasters caused by adverse policies. Animals could die, crops could fail, and the price of commodities could fluctuate. Everyone used the same rocky, potholed roads, suffered the same electricity blackouts, drank the same questionable water, and felt the same disconnection from the wider world. Children in more prosperous families may have been better dressed for the cold, but they used the same schools and playgrounds as all the rest. They had more opportunities to travel to the cities bordering Yauyos, and they might ride in the family car or pickup instead of the public bus or van, but their daily lives were shaped far from city lifeways, like everyone else's.

In fact, some of the most prosperous families had the hardest-working children. This may seem contradictory, but it fits with Katz's findings from a mixed farming and pastoral community in Sudan (2004, 65). There, children of wealthier families started working at younger ages and worked longer hours than the children of poorer families. They did so because of the presence of assets: herds, shops, farmland, vehicles, and tools that afforded many ways of using the labor power of children. In the biographies sample of Yauyos, the children that were most free to wander about town and play were Dina (9) and her three younger siblings. Their parents, day-laborers and odd jobbers, had nothing going on where the children's participation would be required or even possible.

The Costs of Having Children

An extensive literature from economics to philosophy explores adults' perceptions of the economic, time, and opportunity costs of having children (Lancy 2008; Folbre 2008), sometimes weighed against perceptions of children's economic utility or symbolic value (Zelizer 1985). Inspired by these precedents, we asked parents: What does it cost to raise a child in Yauyos? How much do they spend on their children and what do they spend it on? Though specific amounts were hard to calculate, the parents were clear about the types of expenditures they had to be prepared for. The first items that came to mind were a trio: food, education, and clothing.

Although kitchen gardens were ubiquitous, a large swath of the population relied on the market for most of their food. Locally produced items were available at prices lower than in the city. Much came from outside the province, however, at prices elevated by transportation costs and vendors' profits. Infants were almost universally breastfed in Yauyos, but once past infancy, they shared the family's table food. We will discuss the dynamics of access to food and nutrition in chapter 5; here, suffice it to say that food expenditures were a major burden for some families and a touchpoint where parents could practice austerity. Some children complained of receiving little more than noodles; others protested when they saw no trace of meat on their plates.

Clothing was charged with symbolic and emotional significance (see chapter 8), tied in part to its cost. This was an expense directly linked to education. Once children reached school age, families prioritized acquiring enough pieces of the mandatory school uniform for each child to appear to comply with the

FIGURE 4.1. Children in their school uniforms.

rules (figure 4.1). At the outset of the school year, parents would mull over whether children would reuse last year's uniform, inherit that of a sibling, or need a new one. A new uniform was a way for parents to show their pleasure at their children's progress in school. Quality was variable, but the complete uniform might cost anywhere from S/.70 to S/.100 (at the time of fieldwork, around $25–35 US).[3] To save money, canvas or plastic shoes were frequently substituted for the regulation black leather.

Other costs associated with educating children involved school supplies, fees for membership in the parents' association, and the expense of outings and special events (see Anderson and Leinaweaver 2023; Leinaweaver and Anderson 2024). Parents were handed a list at the start of the year indicating what they were expected to buy: paper, pens and pencils, drawing and coloring implements, notebooks, rulers, erasers, pencil sharpeners, workbooks, and textbooks. A complete set was not always feasible. Nilton's elderly parents, in deep economic distress after both experienced major health problems, managed to provide no more than a couple of notebooks for him to begin his first year of secondary school. Younger students borrowed, shared, or simply went without some supplies; older students could copy lesson materials from their schoolmates or use the school library. Parents estimated that they spent about S/.40 ($13) per year per child on supplies and fees. A reasonable budget for the entire school package—uniforms, supplies, activities, and fees—seemed to be around S/.150 ($50) per child per year. Silvia's (14) stepfather said he saved money throughout the three summer months in order to have the S/.600 ($200) he needed to launch his four children at the start of the school year in April. His monthly salary as a municipal government employee was S/.700 ($230).

Other costs were less predictable. Children's health problems (discussed in chapter 5), and the expenditures parents made to resolve them, could vary widely. Diarrhea and severe coughs caused some parents to rush their children off to Huancayo or Cañete, while other parents simply went to the local pharmacy and purchased over-the-counter medicines that had been useful in similar situations before. No planning or budgeting could really be done for these events; as they occurred, families had to resolve them with the resources they had available in the moment.

Parents rarely mentioned toys in their reflections on the expenses associated with having children. As Oscar's mother said: "He plays with toys that he invents in his imagination" (see Anderson 2024). Children made many of their toys out of objects at hand: tops, for example, from seeds and bits of cord. Marbles and chipitaps were traded or won from opponents. Parents might make a spur-of-the-moment purchase from an itinerant vendor on a market day when feeling flush. Knock-off Barbie dolls, volleyballs or soccer balls, tea sets, plastic jungle animals, or jump ropes might arrive that way, or they might come as presents from visiting relatives. Big-ticket items like radios were rare, available only to the very fortunate. Leoncio (11), raised by his grandparents, had an old bicycle. He was promised a replacement by his grandmother the next time she went to Huancayo but, in the end, she had the old one repaired and instead bought him a DVD player, financed with the help of his maternal uncles.

Reaching a position where they could pay for their own school uniforms and supplies was a major stepping-stone on the way to maturity for older children and adolescents. This was the most frequent reason given for them to launch out independently, working in one of the neighboring cities during summer vacation months. But even younger children were arguably making progress toward paying their way in the household economy. The remainder of this chapter describes the many ways they accomplished that.

Children Working and Learning

Many attempts have been made to categorize and quantify the work that rural children do in Peru (Alarcón 2011; Rodríguez and Vargas 2009). Outside observers, and probably the children themselves, would label as work most or all of the activities of Yauyos children in support of their families. Their parents and caregivers would choose a term closer to "helping" (see Orlove 2002, 101–107; Leinaweaver 2008, 92–93). This term draws children's activities into a domestic, voluntary, social sphere and away from the idea of labor. Lancy's phrase, the "chore curriculum" (2008, 235), underscores the learning that children are expected to do in the course of realizing various tasks, as they resolve adults' progressively greater demands and as they gain in age, size, strength, experience, and mental capacity (see also García Rivera 2007, 126; Paradise and Rogoff 2009, 102, 104). Lancy expands the chore curriculum concept to encompass a range of graded learning experiences that correspond to different arenas where children's labor is required, like the "errand curriculum," "cow curriculum," and "fishing curriculum" (2008, 235–271). Yauyos offers yet others: the "mixed herding curriculum," the "childcare curriculum," the "shopkeeping curriculum," the "food cart curriculum." For the very youngest, there was the "brushwood curriculum" and the "guinea pig curriculum."

Though Yauyos parents did not appeal to the concept explicitly, they understood children's work to be empowering. Completing the curriculum would enable children eventually to become competent, self-sufficient adults. It was a parent's and caretaker's job to make that happen. Laziness was not an option. As one of the town mayors said: "There are no children here that can devote all their time to playing." The same man described children aged seven and up as "auxiliary workers." In the most urbanized of our field sites, Yauyos City, field-worker Jhon observed the active movement of people beginning before 7:00 A.M.: lugging baskets of bread for sale, carrying bags, pushing carts and wheelbarrows, all moving their merchandise and tools to the points where they would start the workday. Many had children alongside.

Yauyos households were the scenario for these and many other housekeeping activities, and Yauyos adults had the same difficulties as adults in other contexts to name and describe their domestic labors (see, for example, DeVault 1991). Even more difficult was describing the actions of their children as they became incorporated into those labors. All the children contributed to some degree to the day-to-day tasks of maintaining the household. Sweeping floors (usually hard-packed dirt), clearing away the enameled dishes from the table, collecting household trash in a bucket, folding up the blankets on beds to start the day: their very routineness made them invisible. Adults especially tended to overlook the contributions of younger children whose collaboration was sporadic and spontaneous, rather than a response to commands or requests, and which looked a lot like play (see figure 4.2). Two mothers insisted that their children did little or nothing even as they were performing tasks in full view of the interviewer. In one case it was Elisa (6), who was delightedly stomping on a heap of dried fava beans to aid in removing their husks. The other case was Chino (14), who practically ran the family store in addition to washing clothes and foraging for food for the guinea pigs. Even as he was attending to customers, his mother was saying that children were not really useful until they were sixteen or so.

Children's contributions to meal preparation were notable. Cooking depended almost everywhere on managing wood-burning stoves and open fires and, though

FIGURE 4.2. Sweeping and "helping."

not in charge of the stove, by eight or nine, children were expected to be kitchen assistants. Mirabel started even younger, at age six, as helper to her older sister. For years the two sisters took turns preparing the family meals and helping their mother with occasional catering contracts and gigs in lodging houses. Meal preparation might involve killing chickens or even a lamb, as in the case of Aurora (13), who held the animal down while her mother dispatched it. Field-workers Chiri and Gaby shared meals with various families in Terrazas, and they observed many occasions when all hands were drafted into meal preparation. Whoever was around at the time might be at the stove (most likely the mother), another family member chopping firewood (most likely the father), another grinding garlic, another chopping vegetables, and another running to the bodega for a last-minute purchase. During the week of festivities for Terrazas's town anniversary, eleven-year-old Yeny's parents were busy making and selling snacks to the crowds. The field-workers were paying guests for meals in their household at the time, and they showed up at the appointed hour for afternoon refreshments. Yeny was perched on a high stool, helping her mother stir the purple corn pudding she had on the stove. "Get the sugar and herbs for Gaby's and Chiri's tea," her father ordered her. As if divining what her parents may have been thinking privately, Yeny said, "You had to come just when I'm busiest (Vienen justo cuando estoy ocupada)."

Washing clothes—as we saw with Camila and her mother (chapter 3)—was the activity that was most visible to caretakers. It was the task they could easily point to when asked about children's contributions. Here too, by age eight or nine, children could be expected to be washing their own clothes and perhaps those of other family members (see figure 4.3). Renzo (10), as he changed into a sweater, asked his mother to wash his sweatshirt and pants. "Don't be a pest," she said, "you're too old for that. Instead of being out playing on the street you should have been washing." She said that all her children washed their own clothes from eight years of age on up "but other kids do it from the time they're 6. My kids are little lazybones (vaguitos)." Sometimes it seemed that no matter how much children did, it was never enough. It only pointed to how much more they could be doing.

Age, birth order, capability, and, to an extent, willingness were defining criteria for task assignment. Pamela first began taking her father's lunch out to him in the field when she was five, even though her younger brother Carlos did it only when he was six, she said, because "he didn't walk as well" as she did. Gender had little relevance to tasks assigned during childhood but became far more important in adolescence. This was in part because adolescent boys had expanding opportunities to work for pay outside the home. It also reflected how adolescent girls became increasingly valuable as mothers' assistants, especially if there were young children in the household.[4] Teenage girls could be handed the whole package: managing younger siblings, the household, and a home-based business. (The care of other children—one of the most demanding of children's home-based duties—will be explored in chapter 6.) As a rule, having older sisters was a boon for boys. Jeferson (10) took care of his school uniform, socks, underwear, and tennis shoes while his sisters washed the rest of his clothes. Pascual (3) had Gladis (14) to wash his clothes, walk him to his preschool, and take him out to play. His brother Franklin (10) also benefited noticeably from Gladis's role as caretaker for Pascual and sister Valery's (17) role as house cleaner and general administrator. He had very light duties at home.

FIGURE 4.3. A child washing clothes.

Children's Economic Participation

All children worked, but they did not all have the same duties nor work to the same degree. The type of economy that provided their families' livelihoods greatly influenced whether, how, and how much the children contributed. If their parents and caregivers had complicated lives as part of the productive economy of Yauyos and

Peru, so did the children. Their activities were diverse, sometimes seasonal, sometimes opportunistic, sometimes enjoyable. We have divided them in four categories: herding, farm work, assistance with family businesses, and striking out on their own. A single child could shift among the categories, even combining several on the same day.

Herding: Cattle, Sheep, the Occasional Goat, and Children in Charge

Pamela (9) pastured her family's herd of six sheep and one goat, all seven days of the week. As a rule, children's herding work could be combined with school attendance, and Pamela was no exception: on school days her mother took the animals out in the morning and staked them to a spot in the family's holdings, a mixture of pasture, croplands, and eucalyptus stand some fifteen minutes' walk from town. In the afternoons, Pamela was tasked with supervising the herd and bringing it home to the corral for the night. She often went with her younger brother Carlos (6). They climbed trees, snacked on fruit that grew in the area, took naps, chatted, and did homework. On weekends she might be assigned to take the herd farther away and to stay with it from morning to evening. Expeditions to pasture could also be occasions to meet up with friends. Field-worker Ignacio followed Junior (8) out with his herd of sheep and goats one morning in Los Caminos. As they reached the edge of town, they came across Alejandra (9) and her grandmother, taking out the cows, goats, and sheep. A few steps farther down the road they met up with Iris (16) and Katherine (11) with their family's herd of cows and goats.

Yauyos had, and continues to have, free-range animals. Though some people farmed alfalfa and other forage crops, this was a supplement for use when pastures were drying up. For most of the year, animals had to be taken out daily to areas where they would have grass and water. Children as young as six or seven could be trusted to take a small herd of sheep out to a nearby pasture, keep them in tow as they fed and watered, drive them home, and tie them up or install them in their corral. Cattle were entrusted to older children, as they were harder to control and had to be prevented from invading neighbor's fields and from taking a misstep on narrow paths and almost vertical hillsides. Often the child in charge would make decisions about where the animals could get sufficient food and where they should go for water. Children motivated the animals to move, turn, and stick together with their voices (shouting), switches made from sticks and branches, and stones that they threw at the animals' flanks (see figure 1.4).

Where families had milk cows, children were assistants in the adult tasks of milking, cheese-making, and transporting the milk and cheese back to town. Oscar (10) helped his mother with the family's three cows, all of which had recently given birth. The herd had spent the night in a large field outside the town, and Oscar's first action was to chivy all the animals over from one section to another, through a fence of bushes and dried branches. Once the calves had nursed for a few minutes, Oscar's mother told him to take the calves to the other section so that she could finish milking the mothers. This he accomplished with cries of "Sho, sho" and many small pebbles. While one cow was being milked, the others wandered away. Oscar ran wildly from place to place, attempting to keep order, even as his mother reprimanded him for being slack at his job. His little brother Agustín (2) was part of the group, however, and Oscar took moments off to chase and play with him. For milking cows, stabling the herd at the end of the day might involve putting muzzles or restraints on the calves so that they would not nurse at night. This was also a children's task, even though the calves were strong, and the children might have to accomplish it amid butting and falls.

Stock-raising in Yauyos involved transhumance, seasonal movement of herds between high-altitude and low-altitude pastures tied to the rains. Although it was not for the very young or faint-hearted, many children looked forward to being allowed to participate in the seasonal shift to the highlands. Violeta accompanied Elisa's family on the first leg of the drive from their home base in Pastizales. This was one of the most financially secure families in the community, and the drive involved several dozen head of cattle. The trek took some four hours and entailed climbing three mountain slopes until finally reaching forty-four hundred meters above sea level. Señora Úrsula explained to Violeta that the beasts must be dominated by their human owners. Besides sticks and stones, the tools for so doing were whistling, shouting, and cursing. All three of the children—six-year-old Elisa, ten-year-old Máximo, and thirteen-year-old Esperanza—entered into the task enthusiastically. They whistled to keep cows from straying from the upward path or making their way down into ravines. They shouted words they would never dare to speak at home: "Avanza mierda, qué te pasa carajo (move, piece of s—, what the f—is wrong with you!)". Even little Elisa yelled, "vaca de mierda, avanza (you s—y cow, get moving)" without anyone raising an eyebrow. The humans and animals emerged at last onto a vast plain covered in frost. From there the cattle would continue on alone, relying on memory from years past.

Care and maintenance of animals in a system of communal pasture lands required branding them so that families could track their herds. This was done at *herranzas*, cattle-branding parties, like the one mentioned in chapter 2. Here too was an opportunity for children's participation. Seemingly fearless Flor (10) and her sister Charo (7) were famous for their ability with the lasso. They had taught themselves, and they were frequently called on to use their skill in *herranzas*. Sometimes they could work from a perch on a fence, but on other occasions they were on the ground among the animals and might have to run from charging cows and bulls to shelter in the crowd or an outbuilding. Field-worker Li witnessed their performance at a relatively small and orderly *herranza* involving the herd that belonged to Carolina and her husband:

> After all the guests had eaten, Flor and her younger sister Charo help lasso most of the cows. Some of the adults tried but couldn't do it. Instead, they busied themselves with fetching the ropes back to the girls who took charge of the entire herd, both cows and heifers. Once Flor and Charo

70   CARE AND AGENCY

had gotten their rope around an animal's horns, they shouted, "Tía Carolina!" to let her know that it was ready. Carolina grabbed the cow and called over the vet and her husband. Carolina cut the tail, and her husband held the animal while the vet perforated the ears to insert earrings. He vaccinated each animal and had it drink some water with medication for parasites. Carolina then dribbled a few drops of beer over its back and let it go. The same procedure was applied with the entire herd. Flor and Charo were an essential part of the evening's work. When it was finished, all those present congratulated them on the good job they had done. (Field notes, Li)

For their efforts, Flor and Charo might receive a *propina* (tip) from the *herranza*'s sponsors or be served especially generous plates of food; they could also bathe in the applause and recognition they got in local lore.

Animal biology and the demands of animal care were a fundamental part of the chore curriculum. Children collected food for domestic animals. They might be seen hauling large sacks of corn husks or alfalfa from fields to town, perhaps with the help of a horse or burro. Gathering leaves and grass for guinea pigs or rabbits was a frequent activity for many, accessible even to the youngest. In fact, there was a seamless transition from the days when infants went to the fields and pastures, riding on their mothers' backs, to the toddler years, when they might entertain themselves there with sticks and pebbles, to the moment when they would be entrusted with what adults considered entry-level children's tasks in animal care (figure 4.4). The stock raising, farming, and domestic economies sometimes converged in a way that epitomized the interdependence of all ages, genders, and generations. The field team accompanied one family on a day trip to high-altitude pastures to collect firewood and guano, an essential fertilizer where synthetic substitutes were scarce and expensive. They reserved the use of the municipality's pickup truck for the day and took it in the spirit of a family outing. Adults, older children, and the field-workers filled sacks with animal droppings while the younger ones assembled bundles of firewood. On the way home, they left the sacks of guano off at the various fields the family was cultivating.

Farm Work
Preparing the soil, planting crops, fertilizing, weeding, irrigating, and harvesting were heavy work in the mountainous Andes. Strong arms were needed to maintain the fences, terraces, and irrigation canals. Tools were adapted for working on steep slopes, in small irregular fields, on hard, dry soil strewn with rocks. Two essential tools were the *chakitaklla* (Quechua: foot-plow, hoe) and the *barreta* (steel bar) for digging holes, chipping off rocks, and breaking up clods of dirt. This was considered men's work and usually involved going out early in the morning and staying the entire day. Producing food and feeding others are closely linked to adulthood and personhood in the Andes (Harvey 1998, 77), yet adolescents could

FIGURE 4.4. A child's affection for a baby goat.

take on that role, as did Pepe (14). Both his parents and grandparents owned land, and he was the only boy in his generation. His father, a history teacher in the local school, farmed part-time. His paternal uncle was an agricultural engineer, a specialist in irrigation systems, who provided technical advice on using scarce water and innovating new crops. Pepe participated in planting: corn, alfalfa, and, more recently at the time of our study, avocado trees. He collected alfalfa to feed the guinea pigs. From age seven to eight he helped his grandmother with farming and pasturing. Working in the fields, in contrast to herding, created a risk of missing school. Field-worker Diego ran across another young adolescent one morning, clearly not in school during school hours. He told Diego that he had stayed home because of a cough, but in the afternoon he was out in the field, helping his mother break up clods and level the soil to get ready for planting.

Pepe's other farming-related tasks pointed to the important roles that especially competent and dedicated young people might play. He represented his family group in the organization (*mita*, the turn-taking system; Gelles 2000; Gose 1994) that determined water distribution. Every two weeks, he manipulated the controls: ("Voy cuando me toca el agua, cada 15 días creo que es. (I go when it's my turn to have water released, every 15 days I think)." All the communities had irrigation systems, and one task that older children could be given involved opening and closing the gates in the canals according to the distribution of water agreed on by the organization (Rasmussen 2015). Subject to the programming of turns and hours, this might involve going out late at night or before dawn. Dangers included pumas, the supernatural threat of *condenados* (malevolent spirits, to be discussed in chapter 7; see Fourtané 2015), and real-life human beings with bad intentions; these were considered bad times to be out and about.

Young people had other farming-adjacent tasks as well. Like many other children and adolescents in Los Caminos, Pepe was part of the crews of underage workers that showed up on the plaza when there were trucks to be loaded with sacks of produce. At age thirteen to fourteen he began hiring himself out to work in others' fields. The adolescent Diego encountered playing hooky from school was known to help his mother or father when they were hired as day-laborers to herd cattle. Younger children could be employed as scarecrows when birds attacked the harvest, and they could fit into the security system in other ways. When crops were ready to be harvested, theft was a concern. One option was for owners to leave their house in town and spend the nights in a distant field in a makeshift hut or secondary dwelling. Another option was to involve children as lookouts. Oscar (10), who helped his mother with milking, was commissioned by her to go out to their alfalfa field and check on the state of things when she heard a rumor that someone had attempted to steal part of the crop.

Working in Family Businesses

After herding and farming, the next most common job for children was helping out with a family business. Most often these were bodegas (see figure 4.5). Located in a room, section, or entire first floor of the family home, bodegas were general stores selling a wide variety of dry goods; clothing; over-the-counter medicines; housewares; supplies such as toilet paper, simple tools, sewing notions; and foodstuffs. They offered soft drinks, bottled water, beer, and sometimes other alcoholic drinks. In bins and baskets, they displayed assorted vegetables and fruits, not always in the freshest state. They stocked a variety of candy, chewing gum, and packaged cookies and crackers. Some sold bread, and some offered eggs, chicken, meat, and fish. Most had a refrigerator, although, given the unreliability of the electricity supply, cold conservation was not guaranteed. There were sometimes tables and chairs for consumers to occupy, especially men who came in the evening to purchase beer. Some bodegas were well stocked, chock full of an amazing array of products. Others were small and basic and only opened when a potential customer knocked on a window or door.

Children's tasks in such stores were to monitor people entering and leaving, respond to requests for items off the shelves behind the counter, make sales (including counting pieces and weighing some products), and provide change. They had to memorize the location of various items, know the prices, and do the arithmetic for charging the customers. Customers sometimes bought on credit, and children had to know how and where to note purchases, dates, and amount owed. Most purchases were small, and many of the customers were themselves children, sent on errands by their parents. Children that were helping around the store were

ECONOMIES OF CARE

FIGURE 4.5. Children at a bodega.

thus often dispatching items to their friends and schoolmates. Children could also be employed as a kind of delivery service for their parents' stores. This kind of work, too, was compatible with school; there were always stretches of down time when customers were few and far between, and, as long as they kept track of who entered and exited the space, children, standing at the counter, could do their homework. They might be distracted from their assignments by the television on the counter or mounted on the wall, the sound at maximum volume to attract the attention of passersby and create an atmosphere of conviviality for groups that might gather to partake of a favorite telenovela or a soccer game.

Children that showed a talent and a taste for business could quickly be given broad responsibilities. One of the bodegas in Los Caminos was well supplied and relatively prosperous; it had a monopoly on the soccer jerseys that the local school team wore. On one of the town's fiesta days, this was the only bodega open, and Wilson (14) was at the helm. Field-worker Gabriela dropped in, looking to buy potatoes. There had been no electricity for two days, and the fruit and vegetables were beginning to smell. The floor was strewn with garbage. A cat was batting a ball of crumpled paper in one of the display cases. Wilson was barely visible in the dim light from the open door. He said he was alone. The store owners—his sister, her husband, and their two daughters—had gone to Lima. It seemed from the conversation that it was a frequent occurrence for him to run the store on his own.

Certain features of each locality also shaped what kind of work children did. In Nor Yauyos, for example, because of its tourist attractions, children participated in family enterprises that involved renting out space to visitors. The height of tourist season coincided with midyear vacation from school, freeing Hamilton (13) and Berta (9) to drum up business by going to the plaza when the bus arrived and urging tourists as they disembarked to rent the furnished rooms in their home. The pair's principal contribution was running errands around town to pick up food and other items that the tourists requested.

The consensus among adults was that young children should not expect payment for help they gave to family members nor for minor favors they did for nonfamily. This value was made clear in the breach. Guille's mother was acutely embarrassed, she told the field-workers, because a neighbor had commented how he asked Guille (7) to help him with a simple task—sweeping the sidewalk outside his store—and Guille said that first he had to be paid. His mother was appalled at his aberrant love of money, chalking it up to an early incident when an aunt liked to entertain the family by offering Guille 10 céntimos to dance for them. Children who helped family were occasionally given pin money, but the two things were not overtly linked. Mariano (11), for example, washed dishes and sometimes helped his aunt with herding. He said he bought chewing gum with the money she gave him from time to time.

If children provided more sustained help to distant relatives or nonfamily members, their parents or guardians might receive some recompense. A complicated case is that of Alejandra (9), who was left in the charge of her maternal grandmother when her mother ran away with a lover. Overwhelmed, the grandmother sent the girl to live with a niece, the teacher in charge of Alejandra's class. Alejandra took on a heavy load of housework and herding. At first she was getting a small payment (the teacher had a steady monthly income), but the grandmother arranged for the money to come to her instead, on the grounds that "she needed it." The grandmother may have felt justified when she, in effect, replaced the support she would have gotten from her absent daughter with income brought in by her granddaughter.

Striking Out on Their Own

Working for money was a logical next step for many children as their world expanded to relationships beyond the family. Many had experience selling food items that were prepared at home, especially at sports events and community celebrations. Yeny (11) remembered how she and her brother had sold toasted corn, purple corn drink (*chicha morada*), and stuffed potatoes (*papa rellena*) on the street when they were younger. They earned a tip out of the profits. As the two oldest in the family, they were called on to help in ways that subsequent siblings were spared, given an improvement in family fortunes. This kind of work was part of a process where parents (mothers, in most cases) initially sent their children out to sell items and bring back the earnings but, over time, reduced both their involvement and their claims over profits. Vanessa (10) sold popcorn with a dedication and on a scale that surpassed those of other children. Her mother made the popcorn, but Vanessa paid her for the ingredients, bagging the popcorn in portions of two different sizes that she sold from a big basket. On ordinary days, she would sit with it outside her home, and no one could pass by without being reminded to buy a bag. One day during her town's anniversary celebrations, the demand was brisk, and she had taken in almost S/.25 ($8).

Children found niches where they could earn money by providing personal services. In a household of one of the poorest families of Los Caminos, Dominga (15), the oldest of three children, made a critical contribution to the budget. She worked as a domestic in the school principal's household during the week, also attending school, and she hired herself out as a herder on the weekends. Another hard-working young adolescent was Nilton (12). He offered his services as a porter and could often be seen waiting for customers on a bench in the plaza of Yauyos City, next to the bus stop. He worked regularly for a local distributor delivering various products to stores and restaurants around town: chickens, potatoes, eggs, and others. He went to school in the morning, worked in the afternoon, earned some S/.10 ($3) daily and gave, he said, some of the money to his father.

The dynamics of the local economies gave rise to a certain number of pickup jobs. They were relatively abundant in Los Caminos, with its active traffic in farm produce destined for Cañete and Lima. Trucks arrived at the plaza ready to be loaded with corn, fava beans, and potatoes, whatever might be in harvest season. They would draw an immediate crowd of adolescents, as we see in an extract from Gabriela's field notes:

> Isaac and another boy, about fifteen, were carrying huge sacks of fava beans in from the field. The girls, Iris (16) and a friend, were decanting them into smaller sacks for loading on the truck. Henry had been carrying sacks of corn. He stripped part of the husks and stems away from the cobs before loading them into a sack, which he then emptied onto the bed of the truck. Isaac and his friend were obviously struggling under the weight of the sacks of beans that they hoisted over their shoulders. Each brought one in and immediately went back to the field for another. Still, they laughed and challenged each other to keep up a running pace. Iris and the other girl, some years older, were exchanging jokes with the driver and assistants in charge of the truck. The girls were openly flirtatious; the men were brazenly provocative. (Field notes, Gabriela)

Several of the children in the biographies sample had histories of school-vacation jobs that took them away from home. Often they worked for relatives or at jobs arranged by family members. The work seemed to be welcomed and was frequently orchestrated by the children themselves. In the summer prior to the fieldwork (that is, from December or January to March of 2008), Gladis (14) and her sister were in Lima doing housework for a relative of a Terrazas neighbor.

Aurora (13) was in Cañete, helping an aunt care for her baby and doing farm work. Rufina (15) was a nanny in Lima. Nilton (12) was a watchman at a car park in Lima, while living with a sister in the working-class district of Villa El Salvador. All of his older siblings also worked during the summers in Ica, Cañete, or Lima. Isaac (12), housed by a paternal aunt, worked washing car windows at stoplights, as a ticket-taker on a bus, and at sundry odd jobs. For many children and adolescents throughout the province, especially girls that could be employed in domestic service, their summer jobs began at early ages (Anderson 2007). Gladis was only eight when she spent a summer "helping" an aunt in exchange for clothes.

Even older children earning money considered themselves part of their families' economies. We did not hear of children saving up to satisfy a desire for a bicycle or some electronic item, not even trendy clothes or sneakers.[5] Summer job earnings covered school costs that parents would otherwise have had to pay. In fact, seven-year-old Guille's sin seems not to have been solely that he wanted a tip in exchange for minor services, but that he showed no intention of sharing whatever he earned. Quite the contrary; his mother confided that he had a habit of taking money from her purse or the cash drawer of the restaurant she managed. He was proving to be incapable of putting the interests of his family above his own.

Conclusions

This chapter has documented the complexity of household economies in Yauyos, the uncertainty underlying people's efforts to put together a viable income base, and children's role in it all. A farm and livestock were rarely sufficient to sustain a family. A variety of income streams had to be added, some associated with adult male household members, others with adult female members, and yet others with children, especially older children and adolescents. For several households, agriculture had dropped out of their income stream altogether. Whatever their economic base, not all Yauyos households were equally poor, and a few were relatively prosperous, yet all operated within a context of overarching scarcity of resources and opportunities.

In rural economies of the Andes, children's labor is—unapologetically, unproblematically—one of the family's assets. Performing a variety of chores—pretty much whatever parents and other close elders requested, including self-care, childcare, and animal care—was all normalized as part of a "proper childhood" (Boyden 1997). Children are also the motive behind some, at least, of families' strategies of accumulation. Children built their own capital funds involving livestock, tools, exchange relationships, and a reputation for responsibility, good judgment, and industriousness. Various practices, such as endowing young children with starter herds as gifts from parents, grandparents, or godparents, channeled them toward acquiring the skills needed for prospering in the rural economy and continuing the lifestyle of their forebears.

This chapter has also revealed the substantial scope of children's agency as they performed their various tasks. They had wide berth in deciding how to carry out most chores. Children could and did combine play with work, and most of what they did was not under the direct vigilance of adults. In fact, many seemed to acquire a taste for work and felt a pride in what they did. Several children branched out entrepreneurially with businesses of their own. Older children could decide when they wanted to migrate in search of new working experiences or hire themselves out for a wage locally, although their caregivers continued to have a claim on those wages and how they were spent.

The evidence invites serious reflection on the potential conflicts between children's interests and the interests of their care providers. There were wide differences in the quality of food, clothing, health care, education, and opportunities to travel that the various children received from their parents and guardians. Children had little or no negotiating power over the use of the family budget, though many of them contributed to it. Furthermore, we have offered relatively benign descriptions of children and adolescents helping out around the house, farm, and family business. These descriptions match what we observed, but we also note that they can veer toward abuse and exploitation. In subsequent chapters we consider this issue further: who protects children against their caregivers when their interests clash?

5

Ecologies of Care

Dionisia (12) appeared one day with a sore on her upper lip. She explained that "a spider licked me (araña me ha lamido)." Out of her hearing, a friend clarified the situation: "She eats sweets and doesn't brush her teeth." The changing nutritional context, the presence of other beings that share the environment, the challenges of hygiene and health prevention, and the social stigma of visible illness were all woven together in this interaction. They are all themes of this chapter, as we focus on the embodied dimension of children's care. Our lens expands to take in actors beyond the family and neighborhood, those associated with the Peruvian state and traditional Andean health specialists. Yauyinos, including the youngest among them, could be quite self-sufficient in responding to illness and accidents, but there were occasions when assistance was needed.

Children in our studies in Yauyos were affected by their surroundings, and they in turn contributed to many of the human impacts on the natural world. In chapter 4 we saw the part they played in producing their food. They had a margin of decision over where animals grazed, even over what animals their families raised. They participated in activities that influenced the water supply and that affected patterns of forestation, the propagation of plants and seeds, the selection of crops, and soil composition. They contributed to environmental contamination as they followed the example of their elders, tossing waste wherever they happened to be walking or playing and adding to the piles of plastics and papers that accumulated on the outskirts of the towns. Children recognized that the complexity of their environment and the multiple causes of ill health—germs and contagion, cold and hunger, poverty, embarrassment, and sadness—could all play into a friend's, a family member's, or one's own maladies.

The Andes, like other high-altitude environments, are biologically challenging for human beings, especially vulnerable children (Thomas 1997; Leatherman 1998; Monge and León-Velarde 2003). Human biological and social adaptations to this context encompass several domains: cold (including extreme seasonal temperature variation and contrasts between night and day), ultraviolet radiation, harsh and irregular terrain, and hypoxia, the decreased partial pressure of oxygen, which may affect fetal growth and cause altitude sickness in the elderly (Wiley 2004, 3). Child development is shaped as well by genetic factors (Huicho and Pawson 2003) and high rates of infection by pathogens (Hurtado et al. 2005). Patterns of intrahousehold distribution of resources introduce further variation in the health prospects of different children. The backdrop is the poverty and marginalization of high-altitude regions under prevailing social and political regimes (Goodman and Leatherman 1998; Larme and Leatherman 2003; Koss-Chioino et al. 2003).

In this context, children's "developmental niches" must be understood expansively. Their health and nutrition are part of a social and ecological system in which their caregivers are also implicated. Sharing food is a way of creating relatives in the Andes, so the nourishment of children is not only materially but also symbolically significant (Harvey 1998, 77; Van Vleet 2008, 64–67; Weismantel 1988). The risks surrounding them, from microbes to plastics to unsafe roads to uncomprehending health professionals, can induce major inflections in their life course. Given all the imponderables, we are not surprised by the wide variety of beliefs and explanations concerning bodily functions that crept into conversations about illness and health. Above it all, the mountains hover, alternately threatening and protective, relatives that must also be fed, considered, and cared for, according to Andean world-views (Canessa 2012; de la Cadena 2015; Salas 2019).

Child Nutrition in Rural Yauyos

What gives growing children the energy they require? Small family farms in Yauyos grew potatoes, oats, barley, fava and other varieties of beans, corn, chickpeas, quinoa, and other Andean crops. Some farmers cultivated peas and a few vegetables. Many, especially at lower altitudes, had fruit trees, producing apples, oranges, peaches, and avocados. With animals providing meat, fiber, and wool, as well as milk that could be processed into cheese for consumption or sale, the families of Yauyos could cover many of their basic needs. In addition to fields and pastures located outside the town perimeter, nearly every household had a kitchen garden and a yard or patio where they kept a few domestic animals, typically guinea pigs and fowl, occasionally rabbits and hogs. These were raised for their own consumption or for a quick sale to fellow townspeople or visitors coming through.

Despite this relatively rich resource base, purchased foods, especially rice, sugar, pasta, and bread, were an important part of the diet and have been so for at least a few decades. A study in Terrazas by Sautier and Amemiya (1988), taking place over an entire annual production cycle, weighed servings and asked participants to record the composition of family meals in diaries. This revealed not only the importance of "imported" foods (constituting between 10 percent and 26 percent of different families' caloric intake) but the variability among households (poorer households being more reliant on their own production) and seasonal variation (more consumption of locally produced foods during and in the weeks after harvest). Mine workers in Terrazas had access to well-stocked shelves and subsidized prices at stores within the mining camp. When they came home on weekends, despite the wide range of options available, the food they most frequently brought as a treat for the family was bread (see Weismantel 1988, 139–140).

Boiling is the basic cooking technology underlying the Andean diet (Weismantel 1988). In the communities where we researched, soups were a common means of combining many ingredients into a single dish that was warm and comforting in the mountain climate. They made it possible to use grains, legumes, and tubers that required a long cooking time. A variety of dairy products, relatively cheap and accessible throughout the province, could be put in soups; for example, the *sopa de mantequilla* (butter soup) that was a specialty of Yauyos City. Soups and stews were a vehicle for ensuring that animal products were taken full advantage of. Tripe and other "variety" animal products such as hooves might be cooked into a *patasca*, a soup based on corn and yellow potatoes.

Children's diets in Yauyos, like those of the grown-ups, varied according to the season and the availability of ingredients, whether recently harvested, stored from the previous year, or on the shelves and in the refrigerators of the local bodegas. Breakfast might be fried fish with potato and yucca, perhaps complemented by a cup of oatmeal prepared as a thin gruel with sugar and milk. Lunch for a child coming home from school could be rice with fried cheese or lentils, tripe with rice and yucca, or a watery soup of noodles followed by a plate of rice, boiled or fried potatoes and a small piece of chicken, beef, or mutton. Lunch or an afternoon snack might include mote, large-kernel Andean corn boiled with lye to remove the skins. Supper could be mutton soup, or a combination of reconstituted dried peas and a fried egg, or a portion of canned tuna with fried potatoes. Some meals were followed by a dessert, often a pudding. Cornstarch was used to thicken the puddings, especially the childhood favorite, *mazamorra morada*, made from purple corn.

As this list suggests, carbohydrates were central to the diet in Yauyos, with proteins a complement (figure 5.1). The preferred meat was beef, which was usually available for purchase, but households could rely on a variety of smaller animals they were raising to supply themselves with animal protein.[1] One store owner said she stocked everything her clients needed for preparing their meals, "just no fruits or vegetables." Vegetables are essentially a condiment in traditional Andean cuisine (Weismantel 1988). Fruit, however, was a desired snack. The children of Pastizales waited patiently for bananas, tangerines, and oranges that were unsold or bruised by the end of the market day in their town. They carried out small services for the vendors as a way of earning their reward, helping them to pack their bags and baskets for the trip back down the mountain, sweeping up around the stands, or keeping watch on the merchandise as they waited for the truck or bus. Children of store owners probably got more fruit than the average, but they were expected to limit themselves to the pieces that were at risk of spoiling. Bread was another popular

FIGURE 5.1. Mother and children peeling potatoes.

snack but was not a staple in an area where wheat-growing and milling were not done locally. Each town had a family-run bakery or two, but the artisanal ovens used firewood, and it was hard to make them profitable. Children might use pin-money to buy packages of crackers, cookies, and wafers from the store.[2]

Scarcity and the Risks of Malnutrition

Given the diversity of crops and availability of food, childhood malnutrition should have been rare in Yauyos. In fact, it should be rare in the entire Andean region, yet it is not (Del Pino et al. 2012; Pollitt, León, and Cueto 2007). In Yauyos, as in other parts of the rural Andes, some children were not getting food of the quality and quantity they needed to thrive. Extreme malnutrition was exceptional and there was in general no shortage of animal protein in children's diets in the Nor Yauyos communities, although children in the communities closer to the coast were affected. The greatest child nutrition concern at the time of our research was stunting: children not growing as tall or gaining weight as they should. (It has since been displaced by anemia and obesity. During our fieldwork, no child nor adolescent in Yauyos was obese.) Peru made global headlines for its success at reducing malnutrition and stunting during the 2010s (see Acosta and Haddad 2014), so the rates of child malnutrition we cite here should be considered in context: things are better than they used to be.[3]

A Ministry of Education study in 2005 found that 29 percent of children aged six to nine in both Las Cascadas and Pastizales, and 15 percent in Terrazas, were malnourished (cited in Gil 2013, 63). In our study, we did not measure food intake nor did we access clinical records, but we could rely on a mixture of our own observations, conversations with the children, parent interviews, and, for some communities, comments from personnel of the health centers. On this basis, we evaluated sixteen of the thirty-six children in the biographies sample to be well nourished and eleven to be undernourished. (The remaining nine children were not well nourished, but we could not be sure that their diets were actually deficient.)

The situation of the well-nourished children was the easiest to explain. With two exceptions, their families possessed and actively worked fields where they cultivated a variety of crops. And they had animals; most significantly, milk cows, but also (in varying quantities) sheep, goats, alpacas, guinea pigs, ducks, turkeys, and chickens. The two exceptions were Samuel (6) and Lizbeth (5). Samuel's parents were not from the area originally and did not have land or animals, but they had two professional salaries to spend on the family food budget. Lizbeth's mother, too, had a steady income as municipal secretary. From her second-story office, she could monitor her daughter's activities, making sure she was warmly dressed, and she frequently took her to the health center to forestall any minor illness. Lizbeth was one of the tallest in her preschool class.

The problems experienced by the children that were undernourished were less easy to classify. In a pair of cases the children's poor nutrition appeared to be directly related to their father's alcoholism and the stress that it put on household resources. In other cases, the fault might lie not in the availability of ingredients but in the demands on female caregivers that competed with their food preparation role. (The kitchen was a decidedly female-marked space in this context and, while Andean men can and do cook, they do not routinely prepare entire meals.) With children in school, mothers might have to take the herds out to pasture in the morning. They might prepare the noon meal before they left and have it waiting for the children when they came home from school, though even that required that someone be old enough to light a fire and warm the food, since a cold lunch was unthinkable in this setting.

Renzo's (10) father had recently been hired at the mine ("he carries rocks," one of his sisters described their father's work) and was away for periods of twenty days at a time. His mother was left alone to look after five children, her livestock, and occasional herding jobs. Renzo's teacher said that he fell asleep in class and usually did not want to go out and play with his classmates at recess. If he did, he quickly became exhausted. Like his siblings, he came to school without a midmorning snack. His classmates shared theirs with him. Renzo often stayed for the school lunch, or he took his portion home in a plastic container.

Renzo's low energy could well have been related to anemia and malnutrition, although stress may have also played a role. Low appetite in young people was considered problematic by their caregivers and appeared to us to have socioemotional contours. Yeny (11) lost her appetite and self-confidence following her family's recent move from Huancayo to Terrazas, where she was being mercilessly bullied by her new schoolmates. Tomás (11), being raised by his grandparents yet subject to the discipline of his absent mother, "doesn't like to eat," according to his grandmother. She was worried that he wasn't growing like he should. "I have to take out the belt [i.e., threaten to beat him] in order to make him eat," she said.

Abundance: Windfalls and Special Occasions

Betty's and Lenin's uncle's cow injured itself trying to jump over a stone wall from one terrace to another while tethered by a leg. When their uncle went to fetch it in the late afternoon, it was dead, dangling from the rope. Family members were called out to help with the butchering. Field-workers Diego and Cynthia watched while every member of their host household, down to six-year-old Lenin, came trekking in, one by one, with slabs of meat. Señora Anolia sliced it into strips and prepared it for salting. Unwelcome, unexpected events could be nutritional windfalls, where meat became available for sharing and for sale despite the owners' intentions.

Other, more regular, elements of temporality shaped children's intake, notably weekends and festivities. Weekends everywhere were a time when the points of sale and range of cooked foods available in the towns expanded greatly. *Salchipapa* carts came out onto the street, selling an inexpensive (S/.1, about $0.30) combination of hot dog, fried potatoes, lettuce, and hot sauce. *Anticuchos*, skewers of marinated bull heart, were sold from portable grills. Small restaurants and bars would serve customers until late. Amid the movement of people in the streets and businesses, children could circulate and, in all likelihood, find someone willing to share a plate with them or even buy them a meal. True abundance was associated with celebrations.[4] Fiesta sponsors provided generous portions of meat (slaughtered from their own and supporters' herds), potatoes, and complements, fearful of being criticized if they appeared stingy. Even though children might not get a plate of their own at such an event, adults were often happy to offload the excess amounts they were served. Food vendors also descended on the communities or appeared from within their ranks. A prized item of festive fare for children was candy, as we have seen at *herranzas* (chapter 2).

Fiesta season was followed by the "time of hunger" (*época de hambruna*) in Nor Yauyos. When herds went to high-altitude pastures, daily access to milk and cheese was cut off for many. Mothers might be absent for several consecutive days while they were helping their husbands and sons look after the herds, doing the housekeeping in makeshift shelters, and making cheese. Food preparation at home in town could suffer if grandmothers, aunts, and older daughters were not available to take over.

Filling the Gaps: Social Programs, Subsidies, and Nutritional Supplements

The Peruvian government has been slow to recognize its responsibility in relation to child health and nutrition and slower yet to gear up to where it could successfully administer national programs targeting specific groups and specific nutritional problems (Reyes 2007; Montero and Yamada 2012; Boesten 2010; Petrera and Seinfeld 2007). The programs that existed in Yauyos in 2008 involved subsidies from the national government, locally complemented and applied. They were subject to many contingencies, including the availability of enlightened mayors and willing volunteers.

The most important were school lunch programs, which unfolded with great variation across the communities studied.[5] In Los Caminos, school lunches were available only for preschoolers. On the day the field-workers visited, the menu consisted of rice, potato, and a kind of hot dog made from anchovies that came out of a tin proudly labeled "Wieners from the sea. Government of Peru." Teachers and the volunteer cooks circulated around the tables, encouraging the children to eat and offering them mayonnaise for the hot dog. (Very few finished their meal.) By contrast, the school lunch program in Pastizales was one of the largest and most institutionalized. It fed around one hundred children and adolescents each day, from preschool all the way through high school. Local mothers did the cooking, receiving a payment from the municipality. The children got a complete meal: soup, main course, and dessert, with a menu that often contained legumes and meat. Though the program was well organized, it was slow to get underway. The school year began in April, but the school lunches appeared only in mid-August after the Independence Day holiday and midyear break. Again, this was the time of hunger, a time when families began to feel a more acute need for ensuring their children's midday meal through the schools.

National law required municipal governments to participate in the Vaso de Leche (Glass of Milk) program of free breakfasts (Copestake 2008; Cantor et al. 2018). Initially targeted to preschool children, the program grew to encompass the elderly, disabled, and older children. Local governments received powdered milk, occasionally other supplies such as tinned fish, or the equivalent in funds from the national social assistance budget, but they had to cover the costs of logistics and any complements. Surrounded by producers of milk and cheese, Yauyos mayors might not have chosen this as their preferred strategy for combatting child malnutrition or for ingratiating themselves with their electors. Still, they were obliged to organize something that roughly adhered to the Vaso de Leche guidelines. The committees that oversaw distribution of the rations were a site of leadership for local women and an organizational format of interest to the communities in general. It was not uncommon to see older children walking down the streets, sucking on the corners of the Vaso de Leche powdered milk packets, treating them like a confection. They illustrated one of the persistent challenges of almost all nutritional programs for children in Peru: supplements targeted for the most

ECOLOGIES OF CARE

vulnerable are frequently pooled and shared in collective solidarity (compare Vincent 2021).

Healing Children: Illness and Curing in Rural Yauyos

Children's diets interacted with other factors that influenced their state of health. There were the challenges of keeping warm and the complications of ensuring hygiene. Exposed to ultraviolet radiation, under threat of sunburn, cracked, dry skin was common. Meanwhile, unidentified bacteria and viruses circulating in close-knit communities explained many illnesses in the children of Yauyos. These tended to be low-grade but persistent or recurrent.

Like many of her age-mates, Consuelo (3) had a runny nose almost constantly. Even Lenin (5), with a mother and older sister dedicated to his care, had repeated colds and episodes of bronchitis, "like every child around here does," said his mother. Asked about their children's illnesses, many parents simply said that their colds, coughs, and sore throats were a normal symptom of childhood. They seemed unavoidable when linked to the vicissitudes of ensuring adequate clothing. On one occasion, in the coldest month of July, the Pastizales field team was hanging out with Shirley (10) and her friend Felicitas (8). Felicitas was wearing thin fabric pants, black tennis shoes with holes in them, and a long-sleeved cotton shirt. The team members encouraged her to go home and put on something warmer. "We'll wait for you here," they assured her. Shirley piped up: "Felicitas doesn't have any clothes. Her dad isn't working." Children from the poorest families wore the same clothes for days on end. Many dressed in hand-me-downs that were tattered and ill-fitting. They might have plastic shoes or boots on their feet with no socks, or they might be barefoot. Instead of coats or jackets, most wore, over a t-shirt or long-sleeved turtleneck, synthetic fleece sweatshirts or sweaters knitted by mothers or grandmothers of wool from the family's herd. Many of these garments had served multiple members of the family previously and had holes or were unraveling at the sleeves. Field-worker Sandra felt convinced that most children, most of the time, were simply not warm enough; perhaps their subjective perceptions of cold differed from Sandra's (see Spray 2020).

Along with respiratory illnesses, the other major threat to infants and children in the Andes was diarrhea and digestive tract infections. These were less prominent in the health histories of the biographies sample but clearly a concern, especially for the health workers. Staff of all the health centers fretted over the low levels of hygiene they perceived in the children, in the houses where they lived, and in the surroundings where they worked and played. Keeping the dirt out of a rural environment was—all would agree—an impossible task. Dust and particles blew about, raised by animals' hooves and human movement.

In each of the six communities, some children had dry skin with abrasions and creases where dirt accumulated, hands that were chapped and blackened, and ragged and dirty fingernails. Others had clear skin and clean hands and faces. The difference seemed to lie in parents' policies with respect to baths, handwashing, changing clothes, and the use of products such as shampoo and toothpaste. Anyone who has washed in water from mountain streams can appreciate the challenge for mothers and older siblings in getting young children bathed, and the dread the process awoke in the children. Basic bathing technology for toddlers and young children involved a tub of water that was left to warm in the sun in an inner patio.[6] Boiling water from a kettle on the stove might be added. Bathing involved scrubbing and pouring water over the child's body. Baths would be scheduled for midday or early afternoon when ambient temperatures were warmest.

Crises

Upset stomachs, colds, blisters, and cracked skin could be taken in stride. Rather, it was other health issues that children memorialized in the lists of events they recalled as being scary, even life-changing; moments we viewed as vital conjunctures (Johnson-Hanks 2002). They constituted "conjunctures" insofar as they led to adjustments in the children's behavior or understanding of their place in the world. Falls, road accidents, or dangerous encounters with animals inflected children's subsequent actions. More chronic issues, like stigmatizing diseases or family members with alcoholism or mental illness, could also produce a change of course in children's lives. In some of these cases the children were fully aware of what had happened to them and many, if perhaps not all, of the implications. In other cases—and for some children like Hilario, who had severe autism—they could not have that awareness, and the notion of vital conjuncture could better be applied to the people around them rather than to the children directly.

Herding exposed young people to risks from both the landscape and the animals that occupied it. Given the geography of the region and its uses, falls were an ever-present danger. No matter how skilled people became in navigating mountain slopes and narrow paths, they had frequent need of bonesetters (Oths 2003). Dionisia (12) broke or dislocated bones in her hand when out in the hills with a couple of siblings. An older brother pulled it back into shape but "it hurt a lot," she said. Falls children witnessed could be frightening. Renzo, Dionisia, and their mother were up in the mountains with the herds when the mother fell into a deep ravine. She directed Renzo to round up the sheep and sent Dionisia to town for help. As night drew near, she was able to claw her way out to where she could be rescued. Although children from an early age learned to maneuver around large animals, they were subject to bites, kicks, shoves, and throws from burros and mules. Braulio was nearly killed when the burro he was riding suddenly took off in pursuit of a female in heat.

In some cases, stigma added to the pain. Junior (8) had visible sores, including on his forehead, from leishmaniasis. His classmates teased him to the point where sometimes he refused to go to school. Endemic in Sur Grande, caused by an insect bite, leishmaniasis ran in households, although the severity and persistence of the disease was different among different family members. Junior had been treated the year before at the Cayetano Heredia research hospital, but his family was not able to keep up with the treatment regime, which involved expensive medication and trips to Lima. The local health post was not supplied with effective drugs, and health workers were left to administer what they themselves considered to be an inferior substitute. After the fieldwork ended, we learned that a delegation of mothers and officials from the town had traveled to Lima to request formally that the Cayetano Heredia hospital send a team to combat leishmaniasis in their community. At last notice, their efforts had been successful, and Junior was cured.

Treating Illnesses

Junior's accessing a research hospital was unusual, but interactions with local health workers were a frequent part of childhood (see figure 3.1). When he was around four, Jeferson (10) had been bitten on the face by a neighbor's dog. He had to have several stitches at the health post, as did Oscar (10), after he fell onto rock off a high wall separating his yard from the neighboring field. When a pot of boiling water overturned on Renzo's leg, one of the hazards of children cooking when their parents were absent, his siblings took him to the health post for treatment.

All six communities had health centers provided and managed by the Peruvian Ministry of Health. They were part of the Yauyos-Cañete network of fifty-four health establishments (Reyes 2007). Yauyos, the capital city, had a larger and more complex facility equipped for hospitalizing patients, though not for performing surgeries. Identified as a "hospital" or "clinic" by the locals but officially a second-tier health center, it served some two thousand people in the urban area and some nine thousand in its rural hinterland. Because of their small populations, the other study sites had health centers (*puestos de salud*) that did basic diagnoses, provided primary care, and referred patients to more complex services in the city—Cañete, Huancayo, or Lima—according to need.[7] When Haydee (6) got pneumonia at age two, for example, her family took her to Huancayo for emergency treatment and later to Lima for nebulizing. Ambulances were supplied and maintained by the public health system, but they were notoriously unreliable. They might be in service in far-flung annexes. They might be under repair. The staff that could authorize their use would almost certainly be difficult to contact. Patients' families and neighbors might have to contribute the fuel for the trip. We collected harrowing tales of urgent pleas for ambulances that coincided with fiestas, when the drivers, on government salary and supposedly on call, were too drunk to drive.

With the exception of the facility in the provincial capital, the doctors that served in Yauyos were Serumistas. An extension of the acronym SERUM (Servicio Rural y Urbano Marginal), the title referred to a person who had graduated from medical school, done a year's internship, and took a one-year general medicine assignment in an underserviced part of the country as a way of broadening their experience and gaining credentials that further their career. Similar to the education offerings in the region (Díaz and Ñopo 2016; Oliart 2011), this system condemned the public health service in rural areas to a rapid rotation of key staff. Nurses and technicians served the longest in any given community, but medical hierarchies demanded that doctors or obstetricians direct the centers, despite having the least knowledge of local conditions and least connection to the local population.[8]

The national health system has a long history of misunderstandings and crossed purposes with the rural population (Reyes 2007; Anderson 2001; Yon 2000). Rural health centers may even be underutilized. The reasons are various and sadly predictable: cost,[9] misinformation, lack of trust, discrimination and abuse at the hands of some health workers, and the unfamiliarity of many of their practices, especially those associated with pregnancy and childbirth (Guerra-Reyes 2019; Dierna et al. 1999; Anderson et al. 1999). One Serumista, visiting Bellavista for a day-long health campaign, berated a young mother who presented with her two-month-old. She told the doctor that for the last two days the child had refused to nurse. The doctor observed that the infant was breathing with difficulty and demanded to know how long the problem had been going on. "He hasn't eaten for two days," the mother repeated. "This isn't a problem that's only been going on for two days!" the doctor exploded. Hearing that the mother lived in a nearby annex, he challenged her: "You're that near and you waited until the last moment to bring your child to get medical attention? Your child comes first, only then your fields and your cows!" Pointing to the manta the infant was wrapped in, he told her in a loud voice: "Take that off right now and don't ever swaddle that baby again! (Sácale eso ya y no lo vuelvas a fajar)."[10]

An inevitable contradiction underlay the relationship between the health posts and the townspeople. The townspeople expected effective treatments of illnesses and injuries. Field-worker Gabriela observed that "everybody rushes to the health post to ask for antibiotics" as soon as they feel sick. By contrast, the health centers, with their limited capacity and in line with national policies, were oriented to a public health approach of health promotion, education, and preventive care. They were supplied with a minimal pharmacology of analgesics and other basic medicines. The local health center, for example, did not have the anticonvulsive medicine for epilepsy that Hilario so desperately needed. His mother had to travel to Cañete to get it whenever she could afford it.[11]

Health workers administered some food supplementation programs, especially for infants. They distributed pamphlets and posters, and they organized classes in the local schools and talks for the general public. They vaccinated children and adults; the nurse in Terrazas said children greeted her on the street, not with "Buenos días," but with "Ya me vacuné (I'm already vaccinated)"! Through home visits, they monitored children at risk of malnutrition and anemia. They reported to the Ministry of Health outbreaks of flu, leishmaniasis, and sexually transmitted infections, and they were expected to identify and track all pregnancies, encouraging the mother to deliver in an official health establishment.[12] Health personnel also attempted to identify developmental problems in children that could be referred to more complex services outside the province. Erick (3) had dislocated his jaw during childbirth. He was unable to close his mouth, drooled constantly, and had trouble pronouncing words. The health post, his preschool teacher, and his family worked together to support him, but a definitive solution was beyond their possibilities. Despite the many misunderstandings that could arise, the offerings of the health centers were appreciated, so long as the personnel did not interfere in people's lives in ways they found unjustified (Guerra-Reyes 2019).

In truth, the health post's function in the community was more expansive than its official mandate would suggest. Isaac and his sisters frequently crossed the street to the health post to do their homework and watch TV. Indeed, health posts in rural communities might be the only facility with a television, a warm shower, bright lights, and open spaces in hallways and waiting rooms. They might have the most reliable supply of electricity, including emergency generators. The field team in Pastizales observed a family requesting permission to use the health post's sterilizing equipment as an oven for baking a large potato pie.

At the same time, afflicted yauyinos had many resources they could turn to beyond the official health system. Several of the biographies sample children had family members, especially in the grandparents' generation, who cured with local herbs like chamomile, valerian, gentian, *muña*, *machki*, *toronjil*, and mint (Etkin 2006; Polia 1996). They diagnosed health problems with coca leaves and chewed coca to ward off dangerous spirits when walking at night. Midwives, bonesetters, and lay healers known as *curiosos* and *curiosas* were sought out to alleviate a wide range of medical problems, including the so-called folk diseases familiar in the Latin American literature: *susto*, *empacho*, *nervios*, and others (Campos-Navarro 2006; La Riva González 2013, 373; Pribilsky 2001; Remorini 2013, 420). These healers drew on deeply held Andean beliefs about natural and supernatural forces located in critical places and the need to placate them, often through ceremonious payments involving coca leaves (de la Cadena 2015; Salas 2019; Canessa 2012; Allen 2002). Dante discussed their son's nosebleed with his wife: "The mountain is alive . . . like a person. [Our son] only got grabbed gently because he's an innocent child. But he had a profuse nosebleed. And that is dangerous."

Conclusions

Were people and their health well cared for in Yauyos? In some ways they had a wider range of alternatives for dealing with illness and pain than many urban families. They could explain afflictions in ways that were clearly traceable to things they did and the risks that surrounded them. They had the advantages of healthy, fresh food (very little of it "fast food"). Herbs with medicinal properties grew everywhere. Yauyinos also had family, neighbors, and friends that were concerned about them.

Yet many adults and many children had a delicate health status. Curable conditions likely went undiagnosed since regular preventive exams were not a common practice. Some people lived with disabilities that could have been prevented or alleviated. Many had diets that oscillated between seasonal scarcity and abundance. They were exposed to the elements, and, in some cases, work overloads. Good health and adequate nutrition for rural children, as for grown-ups, were far from universally guaranteed.

Most of the problems we described in this chapter had to do, not with catastrophic disease, but with low-grade, persistent, recurring conditions of suboptimal health.[13] For decades, reducing morbidity and mortality of infants and children in the Andes has been declared a priority of the Peruvian government. Remedying the problems too often decontextualizes and reduces them to biological elements: distributing iron supplements, enhancing the nutritional value of potatoes, preventing water pollution, combating bacteria and parasites, and redirecting childbirth toward health establishments and away from homes (Guerra-Reyes 2019). While these factors are relevant, they miss the broader context. The six localities under study exist in a political context that is fundamentally adverse. Most damning, the attempts at remedies ignore profoundly held beliefs about the etiology of disease and disease processes in the Andes.

We also witnessed, in connection with health, hygiene, and nutrition, a surprisingly broad range of children's agency. Children took themselves off to the health post when they felt they needed to and caregivers were not around or not sufficiently alarmed. They cured the wounds of other children, shared information with them, and counseled them about health prevention. Children expressed their preferences at the family table and had a role in selecting ingredients for meals they helped prepare. Children fished from local streams, picked wild fruits, and scavenged food from street vendors, restaurants, and food carts. They made their tastes for imported items like bread, cookies, and candy known to parents, who—some more than others—sought to indulge those tastes. There were limitations determined by poverty, seasonality, and other factors beyond their control. But even under those circumstances, children were not powerless. Once past a certain age, they were, after all, with few exceptions, producers of food, not simply consumers. Children's direct involvement in their own care, feeding, and healing is a prominent feature of Andean childhood.

6

Practices of Care

The words *cuidar* (to care), *cuidado* (be careful), and *cuidados* (caretaking, precautions) were frequently heard around the province. What does it mean, in Yauyos, to provide care to someone? What causes a person to feel and believe that he or she is being cared for? When and how do people recognize that care is being given generously and appropriately, being shortchanged, or being unjustly withheld? We ask these questions in this chapter, with a focus on the children in our study: who cared for them, whom did they care for, and what forms did that caring take?

We begin by examining "who cares" for children: who takes a position in the circle of care organized around them and how the cast of characters changes as the children move toward adolescence. In Yauyos, the chain of caregivers around a child could be broken by death, migration, or other factors, and the resulting shifts provided evidence for how people thought about obligation and responsibility. In a second section, we examine two faces of care. One is associated with meeting physical needs for food, clothes, health, and safety. This can be glossed under the Spanish verb *atender*, "tend" or "attend to." The other, *preocuparse*, "feel and/or express concern," encompasses a wide range of potential beneficiaries and a wide variety of behaviors. Finally, we discuss how care was evaluated, positively and negatively, and how deficiencies or violations of care were sanctioned. Local understandings of negligence, discipline, and violence come to the fore together with the gap between children's and adults' understandings of care and justice. We end with a consideration of the institutions working in children's defense and a reminder of the ways children can and cannot take matters into their own hands.

Who Cares For the Children?

Care is enmeshed in the context we have charted: both a gendered division of labor (Harris 1978; Oths 1999) and an age hierarchy in which older siblings or cousins care for younger ones (Anderson 1992; Hornberger 1987, 214; Leinaweaver and

Anderson n.d.; Ortiz and Yamamoto 1994; Van Vleet 2008). There was an explicit delegation of caretaking responsibilities: from father to mother, from mother to older children. Husbands might punish their wives for what they deemed deficiencies in the feeding, hygiene, or safekeeping of the couple's children. Older siblings feared their mothers' retribution if younger children in their care fell or injured themselves. These practices were embedded in cycles of long-term reciprocity. Parents cared for their children because their parents had taken care of them (Zegarra 2022). Younger siblings owed care to the older siblings that had given them care. Adult children were expected to care for their elderly parents under the same reciprocal principle (Van Vleet 2008; Leinaweaver 2013; INEI 2016; Vincent 2021; Leinaweaver 2022). The evidence from Yauyos allows us to trace the persistence of these precepts assigning responsibility for care while discovering where and how they have changed.

For details of day-to-day childcare in Yauyos, we draw once again on our sample of thirty-six biographies. We asked field teams to identify each child's caregivers and who should be recognized as "principal" caregiver. To make these evaluations, the field-workers used evidence from observations (who were the children most frequently seen with, who fed them, who comforted them after a slight or a fall), informal conversations, and personal interviews with the sample children's parents and, often, older siblings, besides the children themselves. Teachers, health workers, and local officials also gave insights into the norms of caretaking, the practices they observed in the communities overall, and specific cases of parents that were reputed to be good at their job and others reputed to be negligent. Table 6.1 presents the categories that emerged, sorted by principal caregivers for the thirty-six children and noting whether or not a father figure was regularly present. In a majority of cases (setting aside the self-care category for the moment), the children had a combination of caregivers drawn from the membership of their households.

It will not be surprising, given the cross-cultural significance of the mother-child dyad, that for fourteen out of the thirty-six children, their mothers were their principal caregivers. These fourteen were, in general, younger children. If we add together all the cases in which mothers were at least one member of the child's caregiving team, and consider grandmothers as surrogate mothers, we get an even clearer picture of the fundamental importance of mothers in systems of childcare in rural towns of Yauyos. Alone or as part of a team, mothers were principal caregivers for two-thirds (23) of the thirty-six children. In two of these cases mothers were being assisted by—or had attempted to arrange the assistance of—non-family members. Samuel's (5) mother, a teacher, had briefly hired a local girl to care for him as an infant until he developed persistent diarrhea, and his parents decided to rely exclusively on family. And we describe a case in which Rebeca (18) was effectively an assistant to her employer in the care of three-year-old Consuelo. First, however, we review the three other constellations of care—beyond mothers—that

PRACTICES OF CARE 93

TABLE 6.1

Principal caregivers, children with and without fathers (or surrogates) regularly present in the household (biographies sample)

Principal caregiver(s)	Children in households with mother and father (or surrogates) present	Children in households with no father or surrogate regularly present	Total number of children
Mother	10 (ages 5, 6, 8, 10, 11, 12, 14)	4 (ages 3, 5, 10)	14
Grandmother	1 (age 11)	0	1
Both parents	3 (ages 6, 8, 9)	0	3
Both parents + siblings	1 (age 5)	0	1
Mother + siblings	0	2 (ages 3, 7)	2
Siblings	1 (age 6)	3 (ages 3, 12, 14)	4
Self-care	4 (ages 13, 14, 15)	3 (ages 12, 14, 15)	7
Self-care + mother	1 (age 11)	0	1
Self-care + grandmother	1 (age 11)	0	1
Self-care + siblings/ cousin	2 (ages 9, 10)	0	2
Total children	24	12	36

---

were most significant for children in Yauyos: fathers, siblings, and themselves (self-care).

Care by Fathers

Of the thirty-six children in the sample biographies, twenty-four had fathers (or surrogates: grandfathers, granduncles, or stepfathers) regularly present in the household, while twelve did not.[1] We distinguish between these two situations in table 6.1 on the understanding that fathers played an important role in the organization of care in households where they were daily participants, even where they did not directly attend to the children or even to many of their own needs. A father's presence in everyday activities validated his status as such. One little girl in Terrazas said her father lived in the United States. "I haven't seen him in a long time. I've talked to him on the phone. My mom told me his name: [she shared it]. I don't love him like a real father because he doesn't give me food. One day he gave me a little bit of money. That's why I don't love him" (see Leinaweaver 2015). Cross-culturally, male household heads may greatly influence the standards of care, and they may complicate its provision through their dominance as decision-makers and, often, belief in the priority of their claims (Fuller 2003).

In Yauyos, men clearly knew methods of caring for children, even if many of them were not significantly engaged in caring for their own offspring. Most had gained experience taking care of siblings, nieces, and nephews, when they were young and single. They could step in when emergencies arose, as Jeferson's father did for four months the previous year while the boy's mother was hospitalized in Huancayo. Typically, being an active and involved father depended in part upon the father's line of work and the place where he performed it (Polatnick 1984 speaks of the "opportunity costs" of parenting). Of the biographies sample, children in three households were cared for by both parents, that is, had fathers who shared their day-to-day care with their mothers in full collaboration. These three men were not working primarily as farmers or herders, going out to the fields daily. One was a shopkeeper (caring for Carlos, 6, and Pamela, 9), another an electronics repairman (caring for Camila, 8, and her two siblings), and the third a solderer (caring for Yovana, 5, child of his "old age") with a home-based shop. They were near or at home most of the day, most days, and they were present and available to tend to their children's needs. Many of the fathers and stepfathers of the children in the biographies sample were itinerant. Even Camila's father was not always there: he took jobs wherever he could, sometimes outside the province of Yauyos. Oscar's stepfather worked as a substitute teacher and might be called away for several days or weeks at a time. Dalila's and Elisa's fathers and several others of the fathers were constantly going to the puna to check on their herds. Miners were away for fifteen- or twenty-day rotations.

Stepfathers in Yauyos could be superior to biological fathers in the support they provided. The children born to the single mothers we described in chapter 3 were not treated with any apparent discrimination and in some cases even seemed to be privileged. Stepfathers appeared to respect the close relationship between a mother and a child that had helped each of them through hard times before the stepfather joined the family. The oldest, especially if they were girls, were likely to be their mothers' essential helpers and favored confidants. The firstborn was also likely to be a strong referent and frequent caregiver for younger half-brothers and half-sisters as they came along. Estela (11) fit the description on every point, and she looked on her stepfather as a person in whom she could confide.

A few of the fathers had child support and potential caretaking obligations for children in more than one household. We heard of none that was actively involved in the care of a child that was not residing under the same roof. And, under those circumstances of separate residences, we heard of no biological father that did not drag his feet or otherwise resist the demand for financial support, in the unlikely case that such a demand was made.

Care by Siblings

Examples of sibling care abound in our data (see figure 6.1). Competent and independent Flor (10) and Charo (7), whom we last saw wielding lassoes at an *herranza*, also shared the care of their two younger siblings. Flor carried the most fragile on her back, a baby brother of 6 months. Charo was in charge of Katya (2), similarly tied to her back in a manta or toddling alongside. Their father had the reputation of being a *machista*, a domineering spouse who refused to use contraceptives. This was not the only reference we heard connecting children's roles as caregivers for younger siblings to the parents' unwillingness to control the number of children they had. Additionally, caregiving for successive younger siblings was linked to some of the embodied concerns described in the previous chapter, illustrated in Shirley's comment. Shirley (10) was now in charge of her infant sister Ada, but before that she had been caregiver for her brother, only four years younger than she. She had carried both of them on her back. "That's why I'm so short. It's why I'm not growing," she said, laughing.

Child caregivers responded to the potent signals that guide adults in charge of young children, especially crying. In Pastizales, Bobby (7) was observed with his sister Diana (2). As Li wrote in her notebook, "His sense of responsibility for his little sister was palpable. When the other children moved off to play in another

FIGURE 6.1. Caring for a younger sibling.

space, he stayed by her side and only changed places when his sister cried or got bored. At those times he walked or carried her around and did everything in his power to stop her from crying." In Terrazas, field-worker Gaby recorded an incident in which Pascual (3) was bouncing a tennis ball, when another boy (7) approached him and said, "Can I play with you?" Pascual's older half-brother Franklin (10), with an angry face, pointing his index finger at the child, challenged him: "Watch out if you make my brother cry."

Part of "looking after" related to promoting the everyday safety of those who were less able to understand the consequences of their actions. This kind of protective care, from preventing fights to bundling up a chilly child in an extra layer, was very often performed by older siblings for younger ones. Pascual (3), walking on the street, picked up a discarded bottle of cologne and threw it down, shattering it into pieces. Half-sister Gladis (14) made sure they were swept out of his way. Moments later, when Pascual attempted to get down from a chair that was much too high, Franklin swooped by and lowered him gently to the floor. Protective care might extend to the arena of social reputation, as was the case of Susana (14) and brother David. Their father died of leukemia two years before the fieldwork. As he was dying, he charged David to watch out for his sister, Susana, whose age placed her at risk of going astray or being so perceived. David, eight years old at the time of the study, was faithful to his father's command. On one occasion, as he walked home with the youngest of the three siblings, Erick (3), he saw Susana on a street corner chatting with girlfriends. He launched a dire threat: "Susana, I'm going to kick your butt. Let's go home (ahora te agarro a patadotes. Vamos para la casa)." Little Erick protested what he understood to be an attack on his beloved sister: "No, a mi tata, no."

Some research suggests the existence of formal arrangements of delegation of caretaking responsibilities that entailed swift punishment for older siblings that were neglectful in their duties (Harvey 1998, 75; Ortiz 1989; Lobo 1982), but we did not see that in Yauyos. The assignment of responsibilities seemed to be loose, and child caregivers—rather than the fear of being punished for accidents that might befall their charges—seemed to be motivated by the fun of incorporating younger children in their games, the social norm that made it expectable for them to be with their younger siblings, and perhaps their understanding that childcare involved skills that it was in their long-term interest to acquire.

Care for Oneself

The field-workers identified a substantial number of children as being essentially under their own care, not receiving care from any other person. From the age of thirteen or fourteen, sometimes even earlier, children were expected to be able to *atenderse* (look after themselves, fulfill their daily needs) completely or in large part. Nearly one-third (eleven out of thirty-six) of the biographies sample children cared for themselves, though four of those had some support from other household members. Much of the children's education at home had led up to this. Tina, mother of five ranging from seventeen to five (including Dionisia and Renzo, whom we have met repeatedly) had high expectations for them to learn to be self-sufficient early on. Her philosophy was: "While they're still babies I can be dressing them, too. When they're older, I only have to take care of their bellies (i.e., make cooked food available) and I'm done." Her statement suggested an important nuance to the notion of self-care: meal preparation was still a collective enterprise even in households of self-carers. They were not separately and independently cooking their own food, although they knew how to do it, and many had a major role in supplying the family table.

The field-workers registered the lives of several uncomplaining daughters, self-carers who also collaborated in the care of other family members. These were girls between thirteen and fourteen years of age: Aurora, Nieves, Gladis, Silvia, and Betty. We could also include in that group Maruja (12), the indispensable daughter and granddaughter, keeping shop for her disabled grandmother (see Leinaweaver and Anderson n.d.). These young adolescents followed daily routines, accomplishing multiple tasks that greatly alleviated the burden on their mothers. They were expert at housekeeping duties they had been performing since childhood. They anticipated many of the needs of other family members and intervened proactively.[2]

Meanwhile, and in stark contrast, boys in the same age range were moving away from earlier roles they might have played as helpers in the kitchen and house. Pepe (14) was unable to conform to this gender mandate because his older sister Zenaida (16) had gone to Lima to prepare for her exams for admittance to the police academy. He was left to largely fill her shoes in both his own household and that of his elderly grandparents.[3] Field-worker Ignacio had occasion to observe him as he struggled between his desire to protest, to refuse to help with cooking and serving meals to guests, and his understanding that he was the only person available to do it, at least until his younger sister grew a bit more.

Vital Conjunctures: Breaking the Bonds of Care

Most children were deeply attached to those who tended to them, and some of children's most painful memories reflected changes in the cast of characters they had become accustomed to as their care providers. Given the propensity of adult yauyinos to adapt to challenges through relocating, children were set up for potential hurt. Many of their experiences related to moving and migration fell into the category of vital conjunctures, heightened moments of key changes in children's lives (Hagan, MacMillan, and Wheaton 1996). One such instance was Consuelo's (3) move with her mother to Yauyos City from Cañete, where she was born and grew up and where her father and five-year-old brother still lived. The couple's separation was managed through regular visits back and forth and was made less traumatic by the happy circumstance that the move brought Consuelo closer to her paternal grandfather and other family.

Migrations could occasion major upheavals in children's caretaking arrangements and the context in which they evolved (Leinaweaver 2010a). The authorities of Los Caminos designated a different couple each year to serve as the *ecónomos* (guardians) of the community's herds. In doing so, they tended to lean on the weakest members, those who could not refuse, without regard to their family situation. The couple chosen had to move from town to the upland pastures. At the time of fieldwork, the designated couple was facing their new role with grim resignation. Their older child, attending high school, would stay behind with relatives; the younger one would go with the parents in the hopes that an elementary school could be found for her within reach of the *ecónomos'* hut. If not, she would simply miss a year. Braulio's care network was replaced wholesale when, after finishing primary school in his annex, he was sent away to live with an uncle and his family in Lima. There, he was enrolled in secondary school in one of the city's tougher neighborhoods. He was drawn into gang life, drug and alcohol consumption, and petty thievery. He ended up being sent back and being called on to adapt to a new arrangement again as he became a live-in worker for Señora Pilar at her restaurant and hostel.

Losing important members of their personal networks was probably the most universal experience of movement and change that children in Yauyos had, since almost no family was free of stories of members on the road, members away for a fixed period of time and fixed purpose, members exploring their options, and members long ago lost from view. This phenomenon is also inflected by the long reproductive cycles described in chapter 3, where older siblings could be starting out on new life paths while younger ones were still at home. Yovana and Lizbeth, both five years old, were separated from older brothers and father-figures; Haydee and Dalila, both six years old, were separated from older sisters. Older sisters sometimes left to pursue a career or because of an unwanted pregnancy. Their reasons for leaving were probably less important to their younger sisters than the shifts those departures brought in the distribution of both emotional support and household responsibilities. The migration of an older sister was not only the loss of a friend and a referent for a younger girl. It also meant that the tasks that had been assigned to that sister now fell to the younger one. For both boys and girls, the departures of older siblings, aunts, uncles, or cousins not too distant in age could mean that important bulwarks of protection between the children and their parents had gone with them.

What Is (Good) Care?

Who provided care was something people had opinions about and something that could be, under most circumstances, witnessed or reported. What that care consisted of was similarly a discursively available topic and an ethnographically observable phenomenon. For a restricted circle of beneficiaries, care involved everyday practices of making sure needs were met. In Yauyos these needs fell into primary categories of food, hygiene, safety, and discipline; that is, teaching and promoting good behavior. We call this *atender*, tending to (comparable to Tronto

1993, 103; Thomas 1993, 649; Boris and Parreñas 2010, 1; and Glenn 1992, 1). For a larger circle, care implied attention and concern but no hands-on involvement. It might occasion behind-the-back commentary or criticism. We call this *preocuparse*, being concerned for (compare Tronto 1993, 3; Williams 1997; Borneman 2001, 11). The full gradient of both attentive and concerned actions and intentions fall under the rubric of *cuidado*, the Spanish word for care. We draw our discussion out to consider when care was "something done well" and when it was not; when it met its objectives of helping and safekeeping and when it did not.

Atender: *Care as Meeting Daily Needs*

For many people in Yauyos the daily practices of care involved facilitating others' well-being. Primary among them were feeding (sourcing, preparing, and serving food), attending to personal hygiene and health (including washing and hanging out clothes), and behavioral training (including supervising children's connection to school). Paradoxically, these tasks were not always classified as care when they were not carried out by a dedicated caregiver (Orlove 2002, 101–107; Leinaweaver 2008, 92–93). Rebeca (18) and her brother Nilton (12) shared the residence that their parents had set up in town to enable their children's school attendance (see chapter 3). When asked directly, Rebeca laughed: "Nilton? I don't really take care of him. (Yo no lo cuido.) I help him with his homework, I cook his food, wash his clothes, and iron the ones that need it." She cared in much the same way for five nieces and nephews that also lived in the house, adding the task of giving them baths on some Sundays.

Although Rebeca performed many supporting tasks for her younger kin, she was not present to look after them during the day and could not be counted on to deal with nonroutine needs. She had a job to go to. At work at the municipal hotel, she shared in the care of Consuelo (3), daughter of the administrator. When Consuelo's mother was busy, or simply because Consuelo sought her out, Rebeca dressed her, prepared food, walked her to preschool, and played with her. Rebeca's insistence that she was not really a caretaker to Nilton, or the even younger relatives that shared the household, seems to have sprung from that difference: with her presence, she collaborated in Consuelo's care. This often unspoken element of good care, which went beyond attention to children's needs, consisted of accompanying them, anticipating demands, and guiding them through novel situations.

Perhaps because they needed to be accompanied and assisted in so many of the tasks of daily living, toddlers and preschoolers were favored with affection and patience not customary with older children. Even among the youngest, some children enjoyed especially solicitous care. In cases where the supporting tasks of maintaining the household were shared among several people, we observed light duties for the favored child and enhanced opportunities for relaxing family time together. This phenomenon was exemplified by Erick (3), known about town as one of the healthiest and best-behaved of his age group. Though no father was present in his household, there was both a mother and a grandmother, as well as a great-uncle and two older half-siblings. Erick's mother had a salaried job as a municipal secretary, with regular hours, doing tasks like carrying messages of phone calls from door to door. Each morning, she arose before dawn to tidy the rooms and prepare breakfast. When the sun rose, Erick awoke and called her: "Mamá, mamá." She sang songs to help him get dressed: "Así se pone el zapato, así se pone la media, así se pone el pantalón (that's the way you put on your shoes, socks, pants)." He washed his face and hands at the spigot in the inner patio and then went to the kitchen for breakfast. The meal over, his mother went off to work, his siblings headed for school, and Erick had his grandmother, sometimes the uncle as well, to spend most of the day with, before his mother returned home to sing him goodnight songs. Sometimes, before sleep, Erick, his mother, brother, and sister gathered on their mother's bed to watch television or play a game of Monopoly.

The same themes of a solid arrangement among the adults managing the household, a relatively healthy household economy, and few or no other young children in the family appear in additional cases of children whose care was particularly indulgent. Yovana (5), Lizbeth (5), and Jeferson (10) had all been born years after their nearest sibling and enjoyed the attention of older brothers and sisters without the competition for resources that this usually entailed. Yovana's parents, adult siblings, and preschool teachers were all convinced that she could suffer symptoms such as nosebleeds if she became upset. They conspired to make sure she was happy, and she navigated the various forms of support skillfully. She had a plan in case of disaster. As she told her mother, referencing her older siblings in descending order by age: "When you and my dad die, first Fabio will care for me; when he dies Elena will, and when Elena dies, Ever will. And when Ever dies, who will care for me? I'll tell my teacher to."[4] Lizbeth (5) had the almost unrivaled attention of her mother, suspended momentarily during the past summer while the mother prepared for the exam for her teacher's license. Jeferson, the only boy in his family, was recognized ruefully by his parents as "engreido (pampered)." His two older sisters (15 and 17) were there to do the housework that would otherwise have fallen to him. He had only recently started to wash his own school uniform after his mother heard a radio program cautioning about the negative effects of too much indulgence.[5] Although he had the job of bringing in the family's pair of sheep from a hillside outside the community at 5:00 P.M. every day, his mother did it for him whenever there was a conflict with his school activities.

Finally, solicitous care might be associated with letting one's guard down and permitting feelings of sympathy to rush forth. Yeny (11) was being especially attentive to her sister Karin, not yet two years old. Their mother, already stressed by the four children under her care, was suffering through an unexpected and unwelcome pregnancy. Yeny remembered how she had felt when her brother next in age had come along. She wanted to soften the blow for Karin. Manuela, school librarian, still remembered the way her normally cold and distant father treated her when he was drinking. At those times, "He was more affectionate, he paid more attention to me. He would say, 'Little daughter, what is it you want? Here, take this (some money), it's for you.'" Gift-giving—as we discuss in connection with clothing in particular (chapter 8)—was one way that yauyinos demonstrated their disposition to take care.

Preocuparse *(Being Concerned with or about): Care as Taking Notice*

Criticisms of townspeople for a supposed lack of concern where concern ought to exist were frequently deployed by relative outsiders and persons who, for whatever reason, felt authorized to pass judgment on others. One Bellavista neighbor complained that the elderly deaf woman wandering around town had a daughter, but "she doesn't care about her mother (no le importa); she lives in Lima and can't be bothered." The nuns from the Service and Sacrifice congregation fretted over what they construed as neglected elderly persons in the towns of Sur Grande. The situation illustrated, they said, the underside of parents' wish for their children to find a way out of the rural town; that is, the children forgot about the parents they left behind. "Here, nobody is concerned (acá nadie se preocupa)" (Leinaweaver 2022; Zegarra 2022). As Leinaweaver has argued for the term "gratitude" (2013) in a similar context, the notion of *preocuparse* is most frequently identified through its absence: if "here, nobody is concerned," then care cannot be realized. Similarly, of Henry's parents, the local health workers said: "They are older persons. It seems like they don't take an interest [in Henry's wellbeing] anymore (parece que ya no les interesa). They go to (work) the field and they are tired."

The remark about Henry's parents, resonating with observations we have made in several chapters thus far, suggests that indifference may be a consequence of overwork and exhaustion rather than negligence. Señora Ana offered an insight that suggested indifference might even be a value worthy of cultivation. Her comments emerged in connection with the unexpected research participant Pinocho, a dog who became attached to the field team in Bellavista. They responded by giving it food and water, even trying to figure out how they could give it its first bath. Ana told them that this arrangement was doomed to failure. They would become stressed by the demands of collecting food for Pinocho, just as women in the town were stressed by the limitless obligations to care for their families. It left them no room to grow as persons. She said: "You have to learn to become indifferent."

Caregivers expected the children they looked after to take notice and follow their instructions, though this was variably enforced. As social distance increased, the right and the means for ensuring children's obedience diminished. On one occasion, Leoncio's (11) grandmother and principal caretaker, Carolina, sent him and his two cousins, visiting from Huancayo, to bring her cows from their pasture to the homestead where a veterinarian was on hand to treat them. Carolina waited a while, decided to send their grandfather after them, waited some more, and finally set off herself to meet them. "Nobody pays any attention to me! This boy doesn't obey me anymore." She concluded: "Grandson is not like a child of one's own, is it?" That is, with one's own children one has tools for ensuring obedience;

outside that closed circle, the instruments for achieving compliance are lacking. Yauyinos may have muttered loudly about the bad behavior of children of visitors or neighbors, and they may certainly have commented behind their backs, but they did not strike or seek to correct somebody else's child.

Similarly, people could witness injustices committed against children and serious failures of care, but they did not intervene, not for a lack of concern but because of a lack of authorization. Field-worker Roxana recorded a moment when a fruit and vegetable vendor arrived with her daughter (4) and toddler son from Cañete for the weekly fair in Bellavista. As people spilled off the bus with their packages, the daughter could not prevent the boy from tumbling onto the street, for which she received a blow from their mother. "I bring you along to help, and you only make it worse!" she shouted. Later, as they rested up and waited for the return bus, the mother once again attacked the girl, slapping her face and head several times. She and her brother had fallen when she tried to carry him. "I told you not to pick him up! I told you he was going to fall!" The girl sobbed and rubbed her head. The mother felt called upon to justify herself to Señora Elva, outside whose store this drama was taking place. "She doesn't obey me," she explained. Elva allowed that the girl should have known she didn't have the strength to carry her little brother. The group of three sat on the curb across from the bus stop, the boy on his mother's lap, the girl opposite them and still sobbing. Roxana, on the pretext of buying the last of the avocadoes, asked the woman if that was her daughter. "Of course! I'm not going to discipline somebody else's child (Claro pues, no voy a corregir a hijo ajeno)." Concern could not transform into attention, except where very close relationships were involved.

Obedience, Discipline, and Violence against Children

Even when their tools for enforcement were limited, caretakers expected the children they looked after to heed them. Señora Úrsula obtained a high degree of collaboration from her three children by being in constant motion herself and creating endless opportunities for the children to pitch in. With a large meal to prepare, she asked Elisa (6) to put some chunks of meat in a bowl for keeping in the refrigerator. Elisa objected, saying that her mother had not given her the money she asked for to buy the DVD of a movie she wanted. At that, Úrsula left the kitchen and came back in with a stick. Elisa picked up the bowl immediately and put it in the refrigerator.

Threats of punishments were employed by caregivers as a form of instruction. With a rush of customers—including a clutch of unruly boys—pushing to get into the store as it opened for the afternoon, Pamela's (9) mother shouted out to her: "Don't open the door! If they steal something, I'm going to hit you hard! (¡Que te engañen te voy a dar duro!)" Pamela was expected to absorb a double lesson: how to care for the family business and how to look out for the trickery of boys.

If children persisted in misbehaving, physical punishment could and sometimes did follow. Agripina said she had beaten her son Estanislao (12) repeatedly with a rope that just happened to be the first thing that came to hand. She had told him to go out and get firewood. Instead, she found him bathing in the irrigation canal with his half-brother (3). Without excusing her actions, we can imagine the pressure Agripina was under to get a meal prepared and served to her family of five, just as the firewood ran out. Mothers were often the disciplinary front line, keenly interested in getting the children's compliance in household tasks and sometimes worn thin by the many demands of their roles (Ames 2013a, INEI 2016).

The instances of violence we were told about, including some that the field teams witnessed personally, gave evidence of long chains of interactions that bound children to their caretakers, and local ideas about discipline and punishment as well as violence and resistance. Some of the violence was justified by the children or was at least understandable: they recognized that they had disobeyed an order or misbehaved.[6] Set in the context of an ongoing relationship, even severe punishments did not necessarily destroy the children's trust in the fundamental goodwill of their caretakers. Some of the violence had a contextual explanation while still being reprehensible, as when Isaac's father, dead drunk, threatened everybody in the house with a knife such that they fled to sleep outside. The physical violence against children seemed to fall into three categories: ensuring that assigned tasks were done properly and promptly; retribution for faults; and harassment.

Many of the tasks assigned to children were extremely onerous. They began very early, when children were barely strong enough or able to understand what was wanted and perform it adequately. This created a problem of compliance for the adults (Lobo 1984). Children in Yauyos did get hit with belts, sticks, short whips (the classic three leather strands on a handle called "tres puntos" or "San Martín"[7]), and other implements. It did not happen to all of them, and not often, but the threat was known. Adults—including some teachers—might make a gesture of unbuckling a belt and get an immediate reaction of obedience from a child. Violence might even be used with adolescents. At fifteen, Rufina was almost entirely self-sufficient and managed her affairs, including school and a boyfriend, autonomously. Following in her mother's footsteps, she had started a business making and selling the traditional mantas that identified her community of origin. Rufina explained how she had recently learned to weave with a loom under her mother's tutelage. "My mother hit me, I had to learn, and that's how it is that I know it now (mi mamá me pegaba, tenía que aprender, y es así que ahora sé)."

Following on the threats or enactment of violence to obtain compliance, a second category was acts of violence carried out latterly, as punishment when a child had somehow committed a fault. Chiri and Gaby boarded for meals with a family, recently arrived from Huancayo, that was locally notorious for rough handling of the children. Shoves, shouts, and blows were the equivalent of reasons or explanations in the parents' relations with their children and in the children's relations with one another. Serapio, the father, did odd jobs for the local government, while Agustina, the mother, worked as a day-laborer. Their income was insufficient to provide for their four children, aged thirteen, ten, eight, and almost two, soon to be joined by a newborn. One day the field-workers, Serapio, and the children were waiting for their afternoon tea to be served by Agustina and her aunt. Yeny (10), seated between the two field-workers, suddenly began to cry.

> Turning towards her mother, she said that her dad had hit her with an electrical cable because she was fighting with older brother Marlon in the kitchen. Yeny said Marlon was bothering her and not letting her finish a task that her father had given her. Don Serapio stared straight ahead, looking at the door. Yeny addressed him directly: "You don't hit your sons because they go with you to the field but you do hit me." Their mother directed her words to her husband: "How is it that you hit my daughter?" Her voice was calm, not accusatory. After some 5 minutes Yeny stopped crying and Don Serapio left the house. (Field notes, Chiri)

When it was used as punishment, physical violence, as well as teasing and verbal abuse, was open to disputation. Had a fault actually been committed? Was some punishment justified? Did the severity of the punishment fit the supposed crime? On that day, after Serapio had departed, Agustina explained to the field-workers: "He is patient, quite a bit, but when he blows up, he blows up. He hits the kids really hard. It even scares me." Chiri's field notes continue, demonstrating both the layered interactions between father and daughter, and the ways that the siblings interacted around the possibility and reality of violence:

> On other days when we have eaten with the family, Serapio has been quiet and we hadn't seen him raise his voice at his children. Many times Yeny addresses him affectionately as "papi-li." She smiles and greets him with enthusiasm when he gets home from work, the same as do her brothers. That night Serapio wasn't there for dinner. Marlon found an opportunity to tease his sister, reminding her that her dad had hit her that morning. Yeny stopped eating and said nothing. Sometime later, Yeny announced, "I'm going to dance." She was inspired by a TV program that was playing on the old black and white TV that the family kept in the kitchen. Marlon replied: "You're going to dance just like my dad made you dance." Later yet, Yeny commented on something Marlon said as if calling attention to a mistake or misbehavior. He became very serious: "You don't have the right to correct me." Yeny looked away. (Field notes, Chiri)

Probably the most extreme case of child abuse in all the six towns was that of Guillermina (approximately 8). She was not one of the children in the biographies sample, so we do not know many circumstances of her life, only that she was the oldest in a family with several younger children and a very violent and demanding mother. She used a strategy of running away and hiding under the protection of a neighbor until her mother's wrath died down. A backhanded way of negotiation it was, but it served the purpose of reducing the severity of the blows she received while introducing an element of public shaming. For children to understand that they were in a position to bargain, that they could make their own interpretation of the situation and express their own demands for justice, entailed a high degree of confidence and, as in this case, the availability of allies.

The third way that violence manifested in children's relationships with their caregivers took the form of a kind of casual, ill-tempered harassment. Some parents seemed to use physical and verbal abuse of their children as a way of letting off steam or expressing their impotence, driven more by their own internal states than by the children's behavior. That is what Guille's uncle opined as he observed his seven-year-old nephew become more and more withdrawn and uncontrollable. Fearing his mother's blows, Guille simply avoided her. The uncle thought his sister had a psychological condition that was driving this vicious cycle. Only disturbed people, he said, would resort to beatings in the face of evidence of how counterproductive they were. His assessment of the futility of violence in parent-child relations is in line with modern child psychology and with the consensus reached in recent studies of Andean families. Ames and Crisóstomo (2019) found that many Andean parents may occasionally punish their children physically, and many more argue that it could be necessary and should be within their rights, but very few make a regular practice of it.

These internal community mechanisms did important work in promoting children's safety, yet as we have seen, acts of violence still occurred. The Peruvian government, in view of this, takes some role in protecting children (Luttrell-Rowland 2012; Luttrell-Rowland 2023). Parental actions that might qualify as exploitation of child labor, neglect, and corporal punishment all, in principle, come under the jurisdiction, at the local level, of the Defensoría Municipal del Niño, Niña y Adolescente (DEMUNA). Created in the 1990s, the system of DEMUNAs extends the mandate of the Public Defender (Defensoría del Pueblo) to protect and promote human rights throughout Peru. It complements the work of justices of the peace, mandated to enforce the norms of adequate care for persons under eighteen and other dependents unable to care for themselves. In 2008 it still felt new and unfamiliar to most of the population. In all but major cities, there was no budget to cover specialized staff. Local mayors designated one or another employee to devote a limited number of weekly hours to registering complaints from the public and organizing reconciliation sessions (Ellison 2018).[8]

Of the six towns in our study, Yauyos City had the only fully operating DEMUNA, while Los Caminos had an incipient service.[9] In 2004, the year closest to our study for which they had compiled data, the DEMUNA in Yauyos City had processed some one hundred cases. The leading category of disputes brought before it, here as in the rest of Peru, was claims for child support.[10] Ultimately, the DEMUNA's effectiveness was compromised because children could not represent themselves or take the initiative to open an inquiry. Adults had to perform the paperwork on behalf of children. This was justified as a matter of protecting the children and ensuring that the rules of informed consent were correctly applied. It undoubtedly served as a protection for the DEMUNA and the local government that housed it in case disputes arose among various persons who claimed an interest in a child's welfare. It certainly did not guarantee that the child's voice was heard.

Conclusions

This chapter draws on and dialogues with the anthropological literature on care we reviewed in chapter 1. It resonates with many of the dimensions of care that have been identified and charted in regions of the world very distant from the rural Andes. An obvious one is the interlocking of the practical actions involved in caregiving and the moral norms that provide a backdrop, rationale, and standard for performing care. Providing care to anyone under the conditions of rural life in the Andes is onerous. Yet actual negligence, much less wrongful or ill-intentioned care, was rare in Yauyos. (The exceptions are the topic of chapter 7.)

Caregiving arrangements combined a mix of household members, extended family, community members, visitors, and occasionally official agencies and authorities. Any one of them could be overburdened and overextended. Mothers, especially, often were; many had numerous children under their charge, absent or unhelpful husbands, and a myriad of commitments they undertook to sustain their families' economies. Some actors felt a social mandate to feign ignorance or even to align with other adults against children's needs for care. Some illustrated in Peruvian timbre the syndrome of bureaucratic indifference (Herzfeld 1992). Despite the shortcomings of one and another, the plurality of caregivers, and children's capacity to seek out those most willing to treat them well, gave some assurance that most of the care they experienced would rise to local standards of adequacy.

The evidence from Yauyos confirmed the importance of power and hierarchy in relationships involving care. Pressed by their partners, some women had more children than they might have independently chosen to, and many more were forced to take on greater responsibility for attending to their children and other family members than they considered their fair share. In addition to gender, relative poverty and position in the local system of prestige also influenced the distribution of care, whether the obligation to assume unwanted tasks, such as the *ecónomos*, or the right to receive special consideration, such as was afforded to men from prominent families.

Caring for children everywhere straddles a contradiction. On the one hand, the care, especially of very young and vulnerable children, entails the most meticulous and dedicated of care practices. We have seen, in this chapter and in the preceding one, how infants were breastfed, swaddled, carried almost constantly on the backs first of their mothers (or surrogates) and then those of older siblings. On the other hand, caregivers were charged with teaching, encouraging, and sometimes forcing children to do things for themselves. In Yauyos this principle found extreme expression. We saw the emphasis caregivers placed on children becoming capable of caring for themselves, as early as possible, and in as many ways as possible. Becoming self-reliant, a competent caregiver for oneself and for others, was essential to achieving personhood.

Internal states, the management of emotion, the "disposition" of caregivers, and their hopes for the future have also emerged as important topics in the cross-cultural literature on care. Children in Yauyos appeared to be happy caregivers, most of the time. Caring for siblings, domestic animals, playmates, and home combined, often seamlessly, with play, diversion, and what the children accepted as meaningful learning experiences. Complex feelings came into play when their actions were judged to be deficient and sparked violent reactions from adults. Such situations awakened fear, pain, resentment, and a sense of injustice in the victims. They were also associated with complex feelings on the part of the perpetrators, including memories of having received beatings and unfair accusations when they were children. Perhaps the predominant sensation that the parents transmitted was their lack of control. Unable to control so many of the circumstances of their lives, they struggled to dominate their children and even their own desires.

7

The Limits of Care

The mandates of kinship may silence doubts about who within family networks is deserving of care, but outside of their bounds the question arises: who is truly owed care? At stake is the treatment of persons that are not part of the intimate world of kin and close friends, yet still within sight and hearing. What do adults teach children, both discursively and through their behavior, about their obligations toward persons they do not know well? Who is made into a stranger through practices of exclusion?

Care as it manifests itself in relationships based on descending degrees of proximity and affinity is not central to current theories of care in the social sciences (Hughes 2002; but see Bornat et al. 1997), though it has more purchase within philosophy (O'Neill 2000; Nussbaum 1993). Different collectives make different reckonings of the costs and benefits of limiting or enlarging the sphere of care. Where resources are scarce, the calculation may be especially contentious. At social border zones, the obligation to care is attenuated, qualified, or even extinguished (Appiah 2010). The right to demand care may be in doubt, while the possibilities for refusing care are abundant and often entail no sanctions. Deniers of care can remain anonymous, faceless in the crowd.

The six towns we engaged with were subject to both centrifugal and centripetal forces. With the possible exception of the provincial capital, all were small enough for everyone to recognize everyone else. Though the right to privacy was cherished and gossip was not approved of, people were still generally aware of the relative position, welfare, and needs of other community members. Long-standing norms and institutions governed the rights and obligations of citizens insofar as their behavior affected the welfare of others and the viability of the community per se (compare Canessa 2012; Allen 2002). Yet collective ownership of many resources, with rights and procedures defined partly by law and partly by custom, posed the threat of misuse or abuse (Diez 1999; Puente 2022). Systems of stratification, giving prominence to some kin groups and authority to elders, existed in tense combination with leveling mechanisms: democratic elections to public office, public goods such as education and health care, and assemblies on the plaza for discussion and decision making. The political violence of the 1980s and 1990s in Peru had lasting consequences for an entire generation (Aldana et al. 1994; Villapolo and Vásquez 1999; compare Bellino 2017 in Guatemala), including a silencing of conflicts as a reaction to events that were still painful (Theidon 2004; Poole 1994). Further afield, many dynamics in Peruvian society reinforced the underdevelopment of places like Yauyos and the structural limits on opportunities for their residents (Cotler 2021).

At a level of discourse, few would deny that children are a collective resource and responsibility: "Our children are our future" tripped easily off the tongues of politicians and community leaders. Yet some children in Yauyos were clearly "strangers," not truly incorporated within the sphere of care. Even setting aside extreme cases, the ambiguities and failures of care in the world of adults had consequences for all children. Having traveled to other parts of the country, having tasted its diversity, having seen the effects of social exclusion, and even having been the butt of it, many parents aspired to teach their children the values of tolerance and concern for others. These efforts often fell short.

Care among Neighbors

The concept of social capital gained prominence in the 1990s as a tool for understanding what appeared to be a worldwide erosion of civic engagement and commitment to community. The arguments resonated greatly in Latin America, where failures of social capital helped explain the tendencies toward antidemocratic politics, predatory capitalism, and developmental stagnation. Empirical scholarship from political science suggests that Latin American countries are particularly affected by low levels of trust: in institutions, in political leaders, and interpersonally (Scartascini and Valle Luna 2020; Atria and Siles 2003).[1] Low levels of trust appear to correlate with high levels of inequality, and Latin American societies are among the most unequal in the world (Scartascini and Valle Luna 2020; Jordahl 2007; Ferroni, Mateo, and Payne 2008).[2]

These core concepts were tested for their purchase among rural populations in a baseline survey that was part of the Yauyos Values Study (see chapter 2). The survey asked respondents (N = 383) about the possibility of accepting as neighbors persons belonging to potentially stigmatized groups. The results reflected levels of tolerance among yauyinos, but they also suggest the limits of care. Neighborliness would entail some degree of attention, concern, and possibly concrete help for the neighbors. The findings suggested that differences of place of origin, ethnicity, religion, and politics could be overlooked, but that histories of mental illness or having a prison record were problematic. Other factors that disqualified

TABLE 7.1

Tolerance toward various categories of potential neighbors

Category of person as potential neighbor	Reject the possibility ("no me gustaría") (percentage)	Accept reluctantly ("aceptaría con recelo") (percentage)	Neutral ("me daría igual") (percentage)	Total (percentage)
Someone from outside the community	17.5	17.5	64.9	100.0
Someone of a different race	23.0	16.5	60.5	100.0
Someone of a different religion	29.8	11.5	58.6	100.0
Someone with different political ideas	32.7	18.3	49.0	100.0
Someone that had been in prison	53.5	32.6	13.8	100.0
Someone with a mental illness	61.0	21.2	17.8	100.0
Someone with HIV/AIDS	74.3	14.1	11.5	100.0
Someone with alcohol addiction	79.8	13.6	6.5	100.0
A homosexual	84.3	6.8	8.9	100.0
Someone with a drug addiction	86.1	11.5	2.4	100.0

Source: Values questionnaire, 1999. Internal report, unpublished. N = 383.

persons as potential neighbors for a vast majority of yauyinos were a diagnosis of HIV/AIDS (poorly understood at the time), alcoholism, homosexuality, and drug addiction (table 7.1).

Evidence of mistrust and a lack of community could be found, during our study, in small things like petty theft. Exploring the paths around Los Caminos one afternoon, field-worker Gabriela was out with Katherine (11) and her mother. They passed by a large orchard enclosed on all sides by a wall. Inside were peach trees, owned by a local entrepreneur who had been acquiring land from his neighbors to fill a growing demand for fruit from buyers on the coast. Katherine's mother ordered her over the wall to pick some. The orchard was guarded, though not very effectively. Katherine had to hide momentarily when she heard men's voices up the road. Luckily for her, they did not approach any closer, and Katherine emerged with a manta full of peaches. Her mother took over the load, not before hospitably offering a peach to Gabriela.

Nine-year-old Dina's father had formally been denounced, before the local justice of the peace, for having stolen S/.180 ($60) from Aurelia's bodega. At a hearing to clarify the matter, Dina's father laid the blame on his daughter. Dina addressed her father: "But you told me to take the money. Why are you now asking me how it is that I took it?" A townsman volunteered that Dina and her younger siblings probably had been stealing food wherever they had the chance. Everybody knew, he said, that the parents were neglectful, went off to work and did not leave them enough to eat. Instead of being in school, they would wander the streets, unsupervised. Indeed, in our study this was the couple whose care of their children seemed closest to our understanding of negligence. They rejected the possibility of contraception and the woman—already mother of seven—was pregnant once again during the fieldwork. In practice, Dina was almost a full-time caretaker of her younger siblings. Of the stolen S/.180, the children had spent S/.30 in various shops around town. Their mother had kept the other S/.150. She said she intended to return it, but, more than a year later, she still had not done so. The storekeeper had filed a second complaint.

Theft is a problem with grave implications in small, rural communities that rely for their regular functioning on their members' willingness to respect the norms governing private property, the rights of usufruct, and communal patrimony (Williams 1997). With household members constantly in and out, working and running errands, houses were often left unlocked or closed with a simple padlock or even a hook. Some assets, like standing crops, were impossible to protect. If disputes arose among community members, local norms were the deciding factor (La Rosa Calle 2007). Any intervention from the legal system was unlikely (see Luttrell-Rowland 2023, 68). The provincial capital had a relatively large police station and a jail, but the only police presence in the other five towns was the small detachment in Los Caminos, responsible for patrolling an impossibly huge, mountainous territory.[3]

Petty theft is one end of a continuum that alludes to the roots of mistrust in Andean communities. In the adult world, thefts occurred that were far from petty. Theft of livestock was a constant threat, despite the branding *herranzas* that drew crowds of kin and neighbors as witnesses. It was said that Rufina's family had been ostracized from the annex where she grew up because of accusations of cattle theft against her older brothers. People might encroach on others' fields, and their animals might damage others' crops and terraces. Opportunities were rife for price-gouging by cattle merchants that took animals to distant and more lucrative markets, or by freelance truckers who transported sacks of produce to market. The concerns over misappropriation of a vital and scarce resource, water (Gelles 2000; Li 2015; Rasmussen 2015), were never-ending and justified the omnipresence of water management associations to enforce quotas and turns, as we saw Pepe participating in in chapter 4. Here too, children might be used to surreptitiously manipulate the portals of irrigation canals to divert water to their family's land. Far greater abuses almost certainly occurred when wealthy, well-connected community members negotiated the volumes of water to be allotted to them.

Harriss-White (2003), analyzing the persistence of poverty in village India, gives full berth to the caprices of weather, the insecurity of crop yields, and the unpredictability of commodity prices, even as she documents how farming families struggled to meet expenditures on health, education, and ritual obligations. For small farmers, the impossibility of synchronizing their investments and expenditures with income flows created a dependence on the "nearby rich." These wealthier members of the community could give emergency loans and assistance to their vulnerable neighbors, often tied to promises of loyalty and exclusivity in commercial arrangements that ultimately reinforced their dominion.[4] In Yauyos, such debt was familiar enough: bodegas and restaurants extended credit and kept running tabs for their customers (including preschoolers, in stores selling candy and snacks). In cash-starved economies such as those of rural Yauyos, this was only practical.

Corruption in local government marks another point on the continuum of sources of mistrust. Local government corruption is a major issue in Peru (Cusato 2020; Quiroz 2008; Huber 2008). The pool of interested candidates is small, and elected authorities too often turn out to be incompetent or actively harmful, which translates into mismanaging communal assets, ignoring environmental degradation, and failing to invest in human resources. Many Yauyos towns had absentee mayors and disengaged governors. In Terrazas, Señora Raquel questioned why the municipal government had not yet managed to rebuild the school a year after the earthquake, and indeed, why the school had been damaged at all. She insinuated that there had been corruption in awarding the contract, and she linked that corruption to broader social problems like a failure to engage youth and inspire a strong work ethic.

> If the school had been well built it wouldn't have collapsed. They used inferior materials, thin wires. It's not right. It all fell down. It was a beautiful school, like a school in Lima. It could have been used at night for adult education or technical courses or so many things.
>
> Before, when I was in school, with nothing more than the light of an oil-burning lantern, we were all dedicated to education. We had music classes. The school principal made sure that the pupils had things to do, that they didn't have to go out at night. There have to be things to do in this town at

night, things every student likes. As it stands, what can they do? Just drink. How else can they entertain themselves? They're adolescents.

In my times, the principal organized outings to different places every Sunday. We played sports in different towns, one Sunday here, another Sunday there. Another Sunday we all went out to gather firewood. We collected huge amounts of firewood. We put it in sacks and sold it door-to-door. Now, all the teachers know how to do [to raise money for school activities] is to ask for contributions from every business. I'm tired of it, all the requests. Now they're asking for soft drinks, next it's for a gift, next it's something else. They never make the students work.

In my days they had us sweep the whole town. Every household paid us something. We collected a lot of money. We bought a mimeograph for the school. We did a lot. We never bothered the businesses, we never asked for padrinos. Now nobody wants to work.

Señora Raquel lamented a perceived transformation in both the work ethic and sense of responsibility to one's community. One possible cause is a shift in how people understood the beneficiaries of their efforts, whether the community as a whole or special interest groups. The population of Los Caminos had vivid memories of the times prior to 1985 when they had no land route connecting them to the rest of the province except by foot, mule, or horseback. In order to access a road, they would have to build it themselves. And build it they did, like innumerable other rural communities throughout twentieth-century Peru. Some of the men that had worked in the mines knew how to place dynamite in the crevices of cliffs. Men and women rode or walked to the point where the work had advanced each day with picks, shovels, and mantas for clearing away the dirt and rubble. The women organized brigades to provide food and water. When it was all over, and the first motor vehicles arrived in town, it sunk in that they would, effectively, have to pay to make use of their road. They had to pay a bus fare to travel, and their products were charged a fee for transportation to market. There was a sense of having been made fools of: rather than affirming the principles of equity and opportunity, the road was enriching the owners of taxis and trucks.

One initiative, a possible answer to Señora Raquel's frustrations about the lack of investment in one's local community, was the recent development of fish farms. Trout were abundant in the streams of Nor Yauyos and putting them in pens in the lakes or reservoirs for regular harvesting was considered a way forward. Pastizales had a small communally owned and managed fish farm, and Terrazas had both community-owned farms, administered by the municipal government, and farms that were private investments. When large orders were placed, the mayor hired dozens of people to clean the fish. Viewed optimistically, this could be seen as a case of government and entrepreneurs working together to harvest renewable resources and generate employment. However, the environmental costs are not yet known, and the irregularity of the employment and further enrichment of those with resources to invest in pits and equipment may ultimately mean this initiative is one more in a series that reproduces inequality.

Collateral Damage: Children and the Moral Failings of Adults

Adults in Yauyos were concerned about their standing in the local community, and children were at least sometimes aware of adults' efforts to defend their good name. Moisés, one of seven children, was convinced that part of the reason his family left their old neighborhood on the outskirts of Cañete was that people were talking about his mother behind her back "when she forgot to comb her hair." Children were honored or tainted by the reputation of their parents and caregivers, and people recognized how children could be corrupted by the bad example set by their elders.

In situations in which upholding an adult reputation might entail sacrificing the interests of a child, children could not always rely on their caregivers to take their side. This occurred, for example, when children were accused of a fault and parents accepted the word of an adult accuser over the word of their children. It occurred when disputes arose over the treatment of young girls sent during summer vacations as domestic workers in the homes of distant relatives in the city (Anderson 2007). The girl might complain to her parents of mistreatment, but they were likely to side with the employer, not wishing to disturb relations within the larger family group. It occurred when older men were able to harass and even seduce adolescents without being challenged by other adults, incidents that Gabriela registered repeatedly in her field notes. For many adults, protecting the web of adult relationships took precedence.

The web of adult relationships was critically important because living as an outlier in rural communities of the Andes entailed high costs.[5] Many people walked in fear of the "envy" (*envidia*) of their neighbors. Rebeca (18) told of her grandmother's death in an annex of Yauyos. The cause, she said, was the jealousy of neighbors who observed her bumper harvest. They bewitched both the grandmother and Rebeca's mother, but the mother got help from a curioso in time.

Gender played a significant role in the routes to perdition for yauyinos. Men with a habit of excessive drinking were probably the most visible examples of damaged reputation from the perspective of children. Cousins Maruja (12) and Junior (8) both had fathers that regularly went on alcoholic binges and were famous around town for their level of addiction. Brothers, they were members of a prominent, well-endowed family. Perhaps out of respect for the rest of the kin group, community members were indulgent and full of lamentations for the state they were in, but the men's children were less forgiving. Another harsh condemnation for men was "vagancia (vagrancy, shiftlessness, laziness)", or "no saber trabajar (not knowing how to work)." Men were excoriated behind their backs for being poor providers, especially when infidelity was an aggravating factor.

THE LIMITS OF CARE   115

Female routes to a poor reputation often invoked sexuality out of place. A woman who had an extramarital affair, or was suspected of it, was severely sanctioned, particularly if her partner was a married man. Widow of a miner who was killed in a road accident, mother of seven children, Ricardina had returned with them from the mining camp to make a new beginning in Terrazas. After five years of widowhood, she was anxious for companionship and support. Meanwhile, her father helped her economically, setting her up with a bodega and paying her utility bills. Ricardina began a new relationship in good faith. Although the man had a family in the community, he was not living with them and wanted, he told her, a separation. Still, gossip spread around town. He was the first object of criticism because of his irresponsible attitude toward his established family. But the criticism spread to Ricardina as it became clear that she was pregnant. She was shunned even by her own mother.

In due time, Ricardina gave birth to Pascual. At first she tried to hide the boy and keep him inside, but, as he grew, that became impossible. She registered him for preschool, saying she did not know his father's name. By this time Pascual's father had abandoned the town for Huancayo, leaving the entire problem behind him. But his first family, and their allies, were implacable. On one occasion a group of them came to the door and forced Pascual to state aloud his father's full name and where he lived. Their faction also arranged for Ricardina to be publicly reprimanded by the authorities. People threw her supposed immorality in her face on the street and insulted her and her older daughters in her store until she felt she had no option but to close shop. Her source of satisfaction was that her older daughters had larger goals. One by one they found family members that could help them migrate to Lima or Huancayo and finish their studies, and all were on their way to acquiring a profession. Ricardina had suffered mightily, but by her daughters' success she felt vindicated.

Fear and Powerlessness

Stories of adults in violation of community norms, of adults being sanctioned, resonated in particularly painful ways for their children. Children could be left with a sense of injustice, of the fallibility of adults and their incapacity to align their behavior with the truth. Junior was plunged into despair when he learned that his alcoholic father had sold the family's three cows, including one that was about to calve, for money to continue drinking. In an interesting obverse of Ricardina's travails, Silvia (14) had a good relationship with her father until it became known that he was involved with another woman. He failed to show up for her first communion, and since then she and her mother had had several unpleasant encounters with the mother of her father's out-of-wedlock child. There were many dimensions to her unhappiness in this situation: the loss of respect and trust for her father (actually, her stepfather), sympathy for her mother, fear of the aggressiveness of the other woman—who did not stop at knocking on their door to demand support for her child—and embarrassment for what others might know about it all. She spent many afternoons in the school library in what seemed to be a strategy for avoiding her arguing parents at home and avoiding the streets where she might run across the other woman.

Young people could be actively harmed by the irresponsibility or outright predation of adults. Some troubling insights were shared by the psychologist from Diaconía working in the towns of Sur Grande, who met with adolescents in their final year of secondary school. She observed a pattern of adolescent girls having sexual relations with men in exchange for pocket money or other favors. Several of the high school students acknowledged that girls had sexual relations with bus company employees in exchange for tickets to Cañete. Some pregnancies had come about as a result. An example we were told of fit the pattern for men in resource-laden positions of power. Emma had reportedly been discovered naked in the rented room of the head of the construction crew working on the school. He insisted that she was the one who took the initiative. After all, he said, he was a married man with a daughter of his own. Whatever the case, there were hisses and murmuring in the audience at high school graduation when that same work crew leader appeared as Emma's *padrino*. The hisses seemed to say: How could Emma's mother not have known the true state of affairs between her daughter and the man she was making her compadre?[6]

Poignantly, some children had been convinced by the persons around them that they themselves were simply and irredeemably bad. Overworked Mayra was harsh and unforgiving in her dealings with the middle children of her seven, including Narciso (7). Field-worker Roxana got into a conversation with his entire group of classmates as school let out one day. The most extroverted of them went through the list of Narciso's faults: he was the worst student academically and the worst behaved, he did not obey the teacher, and he hit the girls. Narciso hung his head and began to move away from the group. Roxana, wishing to bolster his self-image, objected and said that he really was a good kid. Narciso looked at her: "I'm not good (no soy bueno)," he insisted.

Children in Yauyos experienced anger, sadness, jealousy, repulsion, impatience, boredom, disappointment, and frustration, as well as being shunned and ignored. Many of the causes have been touched on in earlier chapters. They involved heavy responsibilities (chapter 4), illnesses and accidents (chapter 5), and the disruptions of movement and migration, whether manifested in bullying by classmates at a new school, or broken links in the circle of family and intimates (chapter 6). Such situations and events led to feelings of fear and insecurity that were sometimes intensified by engagement with the supernatural beings that inhabit the Andes. Children in Yauyos, in general, did not seem to be particularly well versed in Andean cosmology; they mainly referred to the large repertory of non-human "earth beings" that inhabit mountains, mines, or lakes (de la Cadena 2015; Salas 2019; Weismantel 2001) under questioning or under the stimulus of walking past places associated with them. However, they learned from those around them

THE LIMITS OF CARE

that the supernatural posed risks. For example, Pamela suddenly suffered a series of nosebleeds; her mother attributed this to her daughter's having been "taken" by the mountain. Aurora's mother, similar to Pamela's, feared the action of vengeful mountain spirits that cause colds and *mal aire*. She explained: "The earth takes you or a mountain picks you up. You have to make a payment to the earth."[7]

Staying safe depended on being careful about the places one went and the times one went there. Town cemeteries did not figure on children's maps of places to be avoided with fear or repugnance; instead, children seemed to associate funerals and burials with festive community events like All Saints' Day, which satisfactorily separated the dead from the living. By contrast, in Bellavista, the plaza and streets of the upper part of the town were reputed to be an area where spiritual forces congregated. *Condenados* haunt spaces like this in the Andes, "condemned" to wander forever because of the sins they committed while living, devouring humans and animals so incautious as to be out alone at night (Isbell 1985, 135; Fourtané 2015). It was best to take the long route and circumvent the points that were most "charged" (*cargados*). The plaza was a place where ritual payments to the earth were made, not only to cure illness but to counteract *daños* (negative witchcraft). The central Plaza Constitución, side-by-side with the church in Yauyos City, was also a site of risk, per Tomás (11), who shared with field-worker Jhon a tale in which several children playing there disappeared suddenly and were never seen again. The priest erected a cross to mark the spot and offered his life on the condition that no other children were ever to disappear from the town again.

We cannot dismiss the possibility that ideas of supernatural beings were stimulated by the presence in our research team of persons that were of foreign origin (Anderson, Leinaweaver, Gabriela, Chris). Ideas about supernatural beings that inhabit the Andes easily blend with tales of strangers who come onto the scene with unknown intentions. The suspicion of outsiders, especially persons from foreign countries, has roots in many Andean versions of tales about beings pretending to be humans who seduce or steal people for various nefarious purposes (the *pishtaco* figure, described elegantly by Weismantel 2001, is the paramount example). Though these ideas were present and children could engage with them when prompted, in most cases they did not seem to feel that such unworldly beings were closely enough involved in their lives to awaken their fears. The plaza in Bellavista was associated not only with supernatural dangers but with the executions perpetrated by Shining Path during the years of political violence. When Pamela spoke of being afraid of going out at night, she mentioned the "night walkers" of Shining Path and the possibility of thoroughly human thieves and kidnappers (see Barrios 2013).

Stranger Children

The technical assistant at the health post was chatting with a pair of women neighbors as they waited for their plates of salchipapa from the cart. The technician's 7-year-old son Tito began to hit and throw stones at Hilario, who happened to be nearby. From time to time his mother called to him to stop, but she did not interrupt her conversation nor make any further move to curtail his behavior. Hilario made no attempt to respond, despite being twice the size of Tito. He simply ran away, trying to shield himself from the blows. The mother shouted to her son that he should leave Hilario alone because he might have a bad reaction. She told him to play instead with another boy his own size who happened onto the scene. (Field notes, Gabriela)

Gabriela, a field-worker who paid particular attention to special needs children and the way they were dealt with in communities of Yauyos, went on to note that Hilario, fourteen years old, had been diagnosed as autistic and epileptic, with severely limited intellectual development. He communicated through gestures, grunts, and movement. Dirty and dressed in tatters, he spent his days wandering around the streets of the town. Children threw rocks at him and teased and insulted him. He could often be found in the plaza, the entrance to the town where the trucks and vehicles came and went, or at the construction site for the new town hall. Dante, wise elder and municipal caretaker, tried to keep an eye out for him, but Hilario had a dangerous habit of running after cars, perhaps reliving the day when his beloved older sister, and first caregiver, left to pursue her plans for a technical career in Lima.

Hilario's family had moved to Lima when he was a toddler, and he had received treatment at one of the country's most prestigious hospitals. His treatment stopped when his pregnant mother was abandoned by his father and could not afford to raise her soon-to-be-three children there. She brought the children back with her to her hometown, anticipating family support and the benefit of what the doctors advised would be a more "tranquil" environment in a rural setting. But the cost of Hilario's medicine was prohibitive, and he needed professional monitoring. He became extremely agitated, however, at any attempt to get him on a bus or van going to Lima. His primary caregiver was his younger sister, a slight girl of twelve who struggled to meet his basic needs and received many blows from much-larger Hilario in the process. She put food out where he could find it and, pushing, coaxing, threatening, and pulling, brought him home at night from wherever he happened to be. Gabriela was convinced he had not had a bath or changed clothes for more than a month. Floundering financially and already anticipating a crisis when Hilario's sister finished high school and would no longer be around to care for him, the mother was considering migrating to Spain, where her brother lived and worked. She would leave Hilario in an institution run by nuns in Lima (Portocarrero and Sanborn 2003).

Hilario was occasionally joined on the plaza by Henry (14–15), another adolescent with a cognitive or emotional disability, though a notably less severe one. He lived with his elderly parents. They could not have maintained their meager herds and modest plantings were it not for Henry's help, which came at the cost of keeping him out of school. Like Hilario's mother, they also considered institutionalizing Henry in Lima. This felt increasingly inevitable because some people in the town worried that he was becoming a threat to the girls. He stared at them for long periods. Some speculated he had harassed girls, or soon would.

Hilario and Henry were children of the community who were in the process of being expelled by the community: they were being made strangers. As such, they were losing their rights to care, and it became thinkable for them to be sent away and institutionalized. They make a fitting close to this chapter about the limits of care and the boundaries that people in Yauyos drew around the sphere of those to whom care is owed. As we noted previously, the Yauyos Values Study in the late 1990s found that persons with mental illness or problems of substance abuse were high on the list of those not acceptable as neighbors. The attitude that predominated, in cases like Hilario and Henry as well as the grown-up alcoholics and predators we have seen thus far, was that there was simply nothing to be done. It is undoubtedly true that rural towns such as those of Yauyos did not have the resources to deal with problems of addiction, physical disabilities, and severe mental illness.[8] It is not true that no such resources existed in other parts of Peru and could not have been brought to bear (Salmon and Bregaglio 2015).

Children might also be excluded, distanced, or made strange in less extreme cases and through everyday practices like the bullying, discrimination, and marginalizaton that showed up on children's playgrounds. We know from an ample body of research the marvelous ingenuity of children as inventors of systems of exclusion to apply to other children (for example, Goodenough 1990). Children in many parts of the world have rituals of contamination ("cooties," being "it") and elaborate ideologies that underlie practices of marginalization (Best 1989; Goodwin 2006). In the towns of Yauyos, certain children were vulnerable to others' teasing, harassment, and sometimes outright aggression. They tended to be children who lacked defenders in the form of older siblings or cousins. They might have physical problems or personal qualities that set them apart. Because the towns were small, children were thrown almost continuously into the company of others; their playmates were their schoolmates and even their next-door neighbors. The victims of bullying had no alternative group or place to hide.

Field-worker Gaby observed eight-year-old Lázaro, who had the reputation of being a bully, on the playground one day after school. Clad in his school uniform with backpack on his back, Lázaro hit his dog across the nose, then picked it up and carried it over to a drainage ditch, where he pitched it into the water. Lázaro pointed and laughed as it struggled to get out, then paused to watch a group of children playing marbles. His dog approached again, playfully nipping his hand. Lázaro responded by grabbing its nose and swinging it side to side. The dog twisted loose and again nipped Lázaro's hand. "Ya no juego (I'm not playing anymore)," he said, and kicked the dog in the stomach. It ran away, yelping. Lázaro now turned his full attention to the marbles game. He stepped in between two boys and kicked away their marbles. "No molestes (don't bother us)," they said. Lázaro sat down to watch for a moment and then asked if he could join the game. Silently, the boys simply moved a few meters away from him. At this Lázaro decided to leave, but, glancing toward his house, he saw that the door was closed and padlocked. He wandered up the street.

Far from adults intervening to stop children's marginalization of others, they might fall in with the children's ideas and practices of distancing.[9] Candelaria (6) was gaining a reputation for aggressiveness among both her peers and the adults. Shirley (10) was protective of her little sister Ada, saying, "Don't touch her. Crazy kids aren't allowed to touch her." Candelaria might tug at Ada or give her a push, but she seemed only to want to give her a kiss. Yet she was unpredictable. On one occasion she bit off a piece of the arm of Shirley's doll and threw it back at her as she ran away. Another time, as parents were delivering their children to school, she ran toward Edgardo, an infant in his mother's arms, and roughly pulled on his arm. "Just wait and see what I'll do to you," said the mother. "My baby is already traumatized; he's afraid of you." Field-worker Violeta asked Candelaria why she did things that made the youngest children cry. She replied, in a poignant echo of Narciso, whom we quoted earlier: "It's because I'm bad."

Children's reasons for setting some of their peers aside as less-than-desirable companions clearly fit into a children's world, where dolls and marbles and being allowed to participate in games were the currency, rather than tokens like sexual orientation or the capacity for judicious self-control. Yet the underlying logic of including some and excluding others has much in common with adult ways. It was as if children were experimenting with various criteria of exclusion in an effort to understand why this was an issue of importance in the adult world. And just as some adults looked on themselves as "strangers" whose claims on the care and esteem of others were dubious, so we have heard two children—Narciso and Candelaria—say explicitly, "I'm bad." The children appeared to take their cues from adults as they drew lines around who was deserving of solicitous care and who was not.

Conclusions

This chapter has explored the sense of community in rural towns of Yauyos and the norms that govern caring among—not exactly "strangers"—but not family members either. No one would question that—even in a single generation—profound changes have taken place in Andean communities, changes that have transformed the collective structures of the past. The rules of affinity and reciprocity gave order and predictability to the relations among and between households. When and how one could draw on the support and assistance of others was known. Transgressions and violations of trust were publicly acknowledged. Community authorities had the power to apply drastic sanctions, including ostracism, to persons who contravened the norms. The authorities themselves were subject to public scrutiny.

That, at least, was how things were supposed to work. But despite institutions, norms, and traditions that seemed as if they ought to nudge toward the contrary, levels of mistrust were high in the towns of Yauyos, just as they are throughout Peru, according to surveys. Analysts of the Andean community today (e.g., Seligmann and Fine-Dare 2018; Cánepa and Lamas 2020) emphasize the force of individualism and the encroachment of market relations on nearly every aspect of life.

Adult norms of behavior were in flux and were often ignored; some transgressions were even flaunted. Adult failings were on full view to children, and the spectacle induced feelings of fear and insecurity. Children had good reason to question the trustworthiness of the world around them, not only as witnesses to adults' unreliability but because of the uncertainties surrounding unseen malevolent forces. Though they received vague and contradictory messages about these matters, they had to consider the possibility of interventions by mountains, springs, and spirits known from traditional Andean cosmology. In this respect and others, this chapter has highlighted the inability of children to control or even comprehend crucial parts of their world.

One controversial method of control that we have foregrounded relates to estrangement: practices like bullying, teasing, and sanctioning that converted community members into strangers beyond the limits of care. Adults in Yauyos were reluctant to admit into the sphere of care persons positioned too far from their accepted models of human beings. Even some children—notably children with clear symptoms of mental illness—were converted into "strangers" and placed at the borders or even outside the bounds of the community's obligation to care. And children made a similar move in their relations among themselves. They marginalized children with whom they played and went to school, seemingly having understood that such exclusion was a normal part of adult life. Exclusion, marginalization, and othering were the processes by which the limits of care were built, mapped, and reproduced.

8

Care and Flourishing

The limits of care, and the unhappy experiences described in preceding chapters, inflected young people's possibilities of joy and flourishing. By mid-adolescence and late adolescence, many young people in Yauyos had concerns about how well things were going for them in the world. We learn this from a survey conducted as part of the Yauyos Values Study. Applying a questionnaire to 160 students in their fourth and fifth (final) year of secondary school (most between 15 and 17 years of age), the surveyors found that a good two-fifths, or 43 percent, of youths considered themselves not very happy. And yet, amid all the challenges we have enumerated in these pages, 55 percent of boys and 60 percent of girls considered themselves to be happy or very happy, as table 8.1 illustrates.

What did yauyino youth need to be happy and to flourish? We referenced as part of our theoretical framework (chapter 1) a number of approaches to notions

---

TABLE 8.1
In general, do you consider yourself happy?

	Total	Boys	Girls
Very happy	16 (10%)	5 (6%)	11 (15%)
Happy	75 (47%)	43 (49%)	32 (45%)
Not very happy	66 (41%)	37 (42%)	29 (40%)
Not at all happy	3 (2%)	3 (3%)	0
Total	160 (100%)	88 (100%)	72 (100%)

Source: Encuesta a Jóvenes Yauyinos, Yauyos Values Study, 1999.

of happiness, hope, quality of life, and human flourishing (Nussbaum 1993; Mattingly and Jensen 2015; Tronto 1993). Widening our lens, we can add the reflections of the contributors to Lamont and Hall's (2009) collection on the characteristics of successful societies. We found many people in Yauyos that would have been quite capable of entering into a dialogue with eminent philosophers about these questions, and who would have added some concepts of their own. They would also have much to say about the barriers to fulfilling the promise of human flourishing in the deep valleys and mountain pastures of Yauyos. In this chapter we consider what elements, what experiences, and what forms of care seemed to contribute to children's happiness and flourishing, and what that flourishing looked like. We have seen enough of individual children to affirm that some were indeed quite happy, while others were troubled and sad. For some the path through adolescence and into young adulthood seemed to be clear. For others it was uncertain.

Flourishing, Yauyos Style

Children's peak experiences of happiness were personal and particular, like their lives and biographies. Each child's sense of self-worth and accomplishment depended on and drew from circumstances distinct from those of any other child. Yet observing children in Yauyos, and participating in their daily lives, gave insights into the kinds of experiences and events that were most often associated with pleasure and fulfillment, even as we noted that many experiences of joy go unspoken. One vast arena for happiness was friendship and play. In Yauyos, as in other worlds of childhood (Lancy 2008, 191–233), it was tacitly assumed that children seek and find joy in their peers and in play. The natural world of hills, rivers, plants, and animals was also a source of pleasure for many children (and indeed adults). Young people, and adults, further derived pleasure from music, responding to a rich and distinctive musical tradition in the Andes (Tucker 2019). For some children, religion and spirituality seemed to open a door to happiness and a meaningful life. Finally, there were explicit expressions of love and appreciation that took the form of hugs and gifts more often than words. These sources of happiness were available, if not always consistently, to all children and adults in the province. Even Guillermina (8) could escape her mother's blows and harassment at times and take refuge in the companionship of her friend Maruja (12), with whom she shared a love of drawing. Guillermina was talented and earned the praise of the occasional sympathetic adult, such as field-worker Gabriela.

Whether on a personal or a collective scale, flourishing for the rural population of Yauyos entailed great challenges. The policymakers and dominant groups in Peru tolerate a vast gap between the conditions of life and the opportunities provided to rural and urban populations. We have seen how large numbers of persons, born in the province but migrants out of it, gave up on the possibility even of surviving in place, much less achieving a sense of flourishing. For children, successfully completing school, becoming "educated persons" (Levinson, Foley, and Holland 1996), opened the possibility of participating fully as citizens in Peruvian society. Implicitly, that entailed resisting and overcoming the discrimination leveled against rural residents (Montero 2006; Huayhua 2010). Weaving together these various themes, this chapter deals with experiences both of pleasure and of pain that were difficult to talk about and often unstated.

Play, Friendship, and Affection

Andean parents have high expectations that their children grow up as "serious" human beings, not careless or thoughtless creatures.[1] Adults in Yauyos recounted memories of their parents and caretakers depriving them of opportunities to play when they were children and punishing them for "wasting time" in useless activities (see Panez and Ochoa 2000; Panez 2004). Sánchez and Valdivia (1994) have proposed that parents undervalue play and underestimate its role in their children's lives and development because most play takes place outside their ken, among siblings and peers. Adults play with infants and very young children—bouncing them on their knee; playing peek-a-boo; offering objects and taking turns. Once past this stage, children play with other children, often far from adult eyes.

Play with peers had its special times and places in all six towns (Anderson 2024). Children's appropriation of some public spaces at certain times of day and early evening was amply tolerated; there, they could play undisturbed (figure 8.1). The plaza in Pastizales, decorated with a fountain, partially enclosed with an iron fence, was the daily meeting place for children of all ages. In shifting combinations, children pursued organized games—telephone (*teléfono malogrado*), hide-and-seek, tag—and assorted other entertainments such as climbing the ornamental trees and riding bicycles in endless circles. Calabash Square in Yauyos City was an ideal space for groups of a dozen or more children to play games or kick around a soccer ball. An open area in Los Caminos, near where buses and vans stopped as they came from the main highway, was used by children for volleyball matches. A tract in Bellavista, planned for a future stadium, was meanwhile a spot where boys went to play soccer. The schools and preschools in each town boasted some simple playground equipment. And games of tops, marbles, or jacks unfolded on doorsteps, sidewalks, or the narrow, steep, unpaved and little-trafficked streets themselves.

There was some variation from town to town in prevailing fashions in children's play. Boys' play in Las Cascadas favored marbles and *chipitaps*. In the other towns, spinning tops was the rage (see figure 1.1). Lucky boys had bicycles in the towns of Nor Yauyos, where plazas with flat surfaces interrupted the steep inclines of some streets. On cobblestones or pavement, girls jumped rope in Terrazas. Construction projects for new community facilities were underway in Los Caminos and Terrazas, and children played among the heaps of sand, stacks of

FIGURE 8.1. Children play in the town plaza.

bricks, piles of rebar, and unfinished walls. They might get warnings and remonstrances from passing adults, but that did not keep them away for long.

Much play was competitive, an opportunity to demonstrate skill and dominance. The common sight of children, arranged in a circle, playing with spinning tops, was an example. Children had a special vocabulary for playing with their tops: the tops "danced," a player "killed" another's top by bumping it out of bounds, and when they got the tops to spin at length with ever-wider movements, the tops were "drunk." A group of boys playing with tops one afternoon, including Moisés's twin Mariano, made liberal use of the slur "maricon" (homosexual) as they commented on each other's skill and luck. One clinched the argument with an ironic exclamation: "Mariano, you got it drunk! It's the only good thing you've done in your life! (¡Lo emborrachaste! ¡Es lo único bueno que has hecho en tu vida!)" Competitive play often featured boys, but two gender transgressive girls excelled at male-coded activities: Pamela (9) was skilled at the top, while Dionisia (12) claimed to have ninety-five marbles that she had won from her mostly male competitors. Dionisia was also in great demand as goalkeeper in boys' soccer games.

Games enjoyed by girls included jump rope and jacks. Some might have sets of playing cards; as one girl commented, "I play cards, that's how I learn to count (yo juego a los casinos, así aprendo a contar)." Some had plush toys. Several had dolls, including the knock-off Barbies that were sold throughout Peru (figure 8.2; see Chin 2001). Five-year-old Lizbeth and her friend played with a set of small plastic animals, another staple in outdoor markets and bodegas, more representative

FIGURE 8.2. Dolls having afternoon snack or "lonche."

of an African savannah or a zoo than Andean fauna. The girls repurposed a zebra as a burro and a buffalo as a cow. With bits of plastic, they built a corral around the animals and gave them water. Lizbeth's pencil case made a suitable place for tying them up for the night.

Many girls enjoyed imitative play: the market, bodega, birthday party, and guinea pig race. To facilitate the imaginary parties, some had collections of miniature plates, cups, pots, and kitchen utensils. Yovana (5) was the protagonist of a birthday party that she, her niece and constant companion, and her friends staged. Yovana was in fact one of the few children that actually had ever had a birthday party with snacks, candles, and a cake. Some children played alone or with imaginary companions, and even "birthday" could be a solitary game. On one occasion Yovana was alone on Calabash Square. She had set up a ring of stones that represented the guests at the party. From the rubbish left behind after the previous night's food carts, plus the usual candy wrappers, leaves, flowers, and assorted papers, she created plates filled with snacks and cake to offer to the guests, one by one.

Art and Song

Children in the rural Andes play with words in riddles, jokes, and tales that they repeat and embroider, in native Andean languages as well as Spanish (La Riva González 2013; Sánchez and Valdivia 1994; Panez and Ochoa 2000; Hornberger 1987).

CARE AND FLOURISHING 127

The children in Yauyos invented poems and songs, told stories, and enjoyed riddles, bestowing nicknames, and other forms of word play and verbal art. This was on full display one afternoon as Señora Aracely was cleaning up after the noon rush hour in the municipal restaurant of Terrazas, accompanied by her daughter Dolores (10), son Cleber (5), their older brother, regular customer Baltasar, and a few other stragglers. Cleber challenged Baltasar: "Say 'uña' (finger or toenail)." "Uña," he said. Cleber replied with a rhyme: "Tú eres la vicuña (You're the vicuña)." Everybody laughed. "Dolores, say 'oro' (gold)," commanded Cleber. "Oro," responded Dolores. Cleber parried with another rhyme: "Tu papá Teodoro (your dad, Teodoro)," which produced a second general round of laughter. Cleber struck again: "Dolores, say 'rocoto' (hot pepper)." Glancing around the room, Dolores shook her head no. Cleber sought a new victim: "Baltasar, say 'rocoto'." Baltasar had also caught on to what was coming and refused to answer. Cleber made a few more attempts to get a response from anyone in the room and finally had to answer his own challenge: "Rasca tu poto (scratch your butt)." The laughter was loud and general. Baltasar tried to reset the trap: "Cleber, say 'rocoto,' pues." Señora Aracely shouted from the kitchen: "Shut up, ah! Look at the bad example Baltasar is setting." After insisting a few times more, Baltasar gave up on eliciting the prohibited words from Cleber, and instead he asked him, "Who teaches you things, Cleber, is it your mother?" "Yes," said the boy. "Well, look at that one," said the mother, amid the general merriment.

Music was omnipresent in the lives of Yauyos youth, circulating with them in radios and CDs. Andean songs can express feelings of longing for the loved person, of disappointment at their treachery, of nostalgia for the home village, of frustration over obstacles in life's path (Turino 1993; Tucker 2019). Music encapsulates an aesthetic experience of compelling significance in the Andes. No fiesta can take place without music in abundance. Different sponsors may contract with different bands to play simultaneously and competitively during community events. Performing music, participating in instrumental ensembles, singing, and dancing were associated with peak events at a community level: fiestas, parades, and public ceremonies. Children were inducted into the musical world of adults from infancy when they went to fiestas on their mothers' backs and danced with them, ever at risk of slipping out of the manta. Many girls looked up to folklore artists such as the singer Sonia Morales, a native of Yauyos who was nationally known at the time of the 2008 study. Some of the young people we knew dreamed of a future in music. Betty (14), for example, displayed in her room the certificates and prizes that she had won singing in competitions at school and in interdistrict events. Accompanied by her father on the guitar, she sang at her town's Independence Day celebration. Rufina (15) imagined herself as lead singer of a band performing Andean folklore music. She had started on the path of entertaining at school events, where girls might be spotted by bands that play the circuit of local fiestas.

Music-making was passed along in family groups, and sons and nephews were incorporated into existing ensembles. Children mentioned among their cherished memories being taught to play an instrument by a father or uncle, like Estela's trumpeter father or Silvia's harpist stepfather, or experimenting with instruments they found around the house.[2] Dina's father was in demand throughout the region to play the *cacho* (literally "horn," a trumpet made from cow's horn, also known as *waqrapuku*), a traditional instrument associated with *herranzas*. He told us, "When I don't have anything to do, I pick up my instrument and start to play, and all four kids start dancing. The youngest one (2) looks at his sister and pulls her out to dance. All four love to dance. Sometimes they turn the radio on, put in a cassette, and all four are dancing. They like to dance huaynos with a background of orchestra or guitar. The little one sees me play the horn and he tries to blow it. I show him how and he makes it sound. He tries getting his mouth around the mouthpiece, too. He tries but he can't do it."

Though not as potent vehicles as music, drawing and painting were significant means of self-expression for some children. Representing persons, scenes, and ideas on paper is not a traditional children's activity in Andean Peru, yet universal access to school has turned it into a skill and entertainment that children are expected to enjoy. Schoolbooks and worksheets depended heavily on illustrations, and children in Yauyos began making pictures in preschool as part of their preparation for reading and writing. The field-workers regularly carried with them materials like notebooks, paper, felt-tip pens, and pencils. Whether they were used to pass the time with individual children while chatting on a park bench or in a group activity, the drawings that resulted tended to be very strongly influenced by classroom staples (heroes, historical figures), to represent local landscapes, or to be inspired by comic books or TV programs such as the popular Japanese animated series Goku. Abstractions were acceptable too. During one drawing session, Chiri asked a girl what her picture meant. "I don't know what it is, but it won second place in the school competition," she said.

Nature

Many children in Yauyos drew pleasure, a feeling of equilibrium and well-being, even an aesthetic sense, from the natural environment. Any child growing up in a rural area has exceptional opportunities to learn about the natural world through their own activities of observation and exploration (de la Torre 1986; Zarger 2010; Katz 2004). Children could be seen stopping at outlooks, climbing up hills for a view of the fields and streams below, pausing to take in the smells and sounds of the outdoors, to appreciate the peace and beauty. Away from town, children could move with a high degree of autonomy.[3] The natural world also offered relief from the bruises of daily living. After a dispute with her mother, Katherine (11) flopped belly-down in a thicket of tall grass, crying and telling everybody to go away.

Learning techniques of orientation and recognizing geographical features were essential survival skills, since getting around efficiently required being able to use not only roads and well-worn paths but shortcuts across trackless hills. Children could and did get lost. A pair of little girls, around seven and four years old, showed up one afternoon in the center of Los Caminos with a small herd of sheep. They had become confused, trying to find their way back to one of the annexes. The animals were put in a corral for the night, and the girls were driven home by a municipal official. The townspeople that witnessed this drama had strong criticism for the parents that had overestimated the abilities of children so young.

Navigating the countryside combined observational talents with memories of places visited with family members or memorialized in local folklore. Field-worker Diego got a taste of this when Braulio (15) invited him to visit his home in a distant annex. Braulio's mother pressed them to stay for a meal, and they were overtaken by darkness trying to get back to town. They stayed on the road for the most part but struck off cross-country on some of the long curves. Along the way, Braulio pointed out features of the landscape. First were the tourist attractions: Cerro San Cristóbal, with a view of the entire village in the valley below; Bosque de Amor, with rivulets and cascades of water among the trees; Laguna Papacocha, covered with totora reeds; a rock wall where people left painted messages (*recuerdos*). On another large rock there was a cross decked out with mantas and flowers, evidently the site of a fatal road accident. Beyond the lake were the fields and pastures that made up part of the community's collective patrimony. Braulio pointed out the parcels that had been assigned to him and that he could return to and work whenever he so decided, an idea that struck him as more attractive than staying in school for three more years until graduation. Several hours later, exhausted, the pair was lucky to get picked up by a passing truck.

Caregivers could enhance children's access to these sources of natural pleasure through accompaniment, instruction, and modeling. Estela's stepfather told her about how he had used his summer pasturing time in the mountains to take solitary walks and clear his mind for the coming school year. Victor (8) had the advantage of his father, Dante, a well-traveled, curious, and communicative older man who took his son along to help him with many tasks that had become difficult for him with age. Older children, especially boys, wandered over the landscape with many sentiments and projects in mind. They might have slingshots for hunting birds or the rabbit-like *vizcachas*, or fishing rods to ply the streams for trout. The fact that children tended to make forays into the countryside in groups of siblings, cousins, or schoolmates suggests that much environmental learning took place between and among children themselves, a pattern identified in other societies (Zarger 2010, 358–359).

Nature provided a setting for significant events that asked to be remembered. Estela (11) organized a trip to the river as a goodbye for Li the day before fieldwork ended. Two of the participants were her goat Vilma and her dog Rambo, with whom she went everywhere. Vilma and Rambo were some of the many pets beloved by children, attachments that adults honored because of their own strong emotional connections to their animals, past and present (compare Luttrell-Rowland 2023, 52). With goat and dog in tow, Li and Estela walked to the river's edge and sat for a long time, watching the water ebb and flow. They followed the shoreline until they found a spot where stones of all sizes, shapes, and colors had collected. Li picked out a few to take back to Lima as souvenirs. Estela picked out several small ones and arranged them to write Li's name on the sand. This was her goodbye gift. At Estela's insistence, with Li's camera, they took photographs of the stones, the animals, the people, and the enveloping hills, pastures, and woods.

Spirituality

Andean cosmology and the nonhuman co-residents of this earth (de la Cadena 2015; Salas 2019; Weismantel 2001), noted in chapter 7, were not the only available sources of spiritual guidance and community for yauyinos. Religious institutions were a minor part of the care of children in Yauyos, but there were many reminders of their possible relevance as the children grew older. Although no child or adolescent reported comforting conversations with a priest or a pastor, Sunday school for Protestants and catechism for Catholics were compelling to many children as openings onto the mysteries of the Christian faith, clearly so important in Peruvian culture. The children's greatest interest was directed to the ceremonies associated with religious beliefs. Li and Violeta observed how the mass for the anniversary of Pastizales was attended primarily by children. Religion, in fact, was closely associated with fiestas, with celebrations of the community and its traditions. As such, it helped to ground the children and to promote a sense of collective life and welfare to be found in places beyond the family.

All rural settlements of any size in Peru have historic churches, built when Catholicism was hegemonic. In recent decades, with the decline in vocations, much of the countryside has been left with empty shells that open their doors for mass and sacraments no more than a few times during the year. In Sur Grande, the nuns of the Service and Sacrifice order were put in charge of the diocese in the absence of priests willing to go and live there. Still, crucifixes and images of Jesus or the Virgin Mary were ubiquitous on the walls of municipal offices, and prayers and references to Christianity were common at public events. Religion with a Catholic tilt was part of the official curriculum in 2008, and catechism classes took place in the schools. In 1957 the Archbishopric of Yauyos was assigned to the jurisdiction of Opus Dei, a particularly conservative movement within the Catholic Church. Though ideologically far removed from the "preferential option for the poor" of post-Medellín Catholicism, Opus Dei in Yauyos incorporated actions to improve the material conditions of the rural population in its ministry.[4] At the same time, anticlericalism had deep roots here as in other parts of the Andes, inherited from generations of coexistence with exploitative priests complicit with landowners and the Guardia Civil. It endured in part due to resentment over the fees parishioners were charged for baptisms, funerals, weddings, and masses.

During the fieldwork, evangelical Protestant organizations came to several of the towns. In July, pastors and lay missionaries of the Iglesia del Movimiento

Misionero Mundial (MMM) visited Yauyos City, distributing small New Testaments, pamphlets, and posters. In August, Los Caminos hosted a group of some twenty volunteers from the Catholic parish in the U.S. that had supported the Cáritas project of postearthquake reconstruction. Sporting identical t-shirts, they set up various games and activities with the children, including soccer and volleyball matches. Most spoke little or no Spanish. For children, the novel encounters, the games, and the rites sponsored by religious organizations were a welcome break in the monotony of daily life. The children knew and cared little for the niceties of doctrinal distinctions among visitors that presented themselves in a generic Christian framework, and it is likely that many of their elders felt the same.

Precious Gifts

What were expressions of love for the children of Yauyos? Providing them with food and shelter were undoubtedly part of it. Listening to them and helping them with their problems were as well. But one key element stands out as a symbol of the love they had earned from adults who, along with other capacities to make decisions over their lives, held the purse strings: this was purchased clothes.

Gaby asked Dionisia (12) how her grandmother showed her love, and Dionisia responded that "She gives me food. She dresses me. When I was five years old, we had a graduation ceremony from preschool to first grade. She bought me a pretty dress and my shoes. They were the most expensive part. I think they cost about 60 soles [$20]." If accurate, this would have been an astronomical sum to pay for a pair of children's shoes, almost equivalent to a week's pay for day-laborers at the time. Dionisia was surely right, however, that her grandmother had made a major effort to please her and to mark a significant occasion. Godfathers, godmothers, uncles, and aunts from the city came for visits on holidays. An appropriate and appreciated gift for them to bring was underwear. This might be a part of children's outfitting that was easy to overlook.

Most of the children could expect new clothes on two occasions throughout the year: Christmas and July Independence holiday. Not receiving the clothes as anticipated put adults' affections in doubt. Gladis (14) was convinced that her mother preferred her sister Valery (17) because she bought clothes for Valery and not for her. Valery had been raised by their maternal grandmother and only joined the household three years ago. The mother may have felt that she owed her a debt for the years of not taking personal care of her (Leinaweaver 2008, 2013, 2022). Gladis was jealous and had opposed her sister's moving in. Gladis, however, could count on the affection of her paternal grandmother who, she explained, bought her the things that her mother did not.

Teens in Yauyos had far too little to spend, and far too little influence over their families' budgets, to get very far into status wars focused on clothing, but they were aware of the prestige overtones of some items. Braulio received an unforgettable token of affection when he briefly lived with his uncle in Lima, who took him to a game at the stadium of their favorite soccer team, Sporting Cristal, and bought him an official team jersey. Brand-name sneakers were out of the realm of possibility but keeping canvas shoes clean and in good repair could give status (Uccelli and García Llorens 2016). Yeni's thirteen-year-old brother Marlon, exempted from any other tasks involving maintaining clothes, washed his sneakers by his own choice. Prestige clothing was not limited to factory-made goods. Prized items were the hand-woven and embroidered mantas with distinctive colors and designs that announced the wearer's local identity. Dionisia's father stopped into a bodega to buy cough drops and was prepared to purchase one "for my Dionisia," but, at learning the price of S/.250 ($85), he handed it back to the shop owner.

With giving of clothes a sign of love, children participated to the extent they could, mindful of their younger siblings and other relatives. Aurora's (13) brother occasionally bought her clothes with the money he made as a stableboy at Aventura Andina. She showed her appreciation by washing his clothes when he came home tired from work. Moisés (11), when new clothes were in the offing, requested that they be in sizes that were big for him so that they could be handed down to his younger brothers as they grew. Jeferson's (10) mother recalled how he had seen her mending a hole in her sweatpants and told her that when he grew up, he would go to work in the mine and buy her a new pair.

Children also gave physical expression to their love in the form of hugs and kisses. Parents, and especially grandparents, were givers and receivers of embraces and other tender acts (Ames 2013a). At a performance in the town stadium, Ponciano (7) made his way to where his grandmother was standing. Perceiving he was too warm, she gently unbuttoned the vest he was wearing and brushed off some leaves. She raised her arms and draped them over Ponciano's shoulders. So linked, both continued watching the show. At an Independence Day celebration, Sonia (6), impeccable in her school uniform, recited the poem "My flag." Coming off the stage, she ran to the section where her classroom group was seated and into the open arms of her mother. Her mother lifted her up and spun her around several times, kissing her on the cheeks. At that sister Camila (8) joined in the embrace, and the three of them hugged and danced.

The field-workers were easily coaxed into physical interactions with the younger children. Kids pestered Chiri for piggyback rides, and he and Gaby appear in many photographs with children sitting on their knees or clinging to their backs. Another way of expressing affection, observed in girls, was combing and arranging the other's hair. Field-worker Li, with long hair and a ponytail, submitting to the tugs and pulls, frequently received these attentions.

Flourishing as Educated Persons and Citizens

Parents in Yauyos had to think of their children's well-being in the present and into the future. Education loomed as the main, if not the only, route to a happy future life. Completing a basic education—through high school—was a minimum requirement; continuing on through a technical institute, one of the growing number of substandard private colleges on offer in Peru, or a recognized university was desirable. Adolescents nearing high school graduation were actively looking into their options: the police academy, nursing school, service in the Peruvian armed forces where technical specialties were offered, schools of culinary arts, teacher training institutes, or college prep courses (see Trivelli and Gil 2021).

In their edited collection of ethnographies of schooling in societies around the world, Levinson, Foley, and Holland (1996) argue that the principal purpose of the schools' existence is the "cultural production of the educated person." The qualities to be instilled in pupils are one thing: knowledge, reasoning, the capacity to communicate, competence in mathematics, and other skills for the work world. An equally important facet of the "educated person" is the response that person elicits in others: respect, recognition, fair treatment, nondiscrimination, and membership in the community of educated persons. While rural Peruvian schools often fell short of these goals (Guadalupe et al. 2017; Oliart 2011; Benavides 2006), there is ample evidence that parents in Yauyos recognized the importance of the symbolic capital schooling afforded (Anderson and Leinaweaver 2023; Leinaweaver and Anderson 2024).

Educated persons would be able to defend themselves from being exploited and humiliated. Above all, educated persons could become active citizens, enabled to take the reins of governance of their local communities and participate constructively in national decisions (Tanaka 1999).[5] In Yauyos, some towns observed the custom of raising the flag in a ceremony on the town plaza on Sunday mornings. Representatives of the professional elite that had successfully run the race to becoming "educated persons" paraded in uniform around the plaza. School principals and teachers, staff of the health post, other government employees, visiting judges and inspectors, and heads of civic organizations all marched with banners representing their institutions. By weekly turns, their designated spokespersons delivered the homily. The messages emphasized the identification of the officials with the community's needs and betterment, together with requests for support and unity in the population. There were the obligatory references to Peru's glorious past, its natural and cultural diversity, and its promise for the future. The arguments were familiar to schoolchildren whose lessons encouraged them to take pride in being part of the nation called Peru.

Mother's Day, Teacher's Day, Campesino Day, Indigenous Languages Day, Children's Rights Day, days celebrating native cultigens like potatoes and quinoa, and days for remembering battles in Peru's wars of independence against Spain or the War of the Pacific[6] were all events that might call for public commemorations with similar messaging. This reached an apogee on Peru's Independence Day, July 28. Our field teams observed the festivities in all six towns: parades, speeches, flag-raising, and a public ceremony whose featured protagonists were children from local schools. In Las Cascadas, children recited poems and dramatized Peru's declaration of independence from Spain in 1821, with a student on horseback dressed as General José de San Martín galloping up to pronounce his well-worn phrase, somewhat garbled on this occasion: "El Perú desde este momento es libre e independiente del yugo español (From this time forward, Peru is free and independent of the Spanish yoke)." This was followed by the governor's remarks, which ended with a peroration: "¡Viva la juventud! ¡Vivan los verdaderos revolucionarios que están presentes! (Long live the youth! Long live the true revolutionaries here today!)"

Educated people, in the interpretation of Harvey (1997, 22) based on observations of many similar events, learned to relate a mythologized past to a happy and hopeful view of the present. Harvey writes of the seemingly unwarranted optimism elicited by mass participation in an Independence Day celebration in the town of Ocongate, Cusco: "The state is represented as a liberating institution that provides work, food, health, wages, order, discipline, and coherence. Democracy is emphasized as the people make a series of statements about their sense of themselves as part of this wider community . . . Everyone in the village is experientially involved in constructing this image of the state" (Harvey 1997, 30). Such events call on the patriotism of the participants and demand that they overlook many shortcomings in their own, often bitter, experience as citizens of Peru. Harvey points to the exclusion of various segments of society that do not march in the parades and are not even named and recognized as valid interest groups. Educated persons, so it seems, learn to overlook such contradictions and play their role as citizens without causing major disruptions.[7]

Play and Communitas

Harvey (1997) emphasizes the dual nature of events such as the Independence Day celebrations, where bullfights, mock battles, clowning, and commercial fairs take their place alongside the speeches, pageants, and parades. In Yauyos as in Cusco and other parts of the Andes, some of the activities made pointed fun of the occasion itself, its pomp and seriousness. They invited the adults to play, and their play was visible and often shared with their children. It is worth remembering that the people involved may have known each other since childhood. They had shared joys and tragedies, friendships and conflicts. The joking and mock aggressions that take place during fiestas can best be understood in that framework. And there is closure: the holiday comes to an end. Where local government budgets and donations from townspeople and "residentes" permit, the celebration may end with a communal meal. In Terrazas, following the Independence Day parade, the entire public lined up for their plates of trout with all the trimmings.

Turner (1974, 2001) proposed the Latin term *communitas* to describe peak moments in human societies when the usual rules are suspended, status positions may be reversed, and common bonds are reaffirmed over the pull of segmentary interests. In Yauyos, becoming sponsors and participants in fiestas *patronales* and *herranzas* could allow marginal and marginalized figures to redeem themselves as

CARE AND FLOURISHING

135

devotees of the faith and defenders of traditions. Men and women could interact without the usual barriers. The spell of communitas could be broken as fights erupted over unresolved disputes, husbands violently gave rein to their resentments against wives and in-laws (Harris 1978; Van Vleet 2008, 161–182), and fiesta sponsors went over their alcoholic limits. But the feeling of unity, equality, and shared joy—Turner's antistructure—persisted.

Pastizales had many community traditions that involved high levels of participation for their preparation, sponsorship, and organization. Many of these expressed a friendly rivalry with neighboring Las Cascadas. Diego made an excursion from his field site there to attend the anniversary celebration of Pastizales's patron saint. One element of the celebration involved a bullfight, though no bull was to be seen. It took place in the sports field by the school. It began with the presentation of the town's authorities, each accompanied by a fanfare from the band. The master of ceremonies read off a "testament" from each of the participants, in case they should not survive the fight. These competed in humor: "First off I leave my wife in the hands of the governor, on the condition that he please keep her fat ("gordita," affectionately), because she really likes meat and potatoes. Next I leave my cows to . . ." and so on. A man had been designated to take the part of the *torero*, while a boy would be the bull. He held a pair of bull's horns up at the level of his forehead. The chase was on between man and "beast" with no respect for the space separating them from the raucous crowd. Meantime a woman, member of the presiding party, began throwing candies into the fray. This was the children's moment, but they had to be quick to pick them up or they would be caught on the horns of the "bull." The bullfight over, everyone joined in the dance. They trailed the band around the plaza and in paying visits to the homes of all the town officials. The children counted and compared the candies they had been able to collect. While the adults ate, drank, and partied, the children took over the streets and the plaza, screaming, laughing, imitating their elders.

From Los Caminos we have Ignacio's record of the fun at an *herranza*. The sponsors hired a group of *huancas* as animators and jesters. Part of their role consisted in bothering the participants by calling them out on actions or characteristics that could be turned into a source of laughter. In Ignacio's case it was his ability to understand and speak some Quechua. The *huancas* tried to trip him into making mistakes and mispronouncing words. As food was being served, they got laughs as they called for a dish to be brought to one or another of the guests by shouting "¡Bacinica! (bedpan, chamber pot)." With not enough plates, spoons, or forks to go around, the *huancas* made a game of approaching people with a demand that they eat faster. And, of course, they actively tried to press liquor on all the guests. One of the group—well known to Ignacio—made a joke of his constant ethnographic presence in the community: "¡Todo el día jodes! ¡Tomando fotos! (Bothering us all day long! Taking pictures!)" And so the night passed for Ignacio (no *herranza* in the countryside would end before dawn): being asked to drink with one after another of the guests, monitoring the camera he lent to participants who wanted

Conclusions

This chapter began with child's play and ended with adult play. In between we had occasion to examine the experiences that brought feelings of happiness, love, security, and well-being to the children of Yauyos. Mixed in were a number of disappointments and resentments. Flourishing meant good lives now and good lives into the future, and education, facilitating migration as an added benefit (Rojas and Portugal 2010), would somehow guarantee that.

Community-wide celebrations were an important reflection of sources of children's well-being. The ludic part of the festivals highlighted the exceptional importance they appeared to have in children's emotional axes. They were a high point in the calendar year and some of the best parts of school. They entailed exciting group activities in planning, marching in the band, memorizing lines, and preparing coordinated costumes alluding to the event being celebrated. Children got new clothes, and old ones were washed, repaired, and pressed. They were congratulated by family members for participating in the programs and going on stage, showing their talents, and conquering their stage fright. They huddled close to siblings, parents, and grandparents in the stands as the day's proceedings went forward. They were swept away in the emotion of being part of a beautiful spectacle in the nighttime parades with tissue-paper lanterns. They got candy, food, maybe even (for adolescents) alcoholic drinks for the first time without anybody noticing or censuring the act.

What contributed most to children's flourishing, understood as their grounding in a secure sense of self, of belonging, of the possibility of joy, of support when needed, and of optimism about the future? Flourishing had to do with circumstances close to hand. Aside from quotidian expressions of mutual commitment in family groups, children shared with their caregivers the intense moments of *communitas* that occurred during public festivals. There, they saw their parents and grandparents, neighbors, and townspeople in general, dance, sing, joke, drink, and eat together. They saw adults who—despite the harshness of their lives—still knew how to play.

A further conclusion to be drawn from the evidence we have reviewed showing the happy, affirming, and affectionate side of children's lives in Yauyos is how little of this is spoken. This is not a place where proclamations of "Love you!" or "Great work!" slip easily from people's lips. On the contrary: Andean parents are famous for withholding praise in the belief it leads children to overestimate their abilities and to put themselves above those around them (Lobo 1982; Bolin 2006). Children and adults in Yauyos expressed their love through actions, not words. But the actions are many and prized. They might involve making visits to grandparents in the countryside, surprising someone with a gift of food, clothes, or even a toy, providing small services, indulging personal tastes and interests, even respecting the privacy of others despite tight living quarters. Powerful memories of childhood experiences keep migrants coming back to the hometown year after year for Independence Day and the fiestas *patronales*. For them, it is an enduring part of flourishing.

9

Conclusions

In this book, we have explored the nested worlds of the children of Yauyos: the intimate realm of home and family, local service providers, larger-scale pictures of the ecology and political economy of Yauyos, and Peru's national sociopolitical system. Care—provided, denied, rejected, shortchanged, misdirected—is relevant at all these levels. The organization of care for children in Yauyos is affected by the marginalization of rural populations in general and the family farming sector in particular. It is also shaped by hierarchies of value, prestige, and recognition determined by powerful urban, and sometimes even international, actors.

Yauyos is the poorest province in the Lima hinterland, so close to the glittering capital, yet so far away in terms of lifestyles and life chances. That has inescapable implications for the future of the province and the children who grow up there. Family farming persists as a livelihood strategy for over two million Peruvian households despite the meager economic rewards. While Peru's booming agrobusiness export sector monopolizes attention, small farmers feed the population. The debates around it have seen a resurgence in recent years but have not been connected to similar debates around childhood and education in rural areas. What roles are the children prepared and motivated to take on as they approach adulthood?

In all probability, many of the children we encountered in Yauyos in 2008 are now part of the exodus that was by that time a well-established trend. We can only speculate about the memories and the meaning for them of the communities where they grew up. There is yet to be a full reckoning of the costs of urban migration for the millions of rural Andeans that have taken that route over the span of decades. Many would have fulfilled their "Peruvian dream," but many others are stuck in the troubled, underserviced, crime-ridden neighborhoods that ring Peruvian cities. In this concluding chapter, we consider the place of Yauyos and the children who live there in larger contexts. In Peru, recognition and misrecognition as well as stigmatization and strategies for overcoming it remain front and center. We consider rural Andean communities, their heritage, and their present reality. Finally, we position the children of Yauyos as valued contributors to emerging scholarship on young people, agency, place, and care.

Tentative, Contingent, Intersubjective Care

We focused our research and analysis on ideas and practices of care, framing our questions around the organization of systems of care in Andean communities and children's involvement in them. We quickly learned, however, that, in Yauyos, the concepts of "system" and "organization," paired with the notion of care, make a poor fit. Much more apt is the concept of care as tinkering (Mol, Moser, and Pols 2010). In the analysis of Mol and her colleagues, care involves "attentive experimentation" (2010, 13): a continuous stream of practices that are tentative and contingent. It entails efforts to understand the needs of care recipients (ambiguously articulated, rarely simple), choosing among possible responses, attempting to prioritize among competing goals and demands, evaluating the results (more guessing and intuition than science), repairing whatever damages may be incurred, and trying to do things better the next time around. No universal rules exist in this setting for determining what is good and what is bad care, although people were willing to share their views. Circumstances are constantly changing, including the evolving relationship between care provider and care receiver, whose roles might be redefined and even eventually reversed.

In Yauyos, participants in care practices included people, plants, animals, soil, water, mountains and other natural features, the dead, and spiritual beings associated with Andean cosmology and Christianity. Also involved were institutions with vague profiles and confusing mandates, their influence emanating from far-off places: the Peruvian government, international cooperation, private philanthropy, and commercial entities. Wishing to help in the best possible way, they may have taken recourse to systems engineers and experts in organizational design, but under the conditions of Yauyos, they were also tinkerers. Like the intimate actors, they worked through complicated agendas, balancing the demands of care as *atender* (meeting daily needs) and care as *preocuparse* (express or feel concern).

Children occupied a variety of places within these schemes. One fundamental determinant of who cared for the children and how that care was dispensed was household composition: who shared in the household and participated in its livelihood strategy. Although boys and men played a role, childcare was identified with women, and many adult women were stretched thin. Household composition was flexible and adjustable, but the changes could go only so far before running up against material resource constraints. Household composition also took into account children's preferences. Children tinkered, too, as they made choices over whose care was most convincing, although their possibilities for choosing where to be when, and in whose company, were not unrestricted (Leinaweaver 2007a).

An important finding from the study in Yauyos concerned the wide variation in experiences of childhood and growing up in small towns that were ostensibly quite homogeneous, and even within a single family. It was rare to hear adults discourse on general precepts about the nature of children and the process of child development, and no overriding mandate obligated parents and other providers to behave equitably toward all the children under their care. To a large degree, the kind of childhood they have depended on the luck of the draw: not birth order per se but rather the life course, the circumstances of the parents when the birth occurred, and the ups and downs they experienced in subsequent years (Johnson-Hanks 2002). Some children were sloughed off during lean times (Leinaweaver 2007b, 2008); others, who came along when income was flowing and no other dependents were making demands on the family budget, were indulged.

People also recognized that children have very different temperaments. They have individual tastes, quirks, strengths, and weaknesses. Some can be trusted to behave responsibly, and some are rebellious. Some are obedient, while some have difficulty interpreting the intentions of their caregivers. Our field data suggest that difficult and needy children may be precisely those that receive the least attention. We saw cases in which care providers seemed to give up in the face of severe health or behavioral problems. Some children suffered extreme violence at the hands of those in charge of their care. In some cases, the customary role of collaborator in the family's livelihood strategy morphed into the outright exploitation of child labor. Adolescent girls and young women who had babies without a publicly recognized partner could be expelled from the circle of care of the household and left to raise the child as best they could. Gaps were opening between the generations. Many elders in the towns appeared to be socially abandoned; many adults felt doubts about who would look after them in old age. Children, sent away to prosper, retained an obligation to their aging relatives that was a source of ambivalence and moral unease.

Much contemporary theory on care has an urban bias, leaving us unprepared to appreciate the place of animals, and the natural world more broadly, in caretaking as experienced by rural children and adults. Harbers (2010), writing about growing up on a Dutch farm, captures the sentiments of the inhabitants of Yauyos as he describes the force of the connection between humans and animals and the profound truth of animals' having an equivalent (though different) status from people (see also Singleton 2010). Farm animals give and receive care, as we have seen in numerous vignettes showing child herders, inseparable animal companions, children gathering food for animals from guinea pigs to cattle, giving animals names, and cursing and berating them when they got out of step. Children suffer at the death or sale of animals they have grown up with, conversed with, and shared lonely hours with at pasture. They are fully aware that their future is tied to the health and increase of the family herds.[1]

Our research illustrates not only how elements of caring have been absent from an agenda set largely in academic circles by persons attentive to a partial

CONCLUSIONS 141

scope of care practices, but also how many of the outsiders that performed various tasks in the towns of Yauyos had only a sketchy understanding of the role of care in this setting. We have seen how medical personnel berated patients that seemed to devote more time to their herds than to their babies. The Catholic nuns that ministered to the diocese of Sur Grande, too, appeared oblivious to animals' food and watering requirements, despite living in the communities and observing daily life. After mass one day, the nuns chided their parishioners for requesting that mass be scheduled for 5:00 P.M. instead of 4:00, since most people were still out with their herds at the earlier hour. Ignacio recorded the nuns' peroration in his notes: "'Couldn't they dedicate just one day out of the week to be with God and with their families? Would their animals die if they didn't make it out to pasture just one day a week?' A woman in the audience found the courage to say 'Yes!' The nuns pretended not to hear her outburst and carried on with their harangue."

The nuns, of course, were there to promote the Catholic God, Jesus, the Virgin Mary, and sundry saints as the primordial source of care for the rural population of Yauyos. When and how do children begin the process of differentiating humans from animals, spirits of the earth, saints and devils, Our Lord of the Earthquakes, Virgin mothers, and the whole panoply of care-related actors that is set before them? Canessa (2012, 160–165) argues that creating such separations is in fact not a desirable or reasonable expectation in the Andes (see also de la Cadena 2015; Salas 2019). Appealing to interpreters of indigenous thought from the Amazon and other locations around the world, he insists that they reject the "false dichotomy between the social lives of people and the environment in which they exist" (Canessa 2012, 162, citing Descola 1994). This entanglement of carers—human and nonhuman, visible and invisible, living and something else—reflects a profound insight into the human condition in its recognition of the existence of multiple carers, all with both positive and negative potential.

Concerning Children's Agency

Childhood studies have become increasingly focused on children's agency, too often unnoticed in earlier scholarship. One of the primary motivations for this study was to understand the scope of, and limits to, children's agency in the rural Andes. We wondered what domains encouraged the exercise of agency, when and how children were disempowered, and what practices guided them toward futures of control, hope, and flourishing (Leinaweaver 2010b). Children in Yauyos, even from a very early age, exercise a wide margin of agency in two domains where this is expected, fostered, and convenient for adults: play and work. The evidence took us to two additional domains where we had not anticipated finding children's broad agency: health and nutrition on one hand, and involvement with nonfamily actors on the other. In this section we consider these four domains.

Play has been given short shrift in this book, crowded out by more urgent topics. Yet it was probably the preeminent domain for children to exercise their agency, in no small part because it was of little interest to adults (Anderson 2024). Grown-ups largely ignored children's play, albeit older children and adolescents— if they happened by—could intervene in what they conceived as defense of their younger siblings' interests and safety. Similar to the groups of children that Goodwin (1990) filmed on the stoops and streets of Philadelphia, participants in the playgroups of Yauyos created their own social organization. They made alliances, established hierarchies, and imposed sanctions for breaking the rules. They bullied and marginalized some of their peers, although complete exclusion was almost impossible because of the small numbers of children that were available as companions, and because the children's society was thoroughly crisscrossed by kinship ties. Although they generally respected conventional gender identities in the roles they played in games and in the types of toys and activities that were associated with them, the children exhibited greater tolerance for transgressions than did adults. Elisa, finding no playmates to be vendors or customers for a girls' game of store one afternoon, convinced her brother to stand in by creating a role for him as truck driver and delivery man. Meanwhile, Pamela's mother did everything she could to keep her daughter away from top-spinning games with the boys; the boys, however, were happy to have her.

Our findings about children's work fit well with the cross-cultural literature that documents children's valuable economic contributions (Lancy 2008). Yauyos children worked hard, both at household chores and as important participants in their families' broader livelihood strategies. By and large, children accepted the logic of reciprocity that underlay their cooperation. Their families provided for their needs, and they recognized and honored that. Children could hardly refuse to perform the duties they were assigned, but their power of decision was surprisingly broad when it came to determining when, where, and how to carry out tasks that were not under direct supervision. Indeed, most of the work that children did was done out of the sight of their elders.

Bodenhorn and Lee (2019, 123) are careful to "recognize the importance of places where children feel safe to explore and investigate out of the range of adults . . . children often have their own cartography that may or may not be shared with adults from the same localities." The work children did frequently demanded initiative, judgment, and creativity. The quality of their performance was seen in the results. Farming, herding, and shop-keeping tasks were easily portrayed as learning exercises and useful preparation for the children's own future. Many clearly enjoyed honing their skills and displaying their initiative.

Children's exercise of agency in relation to their own health care and that of other children was surprising in its scope. They fed themselves, worried about hygiene, and healed their wounds and those of siblings and friends. Children monitored the health and nutrition of other children. Were they dressed warmly enough? Eating enough? Taking baths? Changing clothes? Brushing their teeth? In all this the children adopted a framework well in line with the biocultural synthesis called for by ecologists and medical anthropologists (Goodman and

Leatherman 1998). They already knew that a critical part of maintaining good health was having a strong and caring social network.

Finally, the research uncovered a source of encouragement of children's agency in an unexpected quarter. This involved a category we call nonfamily care providers. Its most important members were teachers, health workers, various missionary and religious groups that came on the scene from time to time, and the occasional NGO. All offered services that ostensibly addressed a care issue. At the same time, they proposed changes and reforms that were unwelcome to many of the adults and whose effects, even if beneficial, would likely only be seen in a distant future. Rather than the slow work of convincing the parents, these entities often bypassed them to deal with the children directly. We saw this with the missionaries who visited the towns (chapter 8). The MMM missionaries said goodbye to Yauyos capital with a gathering of children on Calabash Square. Two young women led them in a game of "San Miguel" before forming a circle and singing religious songs together. The women exchanged kisses and hugs with each child, wished them the best, and promised to return one day soon. Such immediate intimacy with the adults would have been impossible. Some of children's most effective power lies in how they can wield their ostensible irrelevance (Berman 2011, 275).

There were, of course, crucial elements of their lives that the children had absolutely no control over. Among them were fathers who absconded, alcoholism in the family, and parents with mental health challenges. There was the constant backdrop of weather, climate, and the physical dangers of the environment, and the never-ending drain of poverty. But in numerous arenas, many of the children were quite well practiced in the ways of negotiating, cajoling, persuading, and manipulating their care providers into bending to their will.

Emplacing Children in Rural Andean Communities

Place is central in creating what adult onlookers can accept as "proper childhoods" (Boyden 1997, 197–202). By that standard, Yauyos children were having "proper childhoods," by and large, emplaced as they were in households and family groups that made sense by local standards. Even disruptions like migrations or the substitution of a stepfather for a father were understandable in local terms. In their homes the children had plain meals and few creature comforts, but they had routines and a certain stability. For most, the home was a safe space where, within limits, they could express their personalities: radio programs they liked to tune into, clothes they preferred, shared complicities with one or another family member, or secret stashes of things they collected.

Stepping outside their door, the children of Yauyos were met with another familiar scene. The towns were small enough for them to recognize the people that shared their living space.[2] They could make cognitive maps defining family groups, and they knew quite a bit about the histories of neighbors' lives. They knew which adults should be avoided and which might be counted on for help if needed. As Bodenhorn and Lee (2019, 123) explain, "sociality often animates locality—filling it with meaning for these youngsters in different ways and to differing degrees of intensity." As far as children could see—at least the younger ones—local values were relatively consistent. Older residents tried to keep them on the right path: do your homework but do not steal, be lazy, or be carried away by idle dreams. The case of the dog Pinocho offered more instruction: learn to become indifferent, when necessary. Some children had more resources than others, some had more chores and spent more hours working, some had more difficult home situations than others, but nothing was beyond the bounds of comprehensibility.

These familiar surroundings eventually came to embody troubling contrasts with other places more overtly imbued with prestige and opportunities within the geopolitical hierarchies of Peru. At some point all the children became aware of the gap between their circumstances and style of life and those of their contemporaries in nearby cities. Often this came with visits from city cousins, but many yauyino children had themselves been to Lima or Huancayo before they started school. Some of their own family members might well have migrated there, or to Cañete, Ica, or points further beyond. These cities were magnetic. They occasioned constant references in conversations about business trips, shopping, vacations, and visits to the centers of bureaucracy and power of the Peruvian nation. As frequently occurs with migrants who seek validation of their choice, city relatives tended to paint idealized images of their circumstances and surroundings. These were reinforced by observations children made of tourists visiting from Lima in large SUVs and through messages transmitted by the media (see Babb 2011).

The gap between city and countryside was problematic for adults as well. Even the poorest of residents had a portfolio of assets in the rural community—physical, social, juridical, political (Jagannathan 1987)—that they and their children would necessarily lose in a move to the city, where they would also face discrimination and hard daily lives. Parents were torn over where they might have a better future, for themselves and for children whose individual needs and capacities they struggled to calibrate. The comparisons of city and countryside were based on limited information and shot through with uncertainty, but they shaped the imaginings of adults and children alike.

The places children resided were also profoundly affected by processes originating far from their doorsteps. The impact of anthropogenic climate change was ever more apparent to a primarily agricultural population, resembling Katz's observations in an African context that children "were learning the skills and knowledge associated with agriculture, but they were unlikely to have access to land as they came of age. At the same time, they were acquiring an exquisitely detailed knowledge of how to use the local environment even as its resources appeared to be under erasure" (2004, xii). New models of consumption, from fruit to sneakers to propane gas stoves, were taking hold. The prestige of the educated person grew even as that status became increasingly difficult to achieve (Levinson, Foley, and

CONCLUSIONS

Holland 1996). Local childhoods were shaped by global discourses, international laws, and transnational processes (Scheper-Hughes and Sargent 1998; Bornstein 2001; Cole and Durham 2007; Martine et al. 2008), as was clear when organizations such as the Defensoría Municipal del Niño, Niña y Adolescente (DEMUNA) and NGOs working in related spaces introduced the complicated concept of children's rights. Children were caught up in broader patterns of violence and conflict (Boyden and Berry 2004; Morales and Singh 2014). We have seen how, in Yauyos, the havoc caused by Shining Path and the government's response was still present in people's minds. The places they lived in gained meanings, often confusing and ambiguous, from their incorporation into these broader processes.

How Children Saw Their World

Children in Yauyos saw the world differently than their elders, and they saw it differently than most of the researchers that have written about Andean communities. This was partly because of their structurally subordinate position. As standpoint theory predicts, children in Yauyos learned to defend themselves against a too-eager acceptance of adult truths and the consequences that flowed from them: orders and recommendations, verdicts about culpability, punishments and rewards, a pecking order among siblings. This tended to be implicit for younger children, but older children and adolescents were often quite open about how adult versions of reality needed correction, reinterpretation, or outright rejection. The field-workers registered many occasions in which children stated the adult version of things and then added their own, discrepant interpretations. This was nowhere more evident than in the competing visions of education. While parents and teachers made exhortations and speeches showing school to be the means of escaping humiliation and discrimination, the children saw the situation more clearly. Building on their own information-gathering from urban peers, travel to the city, mass media, and other sources, they made a guarded assessment of their chances of getting into college, finishing a college education, and becoming a professional. After all, almost none of their parents had been able to do it and conditions now were far more competitive. Even if they made it through, would that erase the stigma of small-town rural origins (Huayhua 2010)?

Skepticism of what adults presented as truth took root in a soil fed by everyday observations. The children in small, rural towns witnessed the adult world up close with all its warts. In tight living quarters, there were few barriers to what children could see and hear. Children were privy to conversations, disputes, and even violence that might have been easier to hide in other settings. They moved about the towns with few restrictions. They discussed the latest gossip among themselves, and they consulted with a few, select older confidants about how to interpret it. They experienced, often as direct victims, the moral failings of adults: substance abuse, violence, fecklessness, and solipsism. Children were aware of their parents' reputations in local society, and many were embarrassed by them. From the adult point of view, children were underfoot and largely invisible (Berman 2011, 275). From the children's point of view, they were spies working to avoid pain and disaster. As Rogoff (2003, 69) states in a much-quoted summary of children's survival strategies from infancy forward: "(Their) efforts appear similar to those appropriate for anyone learning in an unfamiliar cultural setting: stay near trusted guides, watch their activities and get involved when possible, and attend to any instruction the guides provide."

Children's understandings of the social world around them were not imprinted from patterns that kinship scholars have identified in the region (e.g., Lambert 1977; Mayer 1974; Leinaweaver 2018). Rather, they saw individuals with particular personalities and motivations—say, one grandmother who was quick to laugh and another who stressed obedience; one uncle who pitched in enthusiastically on community projects and another male relative who shirked his duties and evaded the sanctions. The complex political landscape of contemporary Andean communities, where traditional institutions for processing conflicts and imposing peace coexisted with new formats for decision-making that were in principle more inclusive and decentralized, was largely opaque to the children (as it was to many of the less politically involved adults). To degrees corresponding to their different levels of maturity, children grasped the corruption and exploitation that occurred in the towns, the distrust among neighbors and of political leaders, and the internecine fights that never seemed to improve the situation. They saw the inequalities and the abuses of power, and they folded them into their evaluations of the places where they were growing up.

Still and all, children found happiness and love where it was barely visible to adults. Adults in Andean communities look to peak moments of conviviality and release in many of their projects: dancing at the fiestas, getting drunk, enjoying the music, feeling pride in a performance, meeting a ritual obligation, and receiving the adulation of fellow townspeople. While they were thoroughly caught up in the effervescence when celebrations rolled around, the children focused on the pleasures and joys of day-to-day life. Their experiences of happiness and security were tied up with the local environment and the local community in ways the adults did not always remember or understand. Movement, freedom, curiosity, a sense of competence, play, friends (including animal friends), nature, art, music, and spirituality could all bring delight to children. Their "projects" (Ortner 2006), especially those of the younger ones, were built around enhancing the opportunities for pleasure and avoiding the risks of pain, as defined in their world. Those entering adolescence were nurturing projects more recognizable as such in the adult world: Aurora, to travel the globe like the tourists that visited the Aventura Andina resort; Braulio, to take charge of the lands assigned to him; Rufina, to take the stage as a singer of Andean music; others, to pursue careers as chef, police officer, nurse, or teacher. Those most sure of the financial support of their families dared to imagine projects of college and a profession: engineer, lawyer, doctor, or environmental scientist.

What the Future Holds

Many occurrences, large and small, disrupted the course of children's lives in Yauyos, from asthma attacks to the loss of a parent. Moving from one place to another, a mother's new pregnancy, and major illnesses were among the events children talked about. Pushing the analysis beyond what they articulated, we can envision looming points of strain. One concerns the gendered dimensions of the life course. Some girls that were close to the 2008 research were already single mothers just a few years later. Drastic changes have occurred in attitudes and practices involving sexuality and reproduction in Yauyos as in all of Peru, but girls and women are still thrown off course by stigmatization, disinformation, limited options, and vulnerability to resource-rich seducers. The health centers liberally distribute free condoms, but nobody has meaningfully addressed the larger problem of predatory adult males and sexual abusers. To aggravate the problems, there is the increased potential of losing boys' and men's collaboration in family life and childcare and destroying the safeguards that enforced a roughly equal division of labor between men and women. Male violence against women spills into ever-expanding arenas.

A second area where ruptures are to be expected concerns nothing less than the future of rural towns in the Andes (Asensio 2023). The organization and sustainability of family farming is a major part of that. Children's labor is an essential input as things stand, and their labor is vital in many other activities that, taken separately, are marginally profitable but in combination can sustain a family. The much-touted value of formal education is sometimes at odds with the need to acquire the skills for earning a living in the rural landscape, as others have documented in non-Andean settings (Meinert 2003; Serpell 1993; Katz 2004). Many children will not inherit land and herds, and those that do face the uncertainties of climate change, soil degradation, and fickle national and international markets. But forces driving the diversification of the rural economy are also in play. Somehow children must be prepared for eventualities like the option of working virtually in nonfarm occupations from a high-altitude town that has strong and steady internet connections, new approaches to the area's natural endowments, and new ways of accessing the resources of urban Peru and beyond. Rather than the abolition of opportunities for children and adolescents to contribute to their families' prosperity, this calls for new kinds of apprenticeships.

A related area of concern lies in the radical misrecognition of rural Andean cultural processes and further devaluing of associated lifeways, languages, and customs (compare Lear 2006). Potent forces conspired to drain the meaning out of the shared community. As Canessa writes of highland Bolivia:

> As cultural values become undermined, people who had a rich cultural life feel increasingly marginalized. That is, it is not simply that children spend a lot of time in school learning very little at all, but they spend a lot of time

not learning about other things . . . These skills, which are essential for their economic well-being—not to mention cultural reproduction—are valued less and less, while the skills that are valuable for life in urban Bolivia are highly valued. This would not matter so much if they were actually acquiring these skills, but they are manifestly not, and they are taught that the ideas of their parents and grandparents are archaic and irrelevant. The rich set of rituals their parents use to make crops grow and cure animals—rituals that give people a sense of control over the vicissitudes of their lives—are becoming meaningless to young people. In the words of one young woman, "(The mountain spirits) have left us" and another young man said that they "are not powerful anymore." (Canessa 2012, 200)

All of this is exacerbated by the neoliberal practice of making cultural diversity a criterion that qualifies its bearers as state dependents eligible for social programs (e.g., Kymlicka 2009).[3] It was not surprising in these circumstances that some young people in Yauyos showed serious confusions about where they belonged and what they should become.

We Are All Entrepreneurs Now

Andeans have long been recognized as hard-working, innovative, self-reliant, and market savvy, and yauyinos are no exception.[4] Expanding into small businesses was already one of the few options available to small farmers whose crops could fail and whose incomes oscillated annually. Yauyinos have developed tourism and handicrafts businesses, entered into supply chains for urban supermarkets, contracted with fruit exporters, and sold their cattle to feedlots in Cañete. Increasingly, these initiatives entail going against traditional norms and customs. New capitalist economic arrangements come to the fore as entrepreneurs encroach on others' lands and disown community obligations. In recent years, Yauyos, especially its Sur Grande, has come squarely into the line of expansion of Peru's booming agricultural export industry. New technologies have been introduced for managing water, fertilizers, and an itinerant labor force. The agricultural frontier has been pushed back into former desert and new crops have been made possible.

Meanwhile, entrepreneurship—*emprendedurismo* (Cánepa and Lamas 2020)—has become the rallying cry for Peruvian development. In the years after our research in Yauyos, *emprendedurismo* was added to the national school curriculum. Elementary school students were encouraged to think of products they could make and sell. Math exercises were oriented to calculating investments, costs, and profits. Where neither the government nor the private sector has been up to the challenge of providing jobs and opportunities, pulling oneself up by one's bootstraps into self-employment and a perch in the informal sector is touted as the one remaining route to a bright future. But as Cánepa and Lamas observe, "This phenomenon

CONCLUSIONS 149

disproportionately affects the rural population and the 'emerging' middle classes whose struggles the discourse of *emprendedurismo* supposedly celebrates and makes visible. This leads to the question of what it means to govern under a mandate of entrepreneurship in a country of weak institutions and precarious liberties exercised amid corruption, organized crime and violence" (2020, 29, translation ours).

In Yauyos, making small farmers better entrepreneurs was an idea that was promoted by the Valle Grande Institute through its training courses for young men and its medicinal herbs project. An experimental extension was made to women (Zegarra, Higuchi, and Vargas 2018). The Escuela en Alternancia requires that its students have a business plan in order to graduate, and they are expected to spread the ethos of *emprendedurismo* to their parents and relatives on their visits home. In chapter 4 we saw girls running food carts, teenagers managing bodegas whose proprietors were officially older relatives, boys who hunted and fished on consignment, girls who made earrings to sell to schoolmates, and others who made weavings that they offered to tourists. These were all startup business ventures being run by older children and adolescents in our biographies sample and beyond.

The motivation to migrate to the city was undergirded by the promise of an *emprendimiento* (a small business; the tangible fruit of a spirit of *emprendedurismo*) (Golte and Adams 1990; Adams and Valdivia 1991). A first step might involve buying a plot of land and raising a house in a shanty settlement (Skrabut 2018). The house should pay for itself by supporting the business: store, workshop, carpentry, restaurant, beauty salon, whatever it may be. Along the way, any job, however menial, could be acceptable. Moving away and attempting this new life had clear costs in terms of prestige and self-image. Some members of the older generation in Yauyos recalled going from being a well-resourced stock grower to being a cobbler in Lima; or going from ownership of a prosperous store to becoming a short-order cook in a *chifa* (Chinese-Peruvian restaurant) in Huancayo; or going from school librarian in Yauyos to line worker in a Cañete fruit-packing plant. Shame and misrecognition plagued the urban shanty-dwellers and the "informales," the operators of small, unregistered businesses, as much as they tracked rural townspeople (Anderson 2010). And businesses could always fail, as had been the experience of many of the returnees that we met in Yauyos.

Scholarship on the Andean community has documented how a logic of household and a logic of community are simultaneously in play and pose complicated, often contradictory claims for community members (Golte and de la Cadena 1986; Golte 1987). Investing resources, devoting time and energy toward promoting the prosperity of the household, could easily compete with demands for contributing to a collective fund, participating in faenas, and accepting the authorities' decisions about the distribution of farm plots and water, the selection of crops, and the timing of planting and harvesting. The current ascendency of *emprendedurismo* suggests that the logic of household—even a logic of the individual (the lonely Weberian capitalist)—has gained an absolute victory over the logic of community.

And yet farms and communal rights were an essential fallback during the COVID-19 pandemic that began in 2020 (Zegarra et al. 2023). In the face of a collapsing health system and massive death, with the economy practically paralyzed and jobs disappearing daily, many urban dwellers that still had ties to rural communities undertook a reverse migration. With no functioning transport system, contravening the rules of quarantine, they appeared in dramatic news clips as caravans on the sides of roads, walking back to their home villages and towns. There they could at least count on shelter, perhaps reopening houses they had left vacant, and they would be able to grow some food, share a table with their farming relatives, and avoid the high food costs in the city. Meanwhile, local authorities were under orders to stop the spread of infection by closing their borders. Some organized twenty-four-hour patrols to prevent anyone from entering or leaving, while others set up quarantine facilities at the edge of the town and held the return migrants there for periods stipulated by health officials. All found it difficult to turn away brothers and sisters, uncles and aunts, cousins, nieces and nephews, old and cherished neighbors. Often, the patrols turned a blind eye, and under cover of nighttime the returnees could slip through.

The unprecedented situation brought on by COVID-19 made it clear that the rural community and its capacity for collective responses to problems have not lost their relevance. We can even speculate about all that might still be achieved if the community logic were to prevail. With capable and honest leadership, good-faith participation by the townspeople, and effective backing from higher levels of government, we could envision a future of advanced infrastructure, a restored natural environment, and support for children and youth. Basic services like sewer systems and potable water, reliable health and mental health services, clean energy, reforestation of the Andes, and youth organizations and clubs, could all flourish.

The outcome of this thought experiment would be yauyinos—and other rural Andeans—who can make the choice to stay where they grew up and know that they can make a life there. Canessa, based on work in rural Bolivia, argues that "personal identity . . . is so rooted in place and community and the relations of these to agricultural activity. This explains why migrants will go to such pains to maintain fields and attend rituals and fiestas; what is at stake is not merely sentimental links with their place of birth but the very sense of who they are as human beings" (Canessa 2012, 164).

One challenge to achieving this vision is the negative stereotyping of rural populations in Peru, long identified with poverty and indigeneity. Part of children's sense of being well cared for depended upon the recognition that was awarded to the communities they belonged to and the persons they were most intimately connected with. In the deeply unequal and hierarchical national context, many children internalized the lesson that their success and full citizenship would be measured by their ability to "pass" in urban Peruvian society, even to triumph in that society. Besides all else, migrating to the city, and becoming educated, was a destigmatization strategy (Lamont 2009, 155–161; Kymlicka 2009, 250). But it was also a strategy that exposed the migrants to the underbelly of city life, demystifying the touted paragons of national leadership and supposedly open and fair structures of democratic participation. Bombarded by news of crime and corruption, yauyinos had good cause to affirm the superiority of their moral values. Their aesthetic values held their own against the *huachafería* ("kitsch") of much urban cultural production.

The children of Yauyos, and rural Andean Peru more generally, have been thrust by the circumstance of their birth and emplacement onto a complicated stage with innumerable challenges ahead of them. This book has delved into the minutiae of many of those challenges. In closing we must add to them the stands they will be called upon to take in the terrain of the politics of recognition (Fraser and Honneth 2003). As we write, Peru has entered another cycle of political upheaval. Many commentators have remarked on the lack of respect with which the Andean protestors have been treated by members of Congress, journalists, and the public. Too quickly they are put down as violent and backward, as deluded by the promises of communists and terrorists. Clearly, this is a massive, self-serving misreading of their motivations and goals; of their "projects," in Ortner's term. Respect and disrespect are difficult to talk about, and in fact the adult research participants in Yauyos rarely used those words. We have argued that they showed in action their awareness of how the children of the province might be affected by them and might become the victims of misrecognition and discrimination. The older generation did what it could to correct misconceptions and defend their way of being human, against tall odds. Now it is the turn of the children.

ACKNOWLEDGMENTS

Ours has been a collaboration across generations and continents. It benefitted from our differences as much as our similarities. Jeanine was trained as an anthropologist at Cornell University in the 1960s, under the influence of classical Andeanists and before the advent of gender studies. She was aware of the Six Cultures Study and intrigued by John M. Roberts's explorations of games and play. Her entire career has unrolled in Latin America, in a world of conferences, in-house publications, and heavy teaching loads. Jessaca was trained as an anthropologist at the University of Michigan in the 2000s, with a grounding in the "new kinship studies" and feminist anthropology. Her location within U.S. anthropology has contributed to a focus on theory-building, communicating research broadly, and internationalization of scholarship. We share the value of ethnography as our discipline's stellar method and a concern for the application of social scientific knowledge to real-world problems. We have both cherished the many exchanges of knowledge this collaboration has made possible, and have each learned much from one another.

The Wenner-Gren Foundation awarded us an International Collaborative Research Grant, a (now discontinued) funding mechanism in support of "an international anthropology that values and incorporates different national perspectives and resources," including supplemental funding for a training element. Leinaweaver, who at the time that the research was designed was working at the University of Manitoba, was also awarded a CIES Fellowship (the Lima-based CIES stands for "Economic and Social Research Consortium") which supports collaborations between Canadian and Peruvian researchers; this funding enabled the participation of the two Canadian graduate students. Brown University also facilitated Leinaweaver's follow-up travel on this project through Humanities Research Funds. We are indebted to these organizations for their essential financial support of this research.

In chapter 2, we describe the research design and methodology, and introduce the research team. We thank them here as well for their essential important contributions to this work. The students who dedicated themselves to learning child-centered methods and applying them as field-workers and data analysts are: Gabriela Agüero, Cynthia Astudillo, Carlos Chirinos, Diego Geng, Christopher Little, Gabriela Medina, Li Minaya, Violeta Navarrete, Roxana Ocaña, Nadya Padilla, Jhon Sifuentes,

Sandra Torrejón, Ignacio Vargas. Margarita Velasco's role in the data analysis was instrumental. Julio Portocarrero and Helen Palma contributed in numerous ways to the success of the project. Childhood scholars Claudia Fonseca (Brazil), Maritza Díaz (Colombia), and Beatriz Oré (Peru) enriched the students' pre-field training, providing practical pointers and a comparative perspective. Representatives of CODENY (Corporación de Desarrollo del Nor Yauyos), in Lima and in Yauyos, facilitated contacts and information, and provided the field-workers with orientation on their pilot journey to the province. This book would not have been possible without their valued contributions, and we hope to have done justice to the care and thought they put into their work.

We are grateful to fellow panelists, discussants, and audience members at the numerous occasions we have presented aspects of this research. Those include: at a symposium on childhood at the Colombian Anthropology Congress (presented by Leinaweaver, 2009); at the Society for Cross Cultural Research meeting in Charleston (presented by Anderson 2011); at the Society for Latin American and Caribbean Anthropology conference in Oaxaca (presented by Leinaweaver, 2015); at a workshop with the Americas Research Interest Group at the University of Oregon, convened by Kristen Yarris (presented by Leinaweaver, 2016); at a panel we co-convened on research in Yauyos at the LASA conference in New York (presented by Anderson and Leinaweaver, 2016); at the American Anthropological Association conference in Washington, D.C. (presented by Leinaweaver, 2017); and at a virtual workshop on "Transforming Care" convened by Koreen Reece and Diego Maria Malara (presented by Anderson and Leinaweaver, 2023). We have published four shorter discussions of the Yauyos dataset, in Spanish, in Latin American venues. These are cited in our bibliography (Leinaweaver 2010; Anderson 2013; Anderson 2018; Anderson and Leinaweaver 2023), as well as an article in English on education in Yauyos (Leinaweaver and Anderson 2024).

Our thanks go, as well, to our anonymous reviewers for their generous insights, and to the team at Rutgers—Kimberly Guinta, Carah Naseem, Emma-Li Downer, and their many skilled co-workers—who brought this book into being.

Jessaca thanks her colleagues at Manitoba, where her contributions to this project took initial form, and at Brown, where they were completed, for their warm encouragement of this research. She appreciates the many people who have guided her to think about care in more nuanced ways, including Ellen Block, Andrea Flores, Aalyia Sadruddin, Iván Sándoval-Cervantes, Margarita Zegarra, Susan Short, Lynnette Arnold, Erdmute Alber, and Heike Drotbohm. She is grateful to her parents, her siblings, and to Joe and Leo for their support and care throughout the timespan of this project. Jeanine thanks her many colleagues at the Pontificia Universidad Católica del Perú whose conversations, insights, and collaboration have been especially important, in particular Juan Ansión, Carmen Yon, Narda Henríquez, Alejandro Diez, Robin Cavagnoud, and Catalina Romero. She writes, "Silvia Sachún, administrator, was a source of positive energy during the project in Yauyos as she was throughout my years of teaching at the PUCP. Many persons, affiliated with many different institutions, illuminated and inspired me on topics directly related to childhood. Among them are Carmen Vásquez de Velasco, Patricia Oliart, Patricia Ames, and three more specialists that, sadly, are no longer with us: Blanca Figueroa, Fulvia Rosemberg, and Judith Ennew. Finally, I want to thank the late Richard L. May and my sister Geralyn May for their constant support, and Mayu Velasco, Dania Franco, and Margarita Velasco for their untiring willingness to share in my obsessions. Throughout the writing, I could not help but think of my parents, child workers on family farms in the Swedish immigrant communities of western Iowa where they grew up. My mother's tales of how her hands hurt after walking the corn rows and harvesting the cobs was a recurring memory. The children and adults of Yauyos would have sympathized with their experience. To them we owe our greatest debt."

NOTES

CHAPTER 1   CARE, COMMUNITY, AND CHILDREN

1. Historians Carlos Contreras and Marcos Cueto (2000) make numerous references to this centuries-old tradition in their history of Peru since its independence in 1821. See, for example (161–164), the exchanges between intellectuals Alejandro Deustua and Manuel Gonzales Prada at a crucial moment as the country entered the twentieth century, having been soundly defeated by Chile in the War of the Pacific (1879–1883).

2. Hogan (2005, 26–27) criticizes her own discipline of developmental psychology for making the child "context-free, predictable, and irrelevant"; this last, in the sense that adults presumably already know the developmental stages children go through and characteristics associated with them.

3. Eggan criticized the practice, common in early anthropological works, of positing resemblances between beliefs and practices drawn from widely disparate points on the globe, without regard for their context and meaning. "Controlling" the comparisons required demonstrating historical ties, a shared language, geographical proximity, or other evidence of connection between the groups that made elements of their institutions and culture legitimately comparable. The diversity of the Andean region is made commensurate, according to this perspective, by a shared historical process under successive chiefdoms and empires, followed by three centuries of Spanish colonial administration.

4. A landmark was the Institute of Peruvian Studies (Instituto de Estudios Peruanos—IEP) study in the second half of the 1960s of twenty-seven communities located in the Mantaro valley of Junín and the Chancay River Valley (Fuenzalida et al. 1982; Degregori and Golte 1973). In fact, the high-altitude valleys encircling Lima to the east, north, and south have been among those most often used as comparative laboratories (Diez 2001).

5. In selecting the contributors, Ferreira was assisted by Billie Jean Isbell, justly recognized for a long career involving a wide variety of approaches to Andean societies.

6. Studies that incorporate young people as protagonists include Allen (2002), Ames (2013a, 2013b), Babb (1989), Bolin (2006), Bolton et al. (1976), Flores (2010), Grim-Feinberg (2013), Haboud de Ortega (1980), Isbell (1985), Leinaweaver (2007b, 2008), Ortiz (1989), Panez (2004), Panez and Ochoa (2000), Pribilsky (2001), and Van Vleet (2008).

7. Part of Nor Yauyos drains into the Cochas River, which forms part of the Mantaro River basin in the central Andes.

8. We use pseudonyms for five of the localities throughout the book but could not plausibly alter the identity of the provincial capital.

9. What stands of trees exist in Yauyos tend to be eucalyptus, an import from Australia that has replaced native species in much of the Andes. A major government program in

158   NOTES TO PAGES 13–21

the 1990s sought to encourage communities to replant the mountain slopes with trees as a means of soil conservation and temperature moderation.

10. The main road connecting the towns at the lower end of the Cañete valley to those at high altitude was asphalted in the years after our fieldwork. Rainy season runs (most years) late November through February or early March.

11. The exception was the health post, generally constructed with a flush toilet and shower area with a water heater. This was for the staff, but they often allowed visitors (not locals) to use them.

12. Not all residents of the towns were members of the *comunidad campesina*, which was an inherited status that brought with it important rights not only to resources (like communally owned pastures) but to participation in the earnings from businesses, the use of assets such as vehicles, and some government subsidies.

13. In theory, authorities can call on the townspeople for *faenas* involving other projects but, rather than give of their time and energy, people are increasingly likely to pay the fine or hire a worker to replace them.

14. Terrazas, with its nearby mine, used the income to purchase an ambulance, subsidize a restaurant open to townspeople and visitors, supplement the budget of the public health post, and much more.

15. Poverty today is concentrated in the urban slums. Ironically, that is where many Yauyos migrants end up, only to bury—or put on long hold—their dreams of urban prosperity and modernity.

16. At the time of the 2007 national census, 6.5 percent of households in Yauyos had one or more members that had migrated internationally.

17. One-third of the Peruvian population lives in greater metropolitan Lima, including its port city Callao. Common throughout Latin America, primate cities located at estuaries of rivers reflect long histories of export economies tied to a colonial power.

18. Andean towns typically have at least one hotel or hostel, run by the municipal government, which accommodates officials like police or judges, workers on short-term construction and maintenance projects, and other visitors like ethnographers and the occasional investigative reporter.

19. The scenic reserve status meant that the Ministry of the Environment was mandated to monitor the health and numbers of protected species, such as the Andean condor, puma, vizcacha (a native rabbit), vicuña, and fox. In principle, inspectors were deployed to track down illegal artisanal mines and other environmental violations.

20. The museum in Las Cascadas was built around a group of funeral bundles that were found in an excavation in the 1920s. The community has unsuccessfully petitioned the Instituto Nacional de Cultura to research them. They were simply told to preserve the mummies in glass cases as best they could. Showcasing both the influence of Lima beer-drinking customs and the recognition of its picturesque setting and that precolonial heritage, Las Cascadas was the site of a commercial for Cuzqueña beer filmed during the fieldwork.

CHAPTER 2   KNOWING CHILDREN

1. The Consorcio de Investigación Económica y Social (CIES) is a consortium of some fifty Peruvian institutes, think tanks, and universities that produce research on the economy and society, with emphasis on improving public policy. CIES runs an annual research competition and commissions review papers on priority topics and research agendas.

NOTES TO PAGES 22–36 159

2. Even earlier, Yauyos had accumulated a considerable research history. The Huarochirí-Yauyos project (1952–1955) took members of Lima's San Marcos University Ethnology Institute to over two dozen communities under the direction of foundational Peruvian anthropologist José Matos Mar (Matos Mar 1953; Ávalos 1952). Varillas (1965) produced a compilation of local folklore. Fonseca and Mayer (1988) produced an important study of land use, labor, and production systems. A group of French agronomists, economists, and biologists associated with the Institut Français d'Études Andines contributed detailed case studies on topics ranging from household economics and nutrition to migration (Eresue and Brougère 1988).

3. Three sociologists took the leading role in designing, applying, and analyzing the results of the survey: Catalina Romero, Sylvia Matos, and David Sulmont.

4. Many of the mayors were absentee authorities. They lived in Lima or another city and visited their municipal offices irregularly. The pretext that justified this was the need to shepherd projects and petitions through the regional or national bureaucracy. The mayors were rarely available for audiences with their local constituents but were (or so they claimed) furthering local interests.

5. Chris Little, the Canadian anthropology graduate student who joined, had very little command of Spanish and could not share in interviewing or registering conversations. He could, however, be keenly attentive to behaviors and interactions he was able to observe. His presence as an English speaker and non-Peruvian was a complication at times but probably less than might have been the case because of the existence of a tourist site in the town where he was assigned, with regular foreign visitors, and because of the ability of his co-workers to act as intermediaries and "explainers."

6. Anthropologists have often been reticent when it comes to explicating the procedures they use in the design and planning of research studies and, to an even greater extent, those they use in analyzing and interpreting research findings (for counterexamples see Wolcott 1994; Richards 2005; Puddenphatt et al. 2009).

7. FORSUR was the special government entity set up to oversee the reconstruction of the entire area affected by the 2007 earthquake. It was badly administered, and post hoc evaluations have been consistently negative.

8. The largest effort to resolve housing problems came from the Catholic Church charity Cáritas underwritten by USAID. People whose houses were damaged were given prefabricated houses to use until they could repair and rebuild. A small number of those left completely homeless were invited to participate in a longer project that would provide them with earthquake-resistant adobe houses. By August 2008, one year after the earthquake, three people (two women, one man) were the only ones left in the Cáritas self-help home construction project. Several of the USAID prefabricated plywood shelters had been repurposed, some as corrals, one as a workshop for spinning wool and weaving mantas, and another as a room rented out to construction workers there to rebuild the school.

9. Las Cascadas at the time was part of the SAIS Tupac Amaru, a conglomerate of former haciendas and free-standing communities created by the Agrarian Reform of 1969. Because these entities represented alliances of rural producers and were effectively integrating them into capitalist markets, they were a particular target of Shining Path. The SAIS Tupac Amaru was one of the few in the central Andes that survived (CVR 2004, 391). Many people lost property, however; animals were sold at far less than their value, or they were simply left to die of hunger. Residents recall these times as a setback for the entire community.

160　　　NOTES TO PAGES 38-66

10. Chamis is *aguardiente* (grain alcohol) seasoned with lemon and herbs, to which boiling water is added. It is served from a teapot.

11. He was interviewed as part of the Yauyos Values Study in 1998.

CHAPTER 3　INTIMATE CONTEXTS OF CARE

1. Chipitaps (known as "Pogs" in the United States) were one of the favorite entertainments of children in Yauyos during fieldwork. They were small plastic discs, often printed with the image of a character from a Japanese animated series or a Disney cartoon. A kind of tiddlywinks, they could be used in solitary play or competitively, where children tried to win discs off their companions and increase their collections.

2. Some adolescents in unusual circumstances had a bed of their own, such as Braulio, live-in worker at the El Puente restaurant and lodging. Braulio shared a bedroom with his employer, Señora Pilar.

3. Recall that the biographies sample was not representative of the province of Yauyos or any of its towns. We use it to suggest tendencies and to provide a context for the child protagonists.

4. Four of the twelve cases mentioned were adolescents, eighteen years old or under.

5. In the 1960s Peru's total fertility rate was 6.85 children per woman; in 2017 it was 2.5 (INEI 2018, 70; Aramburú and Mendoza 2003, 45). This fertility decline is partly attributable to forced sterilizations during Fujimori's second term (Aramburú 2014, 84), but also relates to greater costs of living emerging from the neoliberal reforms of the 1990s (Boesten 2010). Note also the difference between fertility rates in urban and rural Peru, which is linked "to an increase in national inequality and poverty"; in 2000 rural women had more than twice the number of children as urban women (5.06 vs. 2.37; Aramburú and Mendoza 2003, 48–49, 54).

6. Most of the women used injectable contraceptives, which we learned from their openness and that of the health workers. A wide acceptance of contraception—including abortion—in the Andes has been amply documented by health researchers (Yon 2016, 2000; Reyes 2007). Pregnancy interruption may be attempted by herbal, chemical, or mechanical means. Carmen Yon has found that women fear dangerous pregnancies and difficult births and talk freely about the burden of caring for many children (2000).

7. These children with large families are those we call Jhony, Renzo, Isaac, Rufina, Pascual, Gladis, Dina, Moíses, Nieves, and Nilton.

CHAPTER 4　ECONOMIES OF CARE

1. The government agency INRENA (since reorganized and renamed) was charged with the supervision of protected species, among other environmental protection activities. We were told that it gave permits to three or four of these overseas hunters per year, charging a fee of several thousands of dollars, with the rationale that there was a need for some culling, especially of pumas, that were a real threat to the herds.

2. Peru has a persistent problem of corruption in government, and rural municipalities are among the entities most exposed to it, given the relatively small amounts involved and the lack of effective monitoring systems (Quiroz 2008).

3. The exchange rate was about three Peruvian soles (written as S/.3) to $1 US at this time.

4. Ponce and Escobal (2019) found that antipoverty programs implemented by the Peruvian government in years after our study, with the objective of increasing women's access

NOTES TO PAGES 76–88

to work and income, had the unwanted effect of increasing the time their adolescent daughters spent on housework.

5. The exception may be Aurora (13), who operated a *salchipapa* cart with singular dedication. She had dreams of traveling far away ("to Mexico") after high school. Her attitude toward money and its accumulation may have been influenced by her father and half-brother, who both worked on salary at the Aventura Andina resort.

CHAPTER 5   ECOLOGIES OF CARE

1. Chickens—the most frequent animal protein source for Peruvians up and down the coast—do not do as well at higher altitude, and eating chicken is associated with places like Cañete and Lima. Of all the children in the biographies sample, only Consuelo and Moisés were partial to it. Both had spent their early years in or near Cañete, where chicken and rice are staples, not the beef and potatoes of the Andes.

2. The best protection against caries was the limited presence of sugar in the traditional diet, although this advantage was rapidly being lost. In the older generation, calcium deficiencies and accidents took their toll. Most adults in Yauyos were missing teeth; some were missing nearly all of them.

3. A 1972 national survey of food consumption (Encuesta Nacional de Consumo de Alimentos) found that in the central Andes region, of which Yauyos is a part, 57 percent of children under six years of age were malnourished (Ministry of Agriculture 1979). The Sautier and Amemiya study (1988), cited earlier, focused on four communities in the province, two of which coincide with our study, and found that malnutrition affected a similar number.

4. During the 1980s, Sautier and Amemiya found that Terrazas had three or four days of fiesta every month (1988, 125). The frequency of community-wide festivals has dropped but remains significant.

5. Since 2008 school lunches in marginalized areas of the country, such as rural communities, have been consolidated in a national program (Qali Warma, meaning "healthy child" in Quechua) with central administration and formal procedures for procuring supplies. Things were far more haphazard at the time of the research.

6. In Las Cascadas, possibly following the model of the many tourist hostels that accommodated visitors who came with expectations of a warm, daily shower, several houses had bathrooms including a flush toilet and shower attached to a water heater powered by solar panels.

7. Longer treatments in those cities occurred, though rarely. For example, Rufina (15) had been taken out of school for two years when she needed an operation for cysts in Lima. As a result, she interacted awkwardly with the younger students in her first-year high school class and seemed very unlikely to persist through the four more years it would take to get a secondary school certificate. This healthcare strategy could be very disruptive of children's lives.

8. This care was periodically complemented by health fairs or *campañas de salud integral* (integrated health campaigns). Though usually organized by staff of the health centers, these were sometimes provided by medical students in training, completing course requirements.

9. Under neoliberal reforms, government health centers may charge a small fee for their services, starting at the equivalent of $1 to $2. Recognizing how dissuasive this may be, they often exonerate patients from payment.

NOTES TO PAGES 88–103

10. Swaddling is an adaptive practice used to keep babies warm in cold and high-altitude environments, as it maintains body temperature and prevents them from exposing skin to the elements by wiggling or pulling at wrappings (Remorini 2013, 421; Wiley 2004, 146–156; compare Chisholm 1983, 71–91 on the Navajo cradleboard). Peruvian medical personnel are often, unfortunately, oblivious to the logic of these practices in the Andes.

11. Terrazas municipal government had a fund for the purchase of medicines if community members could demonstrate that they were not able to get them at the health post. In Bellavista, the nuns of Service and Sacrifice received pharmaceutical products and food-stuffs as donations, and they channeled them to community members that had been responsive to the nuns' proselytizing efforts.

12. Around half of the children in the biographies sample in Yauyos were born at home, with a midwife and the woman's relatives, her mother and/or her husband, in attendance. Occasionally it was the maternal grandparents' home, where the mother was visiting or went to give birth. Seven of the children were born in the local health center in the town where the mother lived (for one of them this was at a mining camp). Ten of the children were born in hospitals: five in Huancayo, four in Cañete, and one in Tocache, a border town in the Amazon region where the parents had met. Three of the hospital births involved cesarean sections; of those, two accounted for the only premature babies among the children in the biographies sample.

13. This was, of course, before the COVID-19 pandemic.

CHAPTER 6   PRACTICES OF CARE

1. We use a broad definition of fathers' absence in this table, including cases where there had never been a father in the household, where the father had died, or where the parents had separated, and also cases in which the father regularly worked outside the community in mining, herding, or public works projects, and cases where the father was incapacitated by alcoholism.

2. The only girl of this cohort that rebelled and complained was Rufina (15), who had no younger siblings and whose parents divided their time between their lodgings in town and their house in an annex. Regular routines were hard to discern in her household, and Rufina intended to forge her way on a path far different from her mother's.

3. Chapter 4 showed Pepe's role in the farm economy of both these households. He was an exceptionally busy, strong, competent, and responsible adolescent.

4. "Cuando tú y mi papá se mueran primero me cuidará Fabio; cuando Fabio se muera me cuidará la Elena; y cuando Elena se muera, me cuidará el Ever. Y cuando Ever se muera, ¿quién me cuidará? Le diré a mi profesora que me cuide."

5. His mother said she was considering sending him to a kind of boarding school, the Escuela en Alternancia, where rural students lived in barracks on campus during part of the school year and were expected to be self-reliant. She hoped he could then "aprender a lavar (learn to wash his own clothes)."

6. Rojas (2011) discusses how secondary students justified the violence they experienced in school, highlighting their preference for corporal punishment over any sanctions affecting their grades.

7. A historical figure famous for his peacemaking abilities and Peru's first and only Black saint, San Martín de Porras was mythologized as being capable of getting a dog, a cat, and a mouse to eat from the same plate. This is the ironic origin of the triad so feared by children.

NOTES TO PAGES 105–114

8. Local authorities could also intervene directly in family disputes. The mayor of Pastizales insisted that cases of child abuse were taken up directly by local government: "It goes directly to the gobernador, if it's a minor." We heard of no such case during our fieldwork.

9. Yauyos City also had a Centro de Emergencia Mujer (CEM), part of a network of emergency centers administered by the Peruvian Ministry of Women, which supported women victims of domestic violence through counseling, legal advice, and, in some cases, temporary refuge. Children could receive some of these benefits as dependents of their mothers. We did not hear of any events that activated the Yauyos CEM during our stay in the town.

10. Other cases involved visitation rights for divorced or separated parents, voluntary recognition of paternity, and child custody agreements. The DEMUNA could promote and monitor voluntary agreements; it did not have the force of law to sanction noncompliance. The DEMUNA also facilitated the reduction or waiving of school enrollment fees and parents' association dues for families with limited means, and it ran campaigns for obtaining birth certificates for children that had not been registered in the legally stipulated period. It promoted children's rights and well-being within the community through activities like talks about adolescence and sexuality for young people.

CHAPTER 7   THE LIMITS OF CARE

1. Large-scale comparative surveys like the World Values Survey (https://www.world valuessurvey.org) and Latinbarometer (https://www.latinobarometro.org) find that levels of interpersonal trust are very low in the region.

2. Internationally, high levels of trust are associated with high levels of investment, productivity, and per-capita incomes. Low levels of trust raise transaction costs and impede the development of financial markets. They limit belief in meritocracy and fairness in the operation of government, and they reduce the possibility of effective sanctions on bad behavior (Jordahl 2007).

3. The detachment consisted of four policemen and a captain. They did fifteen-day rotations in the town.

4. We did not pick up on the existence of money lenders in the towns of Yauyos. The real demand for credit would have been associated with preparations for each annual planting season, when fertilizer, seed, and other supplies would have to be acquired. This would have happened in September, October, and November, months after the fieldwork. Given this circumstance, we were unable to observe the strategies farming families used to get access to the capital they needed, or whether this, like insufficient labor force, played into decisions to leave fields fallow or even abandoned. The Peruvian government administers a credit program for small farmers, but it is constantly criticized for mismanagement and a low level of coverage.

5. Persons unable to submit to the rules of sociality in the towns were likely to move away, and they also avoided the neighborhoods of yauyinos in Cañete, Huancayo, and Lima, the residents of which could easily relay information back to friends and relatives at home. References to leavers who simply got lost and were never heard of again were quite common at the time of the 1998–1999 study in Yauyos, before the era of cell phones and TV reality shows featuring reunions of long-estranged family members. Adolescents and young men could run off to join the army or work in a mine. Girls could abscond with a boyfriend or seize an opportunity to join another household as a domestic worker. Some,

in today's Peru, might end up in "prostibars" in the illegal alluvial gold mining zones of Madre de Dios, victims of human trafficking (Grados, Grados, and Medina 2021).

6. On the ambiguities associated with *padrinazgos*, see Shepherd and Barrantes 2023.

7. "El suelo te lleva o un cerro te recoge. Tienes que hacerle pago a la tierra." In other parts of the Andes, the catastrophes that can affect herds and harvests are attributed to unseen forces. They may send frosts and hailstorms, for example, to punish grave faults such as incest or domestic violence. Whole communities pay for the sins of the few (Canessa 2012; Bolton et al. 1976). In Yauyos, people were more likely to speak—at least publicly—of natural disasters, bad luck, or acts of God.

8. According to the 2007 National Census (National Institute of Statistics and Informatics—INEI), 11.8 percent of households in the Region of Lima (excluding the capital city itself) included at least one member with a disability. Households with at least one disabled member skewed urban; 12.6 percent of households in urban localities of the region and 8.2 percent of households in rural towns and annexes included a person with a disability. This may suggest that families are well aware of the limited possibilities of treatment in rural towns. Households with at least one disabled member also skewed toward female-headed households, 13.7 percent of which included at least one person with a disability (as compared to 11.0 percent of male-headed households). The most common disabilities were impaired vision or hearing, limits to use of limbs, and impediments to mobility. We did not see or hear of many cases of disabilities in Yauyos, particularly not among the children, but it is entirely possible that some persons were being cared for at home and effectively hidden from view.

9. Globally, today, adults attempt to intervene in these practices through programs for promoting gender equality, antiracism, and inclusivity for children with different abilities. In 2008, in rural towns of Peru, these strategies were not known nor was this seen to be a responsibility of adults.

CHAPTER 8   CARE AND FLOURISHING

1. Children's play in Andean rural communities became a hot topic in Peru after the internal violence of the 1980s and 1990s, partially blamed by some on the rigors of child socialization. A series of interventions took place that aimed to make children more prosocial and happier, including encouraging play, adult tolerance of it, and even adult participation (Ames 2013a).

2. In Andean musical performances, men tend to be the instrumentalists and women tend to be vocalists, although there are famous male singers in the Andean tradition and many lyrics are written from the male point of view (Tucker 2019).

3. The natural environment was threatening only after dark, for adults as well as children. Avoiding solitary places and sheltering inside at night were reinforced by the tales of *pishtacos* and other supernatural beings that haunted the hills, mentioned in the previous chapter.

4. These irradiated out from the Valle Grande Institute in the city of Cañete and were focused on a long-term effort to improve agricultural production and train local farmers in new technologies.

5. Luykx (1999), in a fundamental study of teacher training in Bolivia, throws doubt on the meaning of citizenship as teachers were being prepared to cultivate it in their students.

6. The War of the Pacific pitted Peru and Bolivia against Chile, which had ample backing from British capitalists interested in the fertilizers produced on the Atacama Desert. Chile prevailed, to the point of occupying Lima and eventually acquiring territory from

NOTES TO PAGES 134–148

both of its opponents. Though fought in 1879–1883, the war still occasions passionate resentments among Peruvians and insistent Bolivian claims for the return of its corridor to the Pacific Ocean.

7. Serpell (1993) presents a searing analysis of the contradictions associated with Western-style education in an African setting.

CHAPTER 9   CONCLUSIONS

1. Wild animals are also implicated; for example, trout are part of the food system and part of the local aesthetic, in that they are good to watch, good to imitate, and good to play with while dipping feet into mountain streams.

2. As noted, Yauyos City may have been an exception because of the large number of rotating employees and temporary visitors that were associated with government administration in the province.

3. This is true to a large extent in Peru. Juntos, a conditional cash transfer program for combatting poverty, and Pensión 65, which supports low-income senior citizens, both limit eligibility to rural areas (Vincent 2021). Under the current rules, given Peru's demography, the bulk of recipients are residents of small towns in the Andes. A minority live in the rural Amazon basin, where ethnic and cultural distinctions are also present. The requirement of rural residence in a majority "indigenous" region is only recently coming under debate.

4. It is worth noting that women tend to be the market specialists in Andean towns and cities (see, for example, Babb 1989; Weismantel 2001). Some Andean women have also had spectacular success as urban entrepreneurs under the rules of neoliberalism.

REFERENCES

Accinelli, Roberto, Cecilia Yshii, Eduardo Córdova, Marita Sánchez-Siera, Celia Pantoja, and Jessica Carbajal. 2004. "Efecto de los combustibles de biomasa en el aparato respiratorio: impacto del cambio de cocinas con diseño mejorado." *Revista de la Sociedad Peruana de Neumología* 48 (2):138–144.

Acosta, Andrés Mejía, and Lawrence Haddad. 2014. "The Politics of Success in the Fight against Malnutrition in Peru." *Food Policy* 44:26–35.

Adams, Norma, and Néstor Valdivia. 1991. *Los otros empresarios: Ética de migrantes y formación de empresas en Lima.* Lima: Instituto de Estudios Peruanos.

Aguirre, Rosario, and Karina Batthyány. 2005. *Uso del tiempo y trabajo no remunerado.* Montevideo: UNIFEM/Universidad de la República.

Aguirre, Rosario, and Sol Scavino. 2018. *Vejeces de las mujeres.* Montevideo: Doble Clic Editoras.

Alarcón, Walter. 2011. *Trabajo infantil en los Andes.* Lima: Instituto de Estudios Peruanos.

Alber, Erdmute, and Heike Drotbohm, eds. 2015. *Anthropological Perspectives on Care: Work, Kinship, and the Life-Course.* Basingstoke, UK: Palgrave Macmillan.

Alberti, Giorgio, and Enrique Mayer, eds. 1974. *Reciprocidad e intercambio en los Andes peruanos.* Lima: Instituto de Estudios Peruanos.

Albó, Xavier. 2019. "Suma qamaña = Convivir Bien. ¿Cómo medirlo?" *Bolivian Studies Journal* 25:99–113.

Alcalde, M. Cristina. 2014. *La mujer en la violencia: Pobreza, género y resistencia en el Perú.* Lima: Instituto de Estudios Peruanos/Pontificia Universidad Católica del Perú.

Aldana, Carmen, María Julia Oyague, and Cecilia Torres Llosa, eds. 1994. *Infancia y violencia 2: Experiencias y reflexiones sobre los niños y la violencia política en el Perú.* Lima: Centro de Desarrollo y Asesoría Psicosocial CEDAPP.

Aldana, Úrsula, and Javier Escobal. 2016. *Los efectos de la migración interna entre el 2007 y el 2014 en el Perú, un análisis a nivel provincial.* Working Paper No. 203. Territorial Cohesion for Development Program. Santiago, Chile: RIMISP.

Alegría, Julio. 2008. "La gestión del agua en el Perú: Antecedentes, situación y perspectivas." In *Los Andes y las poblaciones altoandinas en la agenda de la regionalización y la descentralización*, edited by Hilda Araujo, 127–156. Lima: CONCYTEC.

Allen, Catherine J. 2002. *The Hold Life Has. Coca and Cultural Identity in an Andean Community.* 2nd ed. Washington, DC: Smithsonian Institution.

———. 2016. "Losing My Heart." In *A Return to the Village: Community Ethnographies and the Study of Andean Culture in Retrospective*, edited by Francisco Ferreira, 69–92. London: Institute of Latin American Studies.

Altamirano, Teófilo. 2010. *In Times of Crisis: Migration, Remittances and Development.* Lima: UNFPA/Pontificia Universidad Católica del Perú.

Alzamora, Humberto, Angélica Nué, and Raquel Pastor. 1998. "Diagnóstico del distrito de Yauyos." Unpublished manuscript. Lima: Pontificia Universidad Católica del Perú.

REFERENCES

Amat y León, Carlos. 2012. *El Perú nuestro de cada día*. 2nd ed. Lima: Universidad del Pacífico.

Ames, Patricia. 2013a. *Entre el rigor y el cariño: Infancia y violencia en comunidades andinas*. Lima: Instituto de Estudios Peruanos.

———. 2013b "Niños y niñas andinos en el Perú: crecer en un mundo de relaciones y responsabilidades." *Bulletin de l'Institut Français de Études Andines* 42 (3):389–409.

Ames, Patricia, and Mercedes Crisóstomo. 2019. *Formas de atención y prevención de la violencia contra los niños y niñas en zonas rurales: revisión comparada y estudio de caso en Huancavelica, Perú*. Lima: Instituto de Estudios Peruanos.

Ames, Patricia, and Ana Padawer. 2015. "Dossier: infancias indígenas, identificaciones étnico-nacionales y educación: experiencias formativas cotidianas dentro y fuera de las escuelas." *Anthropologica* 33 (35):5–14. https://doi.org/10.18800/anthropologica.201502.001

Ames, Patricia, and Vanessa Rojas. 2010. *Infancia, transiciones y bienestar en el Perú: una revisión bibliográfica*. Lima: Grupo de Análisis para el Desarrollo GRADE.

Amrith, Megha, and Cati Coe. 2022. "Disposable Kin: Shifting Registers of Belonging in Global Care Economies." *American Anthropologist* 124 (2):307–318. https://doi.org/10.1111/aman.13688

Anderson, Jeanine. 2001. *Tendiendo puentes: Calidad de atención desde la perspectiva de las mujeres rurales y de los proveedores de los servicios de salud*. Lima: Movimiento Manuela Ramos.

———. 2007. *Invertir en la familia: Estudio sobre factores preventivos y de vulnerabilidad al trabajo infantil doméstico en familias rurales y urbanas: el caso del Perú*. Lima: International Labor Organization.

———. 2010. "Incommensurable Worlds of Practice and Value: A View from the Shantytowns of Lima." In *Indelible Inequalities in Latin America*, edited by Paul Gootenberg and Luis Reygadas, 81–105. Durham, NC: Duke University Press.

———. 2012. *La migración femenina peruana en las cadenas globales de cuidados en Chile y España: Transferencia de cuidados y desigualdades de género*. Santo Domingo, Dominican Republic: ONU Mujeres.

———. 2013. "Movimiento, movilidad y migración: una visión dinámica de la niñez andina." *Bulletin de l'Institut Français de Études Andines* 42 (3):453–471.

———. 2016. *Las infancias diversas: Estudio fenomenológico de la niñez de cero a tres años en cuatro pueblos indígenas de la Amazonía peruana*. Lima: UNICEF.

———. 2018. "La etnografía en equipo: experiencias peruanas." In *Trabajo de campo en América Latina: Experiencias antropológicas regionales en etnografía*, edited by Rosana Guber, Volume I, 265–284. Buenos Aires: Sb Editorial.

———. 2020. "What Is Care and What Is Not Caring? The Challenges of Cultural Diversity." *Cuadernos de Relaciones Laborales* 38 (2):305–325.

———. 2024. "Agentes de su propio juego." *Anthropologica* 42 (52).

Anderson, Jeanine, Juan Ansión, Alejandro Diez, Manuel Iguíñiz, Sylvia Matos, Catalina Romero, Denis Sulmont, and Madeleine Zúñiga. 2001. *Yauyos: Estudio sobre valores y metas de vida*. Lima: Ministry of Education, Government of Peru.

Anderson, Jeanine, Alejandro Diez, Diego Dourojeanni, Blanca Figueroa, Oscar Jiménez, Elsy Miní, and Sandra Vallenas. 1999. *Mujeres de negro: la muerte materna en zonas rurales del Perú*. Lima: Ministry of Health, Government of Peru.

Anderson, Jeanine, and Jessaca Leinaweaver. 2023 "La educación rural y sus micro contextos: lecciones de Yauyos." *Revista Peruana de Investigación Educativa* 15 (19) :73–96.

Antrosio, Jason. 2002. "Inverting Development Discourse in Colombia: Transforming Andean Hearths." *American Anthropologist* 104 (4):1110–1122.

Appiah, Kwame Anthony. 2010. *Cosmopolitanism: Ethics in a World of Strangers*. New York: W. W. Norton & Company, Inc.

REFERENCES

Atria, Raul, Marcelo Siles, Irma Arriagada, Lindon J. Robison, and Scott Whiteford, eds. 2003. *Capital social y reducción de la pobreza en América Latina y el Caribe: En busca de un nuevo paradigma.* Santiago, Chile: CEPAL/Michigan State University.

Aramburú, Carlos E. 2014. "Idas y vueltas: los programas de planificación familiar en el Perú." *Revista Latinoamericana de Población* 8 (14):81–103. doi:10.31406/relap2014.v8.i1.n14.4.

Aramburú, Carlos E., and María Bustinza. 2007. "La transición demográfica peruana: implicancias para la conciliación trabajo-familia." *Economía y Sociedad* 63:62–73.

Aramburú, Carlos E., and María Isabel Mendoza. 2003. "La población peruana: perspectivas y retos." *Economía y Sociedad* 50:45–54.

Asensio, Raúl. 2023. *Breve historia del desarrollo rural en el Perú (1900–2020).* Lima: Instituto de Estudios Peruanos.

Ávalos, Rosalía. 1952. "El ciclo vital en la comunidad de Tupe." *Revista del Museo Nacional* XXI:107–184.

Babb, Florence E. 1985. "Women and Men in Vicos: A Peruvian Case of Unequal Development." In *Peruvian Contexts of Change*, edited by William W. Stein, 163–210. New Brunswick, NJ: Transaction Press.

———. 1989. *Between Field and Cooking Pot: The Political Economy of Marketwomen in Peru.* Austin: University of Texas Press.

———. 2011. *The Tourism Encounter.* Stanford, CA: Stanford University Press.

———. 2018. *Women's Place in the Andes: Engaging Decolonial Feminist Anthropology.* Oakland: University of California Press.

Barrios, Eliana. 2013. "Two Decades Later: The Resilience and Post-traumatic Responses of Indigenous Quechua Girls and Adolescents in the Aftermath of the Peruvian Armed Conflict." *Child Abuse and Neglect* 37 (2–3):200–210.

Battaglia, Marianna, and Nina Pallarés. 2020. "Family Planning and Child Health Care: Effect of the Peruvian Programa de Salud Reproductiva y Planificación Familiar, 1996–2000." *Population and Development Review* 46:33–64.

Batthyány, Karina, ed. 2020. *Miradas latinoamericanas a los cuidados.* Mexico and Buenos Aires: CLACSO/Siglo XXI.

Bellino, Michelle J. 2017. *Youth in Postwar Guatemala: Education and Civic Identity in Transition.* New Brunswick, NJ: Rutgers University Press.

Beltrán, Arlette, and Pablo Lavado. 2015. *El impacto del uso del tiempo de las mujeres en el Perú: Un recurso escaso y poco valorado en la economía nacional.* Lima: INEI/Movimiento Manuela Ramos/CISEPA.

Benavides, Martín, ed. 2006. *Los desafíos de la escolaridad en el Perú: Estudios sobre los procesos pedagógicos, los saberes previos y el rol de las familias.* Lima: Grupo de Análisis para el Desarrollo GRADE.

Berg, Ulla, and Karsten Pærregaard, eds. 2010. *El 5to. Suyo.* Lima: Instituto de Estudios Peruanos.

Berman, Elise. 2011. "The Irony of Immaturity: K'iche' Children as Mediators and Buffers in Adult Social Interactions." *Childhood* 18 (2):274–288.

Best, Raphaela. 1989. *We've All Got Scars: What Boys and Girls Learn in Elementary School.* Bloomington: Indiana University Press.

Bodenhorn, Barbara, and Elsa Lee. 2019. "What Animates Place for Children? A Comparative Analysis." *Anthropology & Education Quarterly* 53 (2):112–129.

Boesten, Jelki. 2010. *Intersecting Inequalities: Women and Social Policy in Peru, 1990–2000.* University Park: Pennsylvania State University Press.

Bolin, Inge. 2006. *Growing Up in a Culture of Respect: Child Rearing in Highland Peru.* Austin: The University of Texas Press.

REFERENCES

Bolton, Charlene, Ralph Bolton, Lorraine Gross, Amy Koel, Carol Michelson, Robert L. Monroe, and Ruth H. Munroe. 1976. "Pastoralism and Personality: An Andean Replication." *Ethos* 4:463–481.

Bolton, Ralph. 1977. "The Qolla Marriage Process." In *Andean Kinship and Marriage*, edited by Ralph Bolton and Enrique Mayer, 217–239. Washington, DC: American Anthropological Association.

Bolton, Ralph, and Charlene Bolton. 1975. *Conflictos en la familia andina.* Cuzco, Peru: Centro de Estudios Andinos.

Bolton, Ralph, and Enrique Mayer, eds. 1977. *Andean Kinship and Marriage.* Washington, DC: American Anthropological Association.

Bonilla, Heraclio, Efraín Trelles, Luis Miguel Glave, Scarlett O'Phelan, Nelson Manrique, Alberto Flores Galindo, Víctor Peralta, Ward Stavig, Magdalena Chocano, Iván Hinojosa, and Deborah Poole. 1987. *Comunidades campesinas: Cambios y permanencias.* Lima: Centro de Estudios Sociales Solidaridad.

Boris, Eileen, and Rhacel Salazar Parreñas, eds. 2010. *Intimate Labors: Cultures, Technologies, and the Politics of Care.* Stanford, CA: Stanford University Press.

Bornat, Joanna, Julia Johnson, Charmaine Pereira, David Pilgrim, and Fiona Williams, eds. 1997. *Community Care: A Reader.* 2nd ed. Basingstoke, UK: Palgrave/Open University.

Borneman, John. 2001. "Caring and Being Cared For: Displacing Marriage, Kinship, Gender, and Sexuality." In *The Ethics of Kinship: Ethnographic Inquiries*, edited by J. D. Faubion, 29–46. Lanham, MD: Rowman & Littlefield.

Borneman, John, and Abdellah Hammoudi. 2009. "The Fieldwork Encounter, Experience, and the Making of Truth: An Introduction." In *Being There: The Fieldwork Encounter and the Making of Truth*, edited by Borneman & Hammoudi, 1–24. Berkeley: University of California Press.

Bornstein, Erica. 2001. "Child Sponsorship, Evangelism, and Belonging in the Work of World Vision Zimbabwe." *American Ethnologist* 28 (3):595–622.

Bourque, Susan C., and Kay Barbara Warren. 1981. *Women of the Andes: Patriarchy and Social Change in Two Peruvian Towns.* Ann Arbor: University of Michigan Press.

Boyden, Jo. 1997. "Childhood and the Policymakers: A Comparative Perspective in the Globalization of Childhood." In *Constructing and Reconstructing Childhood*, edited by Allison James and Alan Prout, 190–229. London: Falmer Press.

Boyden, Jo, and Joanna de Berry, eds. 2004. *Children and Youth on the Front Line: Ethnography, Armed Conflict and Displacement.* New York: Berghahn Books.

Braun, Virginia, and Victoria Clarke. 2021. *Thematic Analysis: A Practical Guide.* London: Sage.

Bronfenbrenner, Urie. 1979. *The Ecology of Human Development.* Cambridge, MA: Harvard University Press.

Brougère, Anne Marie. 1988. "Transformaciones sociales y movilidad de las poblaciones en una comunidad del Nor-Yauyos." In *Políticas agrarias y estrategias campesinas en la Cuenca del Cañete*, edited by Michel Eresue and Anne Marie Brougère, 133–158. Lima: Universidad Nacional Agraria/Instituto Francés de Estudios Andinos IFEA.

———. 1992. *¿Y por qué no quedarse en Laraos? Migración y retorno en una comunidad altoandina.* Lima: Instituto Francés de Estudios Andinos IFEA.

Bruschwig, Giles. 1988. "Sistemas de producción de laderas de altura." In *Políticas agrarias y estrategias campesinas en la Cuenca del Cañete*, edited by Michel Eresue and Anne Marie Brougère, 27–52. Lima: Universidad Nacional Agraria/Instituto Francés de Estudios Andinos IFEA.

Buch, Elana D. 2015. "Anthropology of Aging and Care." *Annual Review of Anthropology* 44:277–93.

REFERENCES

Campos-Navarro, Roberto, ed. 2006. *Textos peruanos sobre el empacho.* Lima: Proyecto AMARES / Universidad Nacional Autónoma de México.

Cánepa, Gisela, and Leonor Lamas, eds. 2020. *Épicas del neoliberalismo: subjetividades emprendedoras y ciudadanías precarias en el Perú.* Lima: Pontificia Universidad Católica del Perú.

Canessa, Andrew. 2012. *Intimate Indigeneities: Race, Sex, and History in the Small Spaces of Andean Life.* Durham, NC: Duke University Press.

Cantor, Allison R., Isabella Chan, and Kristina Baines. 2018. "From the Chacra to the Tienda: Dietary Delocalization in the Peruvian Andes." *Food and Foodways* 26 (3):198–222.

Carey, Mark. 2005. "Living and Dying with Glaciers: People's Historical Vulnerability to Avalanches and Outburst Floods in Peru." *Global and Planetary Change* 47 (2–4):122–134.

Carter, William E. 1977. "Trial Marriage in the Andes?" In *Andean Kinship and Marriage*, edited by Ralph Bolton and Enrique Mayer, 177–216. Washington, DC: American Anthropological Association.

Casaverde, Juvenal, Carlos Iván Degregori, Fernando Fuenzalido, Jurgen Golte, Teresa Valiente, and José Villarán. 1982. *El desafío de Huayopampa: Comuneros y empresarios.* 2nd ed. Lima: Instituto de Estudios Peruanos.

Chin, Elizabeth. 2001. *Purchasing Power: Black Kids and American Consumer Culture.* Minneapolis: University of Minnesota Press.

Chisholm, James S. 1983. *Navajo Infancy. An Ethological Study of Child Development.* New York: Aldine Publishing Company.

Collier, Paul. 2007. *The Bottom Billion.* Oxford, UK: Oxford University Press.

Cole, Jennifer, and Deborah Durham, eds. 2007. *Generations and Globalization: Youth, Age, and Family in the New World Economy.* Bloomington: Indiana University Press.

Colloredo-Mansfeld, Rudi. 2016. "Recordkeeping: Ethnography and the Uncertainty of Contemporary Community Studies." In *A Return to the Village: Community Ethnographies and the Study of Andean Culture in Retrospective*, edited by Francisco Ferreira, 149–168. London: Institute of Latin American Studies.

Comisión de la Verdad y Reconciliación (CVR). 2004. *Hatun Willakuy: Versión abreviada del Informe Final de la Comisión de la Verdad y Reconciliación Perú.* Lima: Comisión de la Verdad y Reconciliación.

Contreras, Carlos, and Marcos Cueto. 2000. *Historia del Perú contemporáneo.* 2nd ed. Lima: Instituto de Estudios Peruanos.

Copestake, James. 2008. "Multiple Dimensions of Social Assistance: The Case of Peru's 'Glass of Milk' Programme." *The Journal of Development Studies* 44 (4):545–561.

Cotler, Julio. 2021. *La dominación interna en el Perú.* Lima: Instituto de Estudios Peruanos.

Cusato, Antonio. 2020. "Adquisiciones públicas en el Perú: identificación de pérdidas por no usar los catálogos electrónicos." Working paper, Lima, Consorcio de Investigación Económica y Social CIES.

Degregori, Carlos Iván. 1990. *El surgimiento de Sendero Luminoso.* Lima: Instituto de Estudios Peruanos.

———, ed. 2003. *Comunidades locales y transnacionales: Cinco estudios de caso en el Perú.* Lima: Instituto de Estudios Peruanos.

———. 2015. *Jamás tan cerca arremetió lo lejos: Sendero Luminoso y la violencia política.* Lima: Instituto de Estudios Peruanos.

Degregori, Carlos Iván, and Jurgen Golte. 1973. *Dependencia y desintegración estructural en la comunidad de Pacaraos.* Lima: Instituto de Estudios Peruanos.

de la Cadena, Marisol. 1980. "Economía campesina: familia y comunidad en Yauyos." Lima: Pontificia Universidad Católica del Perú. B.A. thesis.

———. 1988. *Comuneros en Huancayo: Migración campesina a ciudades serranas*. Lima: Instituto de Estudios Peruanos.

———. 2015. *Earth Beings*. Durham, NC: Duke University Press.

De la Torre, Ana. 1986. *Los dos lados del mundo y del tiempo: Representaciones de la naturaleza en Cajamarca indígena*. Lima: Centro de Investigación, Educación, y Desarrollo CIED.

Del Pino, Ponciano, Magrith Mena, Sandra Torrejón, Edith Del Pino, Mariano Aronés, and Tamia Portugal. 2012. *Repensar la desnutrición: Infancia, alimentación y cultura en Ayacucho, Perú*. Lima: Instituto de Estudios Peruanos/Acción Contra el Hambre.

Descola, Philippe. 1994. *In the Society of Nature: A Native Ecology in Amazonia*. Nora Scott, trans. Cambridge, UK: Cambridge University Press.

DeVault, Marjorie L. 1991. *Feeding the Family: The Social Organization of Caring as Gendered Work*. Chicago: University of Chicago Press.

Díaz, Juan José, and Hugo Ñopo. 2016. "La carrera docente en el Perú." In *Investigación para el desarrollo en el Perú: Once balances*, 353–402. Lima: Grupo de Análisis para el Desarrollo GRADE.

Dierna, Rosa, Ximena Salazar, Rosana Vargas, Paola Nacarato, and César Guzmán. 1999. *Salvarse con bien: El parto de la vida en los Andes y Amazonía del Perú*. Lima: Ministry of Health, Government of Peru.

Diez, Alejandro. 1999. "Diversidades, alternativas y ambigüedades: instituciones, comportamientos y mentalidades en la sociedad rural." In *Perú: el problema agrario en debate*, edited by Víctor Agreda, Alejandro Diez, and Manuel Glave, 247–326. SEPIA VII. Lima: Seminario Permanente de Investigación Agraria SEPIA.

———. 2001. "De la comunidad difusa a las comunidades descentradas: Perspectivas analíticas sobre las comunidades de la sierra de Lima desde las etnografías de la segunda mitad del siglo XX." In *Perú: actores y escenarios al inicio del nuevo milenio*, edited by Orlando Plaza, 393–428. Lima: Pontificia Universidad Católica del Perú.

———. 2022. "Comunidades campesinas y estado en el Perú: Relación estructuras de protección, promoción y olvido." *Debate Agrario* 50:119–143.

Dossa, Parin, and Cati Coe, eds. 2017. *Transnational Aging and Reconfigurations of Kin Work*. New Brunswick, NJ: Rutgers University Press.

Earls, John. 2006. *La agricultura andina ante una globalización en desplome*. Lima: Pontificia Universidad Católica del Perú.

———. 2008. "Manejo de cuencas y cambio climático." In *Los Andes y las poblaciones altoandinas en la agenda de la regionalización y la descentralización*, edited by Hilda Araujo, 113–126. Lima: CONCYTEC.

Eggan, Fred. 1954. "Social Anthropology and the Method of Controlled Comparison." *American Anthropologist* 56 (1):743–763.

Ellison, Susan Helen. 2018. *Domesticating Democracy: The Politics of Conflict Resolution in Bolivia*. Durham, NC: Duke University Press.

Eresue, Michel, and Anne Marie Brougère, eds. 1988. *Políticas agrarias y estrategias campesinas en la cuenca del Cañete*. Lima: Universidad Nacional Agraria/Instituto Francés de Estudios Andinos.

Escalante, Carmen, and Ricardo Valderrama. 2016. "Yanque Urinsaya: Ethnography of an Andean Community (A Tribute to Billie Jean Isbell)." In *A Return to the Village: Community Ethnographies and the Study of Andean Culture in Retrospective*, edited by Francisco Ferreira, 125–148. London: Institute of Latin American Studies ILAS.

Escobal, Javier. 2005. "The Role of Public Infrastructure in Market Development in Rural Peru." The Netherlands: Wageningen University. PhD diss.

Escobal, Javier, and Carmen Armas. 2015. "El uso de encuestas y censos agropecuarios para desarrollar una tipología de la pequeña y mediana agricultura familiar en el Perú." In

REFERENCES

Agricultura peruana: Nuevas miradas desde el Censo Agropecuario, edited by Javier Escobal, Ricardo Fort, and Eduardo Zegarra, 15–86. Lima: Grupo de Análisis para el Desarrollo GRADE.

Etkin, Nina L. 2006. *Edible Medicines: An Ethnopharmacology of Food*. Tucson: The University of Arizona Press.

Ewig, Christina. 2006. "Hijacking global feminism: Feminists, the Catholic Church, and the family planning debacle in Peru." *Feminist Studies* 32 (3):632–659. doi:10.2307/20459109.

———. 2010. *Second-Wave Neoliberalism: Gender, Race and Health Sector Reform in Peru*. University Park: The Pennsylvania State University Press.

Feder Kittay, Eva. 2019. *Learning from My Daughter: The Value and Care of Disabled Minds*. Oxford, UK: Oxford University Press.

Ferrando, Delicia. 2002. *El aborto clandestino en el Perú: Hechos y cifras*. Lima: Centro de la Mujer Peruana Flora Tristán/Pathfinder Fund International.

Ferreira, Francisco. 2016. "Introduction: Community Ethnographies and the Study of Andean Culture." In *A Return to the Village: Community Ethnographies and the Study of Andean Culture in Retrospective*, edited by Francisco Ferreira, 1–44. London: Institute of Latin American Studies ILAS.

Ferreira, Francisco, ed., with Billie Jean Isbell. 2016. *A Return to the Village: Community Ethnographies and the Study of Andean Culture in Retrospective*. London: Institute of Latin American Studies ILAS.

Ferroni, Marco, Mercedes Mateo, and Mark Payne. 2008. *Development under Conditions of Inequality and Distrust: Social Cohesion in Latin America*. Washington, DC: International Food Policy Research Institute.

Figueroa, Adolfo. 2000. *Social Exclusion and Rural Underdevelopment*. Lima: Pontificia Universidad Católica del Perú.

———. 2010. "Límites del desarrollo agrario de la sierra peruana." *Economía* 33 (66):157–160.

Flores, Elizabeth. 2010. "Pautas y prácticas de crianza versus pautas y prácticas de enseñanza de niños de preescolar tupinos." Master's thesis. Lima: Pontificia Universidad Católica del Perú.

Folbre, Nancy. 2008. *Valuing Children: Rethinking the Economics of the Family*. Cambridge, MA: Harvard University Press.

Fonseca, César. 1972. "Sistemas económicos en las comunidades campesinas del Perú." PhD diss. Lima: Universidad Nacional Mayor de San Marcos.

Fortes, Meyer. 1958. "Introduction." In *The Developmental Cycle in Domestic Groups*, edited by Jack Goody, 1–14. Cambridge, UK: Cambridge University Press. Papers in Social Anthropology.

Fourtané, Nicole. 2015. *El condenado andino: Estudio de cuentos peruanos*. Lima and Cusco: Instituto Francés de Estudios Andinos IFEA/Centro de Estudios Regionales Andinos Bartolomé de las Casas CBC.

Fraser, Nancy, and Alex Honneth. 2003. *Redistribution or Recognition? A Political-Philosophical Exchange*. London: Verso.

Frekko, Susan, Jessaca Leinaweaver, and Diana Marre. 2015. "How (Not) to Talk about Adoption: On Communicative Vigilance in Spain." *American Ethnologist* 42 (4):703–719.

Fuller, Norma. 2003. "The Social Constitution of Gender Identity among Peruvian Males." In *Changing Men and Masculinities in Latin America*, edited by Matthew C. Gutmann, 134–152. Durham, NC: Duke University Press.

Fuenzalida, Fernando, Teresa Valiente, José Luis Villarán, Jurgen Golte, Carlos Iván Degregori, and Juvenal Casaverde. 1982. *El desafío de Huayopampa: Comuneros y empresarios*. Lima: Instituto de Estudios Peruanos.

García Rivera, Fernando. 2007. "Coexistencia de prácticas socioculturales locales y nacionales en contextos comunitarios y escolares de una localidad andina del Peru." *Signos Lingüísticos* 5:119–137.

Geertz, Clifford. 1973. *The Interpretation of Cultures*. Boston: Beacon Books.

Gelles, Paul. 2000. *Water and Power in Highland Peru: The Cultural Politics of Irrigation and Development*. New Brunswick, NJ: Rutgers University Press.

Gil, Vladimir. 2013. *Estudio de la vulnerabilidad e impacto del cambio climático sobre la Reserva Paisajística Nor Yauyos Cochas (Vía RPNYC)*. Lima: Fundación para el Desarrollo Agrario.

Glave, Manuel, and Karla Vergara. 2016. "Cambio global, alta montaña y adaptación: una aproximación social y geográfica." In *Investigación para el desarrollo en el Perú: Once balances*, 445–507. Lima: Grupo de Análisis para el Desarrollo GRADE.

Glenn, Evelyn Nakano. 1992. "From Servitude to Service Work: Historical Continuities in the Racial Division of Paid Reproductive Labor." *Signs* 18 (1):1–43.

———. 2010. *Forced to Care: Coercion and Caregiving in America*. Cambridge, MA: Harvard University Press.

Golte, Jurgen. 1987. *La racionalidad de la organización andina*. 2nd ed. Lima: Instituto de Estudios Peruanos.

———. 2000. "Economía, ecología, redes. Campo y ciudad en los análisis antropológicos." In *No hay país más diverso: Compendio de antropología peruana*, edited by Carlos Iván Degregori, 204–234. Lima: Red para el Desarrollo de las Ciencias Sociales en el Perú.

Golte, Jurgen, and Norma Adams. 1990. *Los caballos de Troya de los invasores: Estrategias campesinas en la conquista de la gran Lima*, 2nd ed. Lima: Instituto de Estudios Peruanos.

Golte, Jurgen, and Marisol de la Cadena. 1986. "La codeterminación de la organización social andina." Working paper 13, Lima, Instituto de Estudios Peruanos.

Gonzáles de Olarte, Efraín, and Juan Manuel del Pozo. 2018. "El espacio importa para el desarrollo humano: El caso peruano." Working paper 462, Lima, Pontificia Universidad Católica del Perú, Department of Economics.

Goodenough, Ruth Gallagher. 1990. "Situational Stress and Sexist Behavior among Young Children." In *Beyond the Second Sex: New Directions in the Anthropology of Gender*, edited by Peggy Reeves Sanday and Ruth Gallagher Goodenough, 225–251. Philadelphia: University of Pennsylvania Press.

Goodman, Alan H., and Thomas L. Leatherman. 1998. "Traversing the Chasm between Biology and Culture: An Introduction." In *Building a New Biocultural Synthesis: Political-Economic Perspectives on Human Biology*, edited by Alan H. Goodman and Thomas L. Leatherman, 3–41. Ann Arbor: University of Michigan Press.

Goodwin, Marjorie Harness. 1990. *He-Said-She-Said: Talk as Social Organization among Black Children*. Bloomington: Indiana University Press.

———. 2006. *The Hidden Life of Girls: Games of Stance, Status, and Exclusion*. Malden, MA: Blackwell Publishing.

Gorriti, Gustavo. 1999. *The Shining Path: A History of the Millenarian War in Peru*. Chapel Hill: University of North Carolina Press.

Gose, Peter. 1991. "House Rethatching in an Andean Annual Cycle: Practice, Meaning, and Contradiction." *American Ethnologist* 18:39–66.

———. 1994. *Deadly Waters and Hungry Mountains: Agrarian Ritual and Class Formation in an Andean Town*. Toronto: University of Toronto Press.

Grados, Claudia, María Grados, and Claudia Medina. 2021. "Balance actual de la trata, explotación sexual y violencia en zonas de minería informal de Madre de Dios y Piura." Working paper, Lima, Consorcio de Investigación Económica y Social CIES. https://econpapers.repec.org/RePEc:bbj:invcie:694.

Graeber, David. 2015. *The Utopia of Rules*. Brooklyn, NY: Melville House.

Greene, Sheila, and Malcolm Hill. 2005. "Researching Children's Experience: Methods and Methodological Issues." In *Researching Children's Experience: Approaches and Methods*, edited by Sheila Greene and Diane Hogan, 1–21. Thousand Oaks, CA: Sage Publications.

Greene, Sheila, and Diane Hogan, eds. 2005. *Researching Children's Experience: Approaches and Methods*. Thousand Oaks, CA: Sage Publications.

Grim-Feinberg, Kate. 2013. "Cultural Models of Respectful Subjectivity among Primary School Children in Post-Conflict Ayacucho, Peru: An Embodied Learning Analysis." PhD diss. Urbana: University of Illinois.

Guadalupe, César, Juan León, José Rodríguez, and Silvana Vargas. 2017. *Estado de la educación en el Perú: Análisis y perspectivas de la educación básica*. Proyecto FORGE. Lima: GRADE.

Guerra-Reyes, Lucía. 2019. *Changing Birth in the Andes: Culture, Policy and Safe Motherhood in Peru*. Nashville, TN: Vanderbilt University Press.

Haboud de Ortega, Marleen. 1980. "La educación informal como proceso de socialización en San Pedro de Casta." Pontificia Universidad Católica del Perú. *Debates en Antropología* 5:71–114.

Hagan, John, Ross MacMillan, and Blair Wheaton. 1996. "New Kid in Town: Social Capital and the Life Course Effects of Family Migration on Children." *American Sociological Review* 61:368–385.

Hammersley, Martyn. 2017. "Childhood Studies: A Sustainable Paradigm?" *Childhood* 24 (1): 113–127.

Harbers, Hans. 2010. "Animal Farm Love Stories: About Care and Economy." In *Care in Practice: On Tinkering in Clinics, Homes and Farms*, edited by Annemarie Mol, Ingunn Moser, and Jeannette Pols, 141–170. Bielefeld, Germany: Transcript.

Harding, Sandra. 2004. "Introduction: Standpoint Theory as a Site of Political, Philosophic and Scientific Debate." In *The Feminist Standpoint Theory Reader: Intellectual and Political Controversies*, edited by Sandra Harding, 1–15. New York: Routledge.

Harkness, Sara, and Charles M. Super. 1994. "The Developmental Niche: A Theoretical Framework for Analyzing the Household Production of Health." *Social Science and Medicine* 38:217–226.

Harris, Olivia. 1978. "Complementarity and Conflict: an Andean View of Women and Men." In *Sex and Age as Principles of Social Differentiation*, edited by J. S. La Fontaine, 21–40. London: Academic Press.

———. 2000. "Andean Anthropology in the Fulcrum of History." In *To Make the Earth Bear Fruit: Ethnographic Essays on Fertility, Work and Gender in Highland Bolivia*, 1–24. London: Institute of Latin American Studies.

Harriss-White, Barbara. 2003. *India Working: Essays on Society and Economy*. Cambridge, UK: Cambridge University Press.

Harvey, Penelope. 1997. "Peruvian Independence Day: Ritual, Memory, and the Erasure of Narrative." In *Creating Context in Andean Cultures*, edited by Rosaleen Howard-Malverde, 21–44. Oxford, UK: Oxford University Press.

———. 1998. "Los 'hechos naturales' de parentesco y género en un contexto andino." In *Gente de carne y hueso: las tramas de parentesco en los Andes*, edited by Denise Y. Arnold, 69–82. La Paz, Bolivia: ILCA/CIASE.

Henríquez, Narda. 2005. *Red de redes para la concertación: La experiencia de la Mesa de Concertación para la Lucha contra la Pobreza*. Lima: Mesa de Concertación.

Henríquez, Narda, and Christina Ewig. 2013. "Integrating Gender into Human Security: Peru's Truth and Reconciliation Commission." In *Gender, Violence, and Human Security: Critical Feminist Perspectives*, edited by Aili Mari Tripp, Myra Marx Feree, and Christina Ewig, 260–283. New York: New York University Press.

REFERENCES

Herzfeld, Michael. 1992. *The Social Production of Indifference*. Oxford, UK: Berg.

Hirschfeld, Lawrence C. 2002. "Why Don't Anthropologists Like Children?" *American Anthropologist* 104 (2):611–627.

Hogan, Diane. 2005. "Researching 'The Child' in Developmental Psychology." In *Researching Children's Experience: Approaches and Methods*, edited by Sheila Greene and Diane Hogan, 22–41. Thousand Oaks, CA: Sage Publications.

Hondagneu-Sotelo, Pierrette. 2001. *Doméstica: Immigrant Workers Cleaning and Caring in the Shadows of Affluence*. Berkeley: University of California Press.

Hornberger, Nancy H. 1987. "Schooltime, Classtime, and Academic Learning Time in Rural Highland Puno, Peru." *Anthropology & Education Quarterly* 18:207–221.

Horsfield, Margaret. 1998. *Biting the Dust (the Joys of Housework)*. New York: Picador USA.

Huayhua, Margarita. 2010. "Runama Kani icha Alquchu?: Everyday Discrimination in the Southern Andes." PhD diss., University of Michigan.

Huber, Ludwig. 2002. *Consumo, cultura e identidad en un mundo globalizado: Estudios de caso en los Andes*. Lima: Instituto de Estudios Peruanos.

———. 2008. *Romper la mano: Una interpretación cultural de la corrupción*. Lima: Instituto de Estudios Peruanos/Proética.

Hughes, Christina. 2002. *Key Concepts in Feminist Theory and Research*. London: Sage Publications.

Huicho, Luis, and Guy Pawson. 2003. "Crecimiento y desarrollo." In *El reto fisiológico de vivir en los Andes*, edited by Carlos Monge and Fabiola León-Velarde, 315–352. Lima: Instituto Francés de Estudios Andinos IFEA/Universidad Peruana Cayetano Heredia.

Hurtado, A. Magdalena, Carol A. Lambourne, Paul James, Kim Hill, Karen Cheman, and Keely Baca. 2005. "Human Rights, Biomedical Science, and Infectious Diseases among South American Indigenous Groups." *Annual Review of Anthropology* 34:639–665.

INEI. 2016. *Encuesta nacional sobre relaciones sociales ENARES 2013 y 2015: principales resultados*. Lima: Instituto Nacional de Estadística e Informática, Government of Peru.

———. 2018. *Perú: perfil sociodemográfico*. Lima: Instituto Nacional de Estadística e Informática, Government of Peru.

———. 2022. *Perú: Estadísticas de la Emigración Internacional de Peruanos e Inmigración de Extranjeros, 1990–2021*. Lima: Instituto Nacional de Estadística e Informática, Government of Peru.

Isbell, Billie Jean. 1976. "La otra mitad esencial." *Estudios Andinos* 5 (1):37–56.

———. 1985. *To Defend Ourselves: Ecology and Ritual in an Andean Village*. 2nd ed. Prospect Heights, Ill.: Waveland Press.

———. 2016. "Reflections on Fieldwork in Chuschi." In *A Return to the Village: Community Ethnographies and the Study of Andean Culture in Retrospective*, edited by Francisco Ferreira, 45–68. London: Institute of Latin American Studies ILAS.

Jagannathan, N. Vijay. 1987. *Informal Markets in Developing Economies*. Oxford, UK: Oxford University Press.

James, Allison, and Alan Prout, eds. 1997. *Constructing and Reconstructing Childhood*. London: Falmer Press.

Johnson-Hanks, Jennifer. 2002. "On the Limits of Life Stages in Ethnography: Toward a Theory of Vital Conjunctures." *American Anthropologist* 104 (3):865–880.

Jordahl, Henrik. 2007. *Inequality and Trust*. Working Paper IFN 715, August 21, Stockholm, Sweden, https://dx.doi.org/10.2139/ssrn.1012786

Katz, Cindi. 2004. *Growing Up Global: Economic Restructuring and Children's Everyday Lives*. Minneapolis: University of Minnesota Press.

Keith, Robert G., Fernando Fuenzalida, José Matos Mar, Julio Cotler, and Giorgio Alberti. 1970. *La hacienda, la comunidad y el campesino en el Perú*. Lima: Instituto de Estudios Peruanos.

REFERENCES

Koss-Chioino, Joan D., Thomas Leatherman, and Christine Greenway, eds. 2003. *Medical Pluralism in the Andes*. London and New York: Routledge.

Kymlicka, Will. 2009. "The Multicultural Welfare State?" In *Successful Societies: How Institutions and Culture Affect Health*, edited by Michèle Lamont and Peter A. Hall, 226–253. Cambridge, UK: Cambridge University Press.

Lamb, Sarah. 2000. *White Saris and Sweet Mangoes: Aging, Gender, and Body in North India*. Berkeley: University of California Press.

Lambert, Bernd. 1977. "Bilaterality in the Andes." In *Andean Kinship and Marriage*, edited by Ralph Bolton and Enrique Mayer, 1–27. Washington, DC: American Anthropological Association.

Lamont, Michèle. 2009. "Responses to Racism, Health, and Social Inclusion as a Dimension of Successful Societies." In *Successful Societies: How Institutions and Culture Affect Health*, edited by Michèle Lamont and Peter A. Hall, 151–168. Cambridge, UK: Cambridge University Press.

Lamont, Michèle, and Peter A. Hall, eds.. 2009. *Successful Societies: How Institutions and Culture Affect Health*. Cambridge, UK: Cambridge University Press.

Lancy, David. 2008. *The Anthropology of Childhood: Cherubs, Chattel, Changelings*. Cambridge, UK: Cambridge University Press.

La Riva González, Palmira. 2013. "Watuchi: Enigmas y saberes infantiles en los Andes del sur del Perú." *Bulletin de l'Institut Français d'Études Andines* 42 (3):369–388.

La Rosa Calle, Javier, ed. 2007. *Acceso a la justicia en el mundo rural*. Lima: Instituto de Defensa Legal.

Larme, Anne C., and Thomas Leatherman. 2003. "Why *sobreparto*? Women's Work, Health, and Reproduction in Two Districts in Southern Peru." In *Medical Pluralism in the Andes*, edited by Joan D. Koss-Chioino, Thomas Leatherman, and Christine Greenway, 191–208. London: Routledge.

Lear, Jonathan. 2006. *Radical Hope: Ethics in the Face of Cultural Devastation*. Cambridge, MA: Harvard University Press.

Leatherman, Thomas L. 1998. "Illness, Social Relations, and Household Production and Reproduction in the Andes of Southern Peru." In *Building a New Biocultural Synthesis: Political-Economic Perspectives on Human Biology*, edited by Alan H. Goodman and Thomas L. Leatherman, 245–267. Ann Arbor: University of Michigan Press.

Leinaweaver, Jessaca. 2007a. "Choosing to Move: Child Agency on Peru's Margins." *Childhood: A Global Journal of Child Research* 14 (3):375–392.

———. 2007b. "On Moving Children: The Social Implications of Andean Child Circulation." *American Ethnologist* 34(1): 163–180. doi: 10.1525/ae.2007.34.1.163.

———. 2008. *The Circulation of Children: Kinship, Adoption and Morality in Andean Peru*. Durham, NC: Duke University Press.

———. 2009. "Raising the Roof in the Transnational Andes: Building Houses, Forging Kinship." *Journal of the Royal Anthropological Institute* 15(4):777–796. 10.1111/j.1467-9655.2009.01584.x.

———. 2010a. "Outsourcing Care: How Peruvian Migrants Meet Transnational Family Obligations." *Latin American Perspectives* 37 (5):67–87.

———. 2010b. "Agencia infantil y la organización social y cultural del cuidado en Yauyos, Perú." In *Contribuciones a la antropología de la infancia*, edited by Maritza Díaz and Socorro Vásquez, 41–60. Bogotá, Colombia: Editorial Javeriana.

———. 2013. "Toward an Anthropology of Ingratitude: Notes from Andean Kinship." *Comparative Studies in Society and History* 55 (3):1–25.

———. 2015. "Transnational Fathers, Good Providers, and the Silences of Adoption." In *Globalized Fatherhood*, edited by Marcia Inhorn, Wendy Chavkin, and José-Alberto Navarro, 81–102. New York: Berghahn Books.

———. 2018. "Kinship, Households, and Sociality." In *The Andean World*, edited by Linda J. Seligmann and Kathleen S. Fine-Dare, 235–248. New York: Routledge.

———. 2022. "Counter-Demography: Situated Caring for the Aged in Andean Peru." *Medical Anthropology* 41:6–7: 630–644. Doi: 10.1080/01459740.2021.1988595.

Leinaweaver, Jessaca, and Jeanine Anderson. n.d. "Child Care and Children Caring in Yauyos." Unpublished manuscript.

Leinaweaver, Jessaca, and Jeanine Anderson. 2024. "Working Together, Learning Apart: A Multicommunity Study in Rural Peru." *Ethnography and Education* 19 (2):175–193. https://doi.org/10.1080/17457823.2024.2339859.

Lennox, Erin. 2015. "Double Exposure to Climate Change and Globalization in a Peruvian Highland Community." *Society & Natural Resources: An International Journal* 28 (7):781–796.

Levinson, Bradley A., Douglas E. Foley, and Dorothy C. Holland, eds. 1996. *The Cultural Production of the Educated Person: Critical Ethnographies of Schooling and Local Practice*. Albany: State University of New York Press.

Li, Fabiana. 2015. *Unearthing Conflict: Corporate Mining, Activism, and Expertise in Peru*. Durham, NC: Duke University Press.

Lobo, Susan. 1982. *A House of My Own: Social Organization in the Squatter Settlements of Lima, Peru*. Tucson: University of Arizona Press.

Long, Norman, and Bryan Roberts. 1984. *Miners, Peasants and Entrepreneurs: Regional Development in the Central Highlands of Peru*. Cambridge, UK: Cambridge University Press.

Low, Setha, and Denise Lawrence-Zúñiga, eds. 2003. *The Anthropology of Space and Place: Locating Culture*. Malden, MA: Blackwell Publishing.

Luttrell-Rowland, Mikaela. 2012. "Ambivalence, Conflation, and Invisibility: A Feminist Analysis of State Enactment of Children's Rights in Peru." *Signs* 38 (1):179–202.

———. 2023. *Political Children: Violence, Labor, and Rights in Peru*. Stanford, CA: Stanford University Press.

Luykx, Aurolyn. 1999. *The Citizen Factory: Schooling and Cultural Production in Bolivia*. Albany: State University of New York Press.

Mallon, Florencia E. 1983. *The Defense of Community in Peru's Central Highlands: Peasant Struggle and Capitalist Transition, 1860–1940*. Princeton, NJ: Princeton University Press.

Mannheim, Bruce. 1991. *The Language of the Inka since the European Invasion*. Austin: University of Texas Press.

Martine, George, Gordon McGranahan, Mark Montgomery, and Rogelio Fernández-Castilla, eds. 2008. *The New Global Frontier: Urbanization, Poverty and Environment in the 21st Century*. London: Earthscan.

Matos Mar, José. 1953. "El proyecto Yauyos—Huarochirí." *Revista del Museo Nacional* 22:179–190.

———. 2004. *Desborde popular y crisis del Estado*. Lima: Fondo Editorial del Congreso del Perú.

Mattingly, Cheryl. 2010. *The Paradox of Hope: Journeys through a Clinical Borderland*. Berkeley: University of California Press.

Mattingly, Cheryl, and Uffe Juul Jensen. 2015. "What Can We Hope For? An Exploration in Cosmopolitan Philosophical Anthropology." In *Anthropology and Philosophy: Dialogues on Trust and Hope*, edited by Sune Liisberg, Esther Oluffa Pedersen, and Anne Line Dalsgård, 24–55. New York: Berghahn Books.

Mayer, Enrique. 1974. "Las reglas del juego en la reciprocidad andina." In *Reciprocidad e intercambio en los Andes peruanos*, edited by Giorgio Alberti and Enrique Mayer, 37–65. Lima: Instituto de Estudios Peruanos.

———, ed. 1988. *Comunidad y producción en la agricultura andina*. Lima: FOMCIENCIAS.

———. 2003. *The Articulated Peasant: Household Economies in the Andes*. Boulder, CO: Westview Press.

REFERENCES

Meinert, Lotte. 2003. "Sweet and Bitter Places: The Politics of Schoolchildren's Orientation in Rural Uganda." In *Children's Places: Cross-Cultural Perspectives*, edited by Karen Fog Olwig and Eva Guilløv, 179–196. London: Routledge.

Meléndez, Guido, and César Huaroto. 2014. *Evaluando las complementariedades de proyectos de infraestructura rural: El impacto conjunto de electrificación y telecomunicaciones en el bienestar del hogar y la formación de capital humano.* Lima: Consorcio de Investigación Económica y Social CIES.

MIMDES/INEI. 2011. *Encuesta Nacional de Uso del Tiempo: Principales resultados.* Lima: Ministry of Women and Social Development, Government of Peru.

Ministerio de Agricultura. 1979. *Encuesta Nacional de Consumo de Alimentos.* Lima: Ministry of Agriculture, Government of Peru.

Mol, Annemarie. 2008. *The Logic of Care: Health and the Problem of Patient Choice.* London: Routledge.

Mol, Annemarie, Ingunn Moser, and Jeannette Pols, eds. 2010. *Care in Practice: On Tinkering in Clinics, Homes and Farms.* Bielefeld, Germany: Transcript.

Molina Serra, Ainhoa. 2017. "Esterilizaciones (forzadas) en Perú: Poder y configuraciones narrativas." *AIBR: Revista de Antropología Iberoamericana* 12 (1):31–52. doi:10.11156/aibr.120103.

Monge, Carlos, and Fabiola León-Velarde, eds. 2003. *El reto fisiológico de vivir en los Andes.* Lima: Instituto Francés de Estudios Andinos IFEA/Universidad Peruana Cayetano Heredia.

Montaño, Sonia, and Coral Calderón, eds. 2010. *El cuidado en acción: Entre el derecho y el trabajo.* Santiago, Chile: Economic Commission for Latin America and the Caribbean/UNIFEM.

Montero, Carmen. 2006. "La exclusion educativa de las niñas del campo: ¿pasado o presente?" In *Las brechas invisibles: Desafíos para una equidad de género en la educación*, edited by Patricia Ames, 203–231. Lima: Instituto de Estudios Peruanos.

Montero, Ricardo and Gustavo Yamada. 2012. "Exclusión y discriminación étnica en los servicios públicos en el Perú." In *Discriminación en el Perú: Exploraciones en el Estado, la empresa y el mercado laboral*, edited by Francisco Galarza, 219–278. Lima: Universidad del Pacífico.

Montgomery, Heather. 2009. *An Introduction to Childhood: Anthropological Perspectives on Children's Lives.* Malden, MA: Wiley-Blackwell.

Morales, Alvaro, and Singh, Prakarsh. 2014. "The Effect of Civil Conflict on Child Abuse: Evidence from Peru." HiCN (Households in Conflict Network) Working paper 187, University of Sussex, UK, Institute of Development Studies.

Moran-Ellis, Jo and E. Kay Tisdall. 2019. "The Relevance of 'Competence' for Enhancing or Limiting Children's Participation: Unpicking Conceptual Confusion." *Global Studies of Childhood* 9 (3):212–223.

Nué, Angélica. 2000. "Percepciones y autopercepciones de ancianos en la Comunidad de Santa Cruz de Andamarca." *Anthropologica* 18:153–173.

Nussbaum, Martha C. 1993. "Non-Relative Virtues. An Aristotelian Approach." In *The Quality of Life*, edited by Martha C. Nussbaum and Amartya Sen, 242–269. WIDER Studies in Development Economics. Oxford, UK: Clarendon Paperbacks.

———. 1995. "Human Capabilities, Female Human Beings." In *Women, Culture and Development: A Study of Human Capabilities*, edited by Martha C. Nussbaum and Jonathan Glover, 61–104. Oxford, UK: Clarendon Press.

Oliart, Patricia. 2005. "Género, sexualidad y adolescencia en la provincia de Quispicanchi." In *Quispicanchi: Género y sexualidad*, edited by Patricia Oliart, Rosa María Mujica, and José María García, 9–45. Lima: Instituto Peruano de Educación en Derechos Humanos y La Paz (IPEDEHP)/Fe y Alegría.

———. 2011. *Políticas educativas y la cultura del sistema escolar en el Perú.* Lima: Instituto de Estudios Peruanos/TAREA.

REFERENCES

Olthoff, Jacobijn. 2006. *A Dream Denied: Teenage Girls in Migrant Popular Neighbourhoods, Lima, Peru* Amsterdam: Dutch University Press.

Olwig, Karen Fog, and Eva Gulløv, eds. 2003. *Children's Places: Cross-Cultural Perspectives.* London: Routledge.

O'Neill, Onora. 2000. *Bounds of Justice.* Cambridge, UK: Cambridge University Press.

Orlove, Benjamin. 1974. "Reciprocidad, desigualdad y dominación." In *Reciprocidad e intercambio en los Andes peruanos*, edited by Giorgio Alberti and Enrique Mayer, 290–321. Lima: Instituto de Estudios Peruanos.

———. 2002. *Lines in the Water: Nature and Culture at Lake Titicaca.* Berkeley: University of California Press.

Ortiz Rescanierre, Alejandro. 1989. "La comunidad, el parentesco y los patrones de crianza andinos." *Anthropologica* 7:135–170.

Ortiz Rescanierre, Alejandro, and Jorge Yamamoto. 1994. *Un estudio sobre los grupos autónomos de niños.* Lima: Fundación Bernard Van Leer/Ministry of Education, Government of Peru.

Ortner, Sherry B. 2006. "Power and Projects: Reflections on Agency." In *Anthropology and Social Theory: Culture, Power, and the Acting Subject*, 129–153. Durham, NC: Duke University Press.

Osterling, Jorge P. 1980. *De campesinos a profesionales: Migrantes de Huayopampa en Lima.* Lima: Pontificia Universidad Católica del Perú.

Ostrom, Elinor. 1990. *Governing the Commons.* Cambridge, UK: Cambridge University Press.

Oths, Kathryn S. 1999. "*Debilidad*: a Biocultural Assessment of an Embodied Andean Illness." *Medical Anthropology Quarterly* 13:286–315.

———. 2003. "Setting It Straight in the Andes. Musculoskeletal Distress and the Role of the Componedor." In *Medical Pluralism in the Andes*, edited by Joan D. Koss-Chioino, Thomas Leatherman, and Christine Greenway, 63–91. London: Routledge.

Pærregaard, Karsten. 1997. *Linking Separate Worlds: Urban Migrants and Rural Lives in Peru.* Oxford, UK: Berg.

———. 2020. "Searching for the New Human: Glacier Melt, Anthropogenic Change, and Self-reflection in Andean Pilgrimage." *HAU Journal of Ethnographic Theory* 10 (3):844–859.

Pajuelo, Ramón. 2000. "Imágenes de la comunidad: Indígenas, campesinos y antropólogos en el Perú." In *No hay país más diverso*, edited by Carlos Iván Degregori, 123–179. Lima: Red para el desarrollo de las ciencias sociales en el Perú.

Panez, Rosario. 2004. *El lenguaje silencioso de los niños: Un estudio peruano sobre los Derechos del Niño desde su producción creativa.* Lima: Panez & Silva Ediciones.

Panez, Rosario, and Socorro Ochoa. 2000. *Cultura recreacional andina.* Lima: Panez & Silva Ediciones.

Paradise, Ruth, and Barbara Rogoff. 2009. "Side by Side: Learning by Observing and Pitching In." *Ethos* 37 (1):102–138.

ParksWatch. 2003. "Park Profile Peru Nor Yauyos—Cochas Landscape Preserve." Accessed July 1, 2015. https://www.parkswatch.org.

Parodi, Carlos. 2000. *Perú 1960–2000: Políticas económicas y sociales en entornos cambiantes.* Lima: Universidad del Pacífico, Centro de Investigación.

Pérez Orozco, Amaia, Denise Paiewonsky, and Mar García Domínguez. 2008. *Cruzando fronteras: migración y desarrollo desde una perspectiva de género.* Madrid: Instituto de la Mujer/ Santo Domingo: UN-INSTRAW.

Petrera, Margarita, and Janice Seinfeld. 2007. *Repensando la salud en el Perú.* Lima: Universidad del Pacífico.

Platt, Tristán. 2016. "Avoiding 'Community Studies': The Historical Turn in Bolivian and South Andean Anthropology." In *A Return to the Village: Community Ethnographies and the Study*

REFERENCES

of Andean Culture in Retrospective, edited by Francisco Ferreira, 199–232. London: Institute of Latin American Studies.

Polatnick, M. Rivka, 1984. "Why Men Don't Rear Children: A Power Analysis." In *Mothering: Essays in Feminist Theory*, edited by Joyce Trebilcot, 21–40. Totowa, NJ: Rowman & Allanheld.

Polia Meconi, Mario. 1996. *"Despierta, remedio, cuenta . . .": adivinos y médicos del Ande.* Volumes I and II. Lima: Pontificia Universidad Católica del Perú.

Pollitt, Ernesto, Juan León, and Santiago Cueto. 2007. "Desarrollo infantil y rendimiento escolar en el Perú." In *Investigación, políticas y desarrollo en el Perú*, 485–535. Lima: Grupo de Análisis para el Desarrollo GRADE.

Ponce, Carmen, and Escobal, Javier. 2019. *Reshaping the Gender Gap in Child Time Use: Unintended Effects of a Program Expanding Economic Opportunities in the Peruvian Andes.* Lima: Grupo de Análisis para el Desarrollo GRADE.

Poole, Deborah, ed. 1994. *Unruly Order: Violence, Power, and Cultural Identity in the High Provinces of Southern Peru.* Boulder, CO: Westview Press.

Portocarrero, Felipe and Cynthia Sanborn, eds. 2003. *De la caridad a la solidaridad: Filantropía y voluntariado en el Perú.* Lima: Universidad del Pacífico.

Pribilsky, Jason. 2001. "Nervios and 'Modern Childhood': Migration and Shifting Contexts of Child Life in the Ecuadorian Andes." *Childhood* 8 (2):251–273.

———. 2009. "Development and the 'Indian Problem' in the Cold War Andes: 'Indigenismo,' Science, and Modernization in the Making of the Cornell-Peru Project at Vicos." *Diplomatic History* 33 (3):405–426.

Puddephatt, Antony J., William Shaffir, and Steven W. Kleinknecht, eds. 2009. *Ethnographies Revisited: Constructing Theory in the Field.* New York: Routledge.

Puente, Javier. 2022. *The Rural State: Making Comunidades, Campesinos, and Conflict in Peru's Central Sierra.* Austin: University of Texas Press.

Quijano, Aníbal. 2011. "Buen Vivir: entre el desarrollo y la des/colonialidad del poder." *Ecuador Debate* 84:77–88.

Quiroz, Alfonso. 2008. *Corrupt Circles: A History of Unbound Graft in Peru.* Baltimore, MD: Johns Hopkins University Press.

Rasmussen, Mattias Borg. 2015. *Andean Waterways: Resource Politics in Highland Peru.* Seattle: University of Washington Press.

Ray, Raka, and Seemin Qayum. 2009. *Cultures of Servitude: Modernity, Domesticity, and Class in India.* Stanford, CA: Stanford University Press.

Remorini, Carolina. 2013. "Estudio etnográfico de la crianza y de la participación de los niños en comunidades rurales de los Valles Calchaquíes septentrionales (noroeste Argentino)." *Bulletin de l'Institut Français d'Études Andines* 42 (3):411–433.

Reyes, Esperanza. 2007. *En nombre del Estado: Servidores públicos en una microrred de salud en la costa rural del Perú.* Lima: Universidad Peruana Cayetano Heredia.

Richards, Lyn. 2005. *Handling Qualitative Data: A Practical Guide.* Thousand Oaks, CA: Sage.

Richardson, Laurel. 1998. "Writing: A Method of Inquiry." In *Collecting and Interpreting Qualitative Materials*, edited by Norman K. Denzin and Yvonna S. Lincoln, 345–371. Thousand Oaks, CA: Sage.

Rivera, Juan Javier. 2005. "Killing What You Love: An Andean Cattle Branding Ritual and the Dilemmas of Modernity." *Journal of Anthropological Research* 61 (2):129–156.

Rodríguez, José, and Silvana Vargas. 2009. *Trabajo infantil en el Perú: Magnitud y perfiles vulnerables.* Informe Nacional 2007–2008. Lima: International Labor Organization / INEI.

Rodríguez, Pablo, and María Emma Mannarelli, eds. 2007. *Historia de la infancia en América Latina.* Bogotá: Universidad Externado de Colombia.

Rogoff, Barbara. 2003. *The Cultural Nature of Human Development*. Oxford, UK: Oxford University Press.

Rojas, Vanessa. 2011. *"Prefiero que me peguen con palo . . . las notas son sagradas": Percepciones sobre disciplina y autoridad en una secundaria pública en el Perú*. Lima: Grupo de Análisis para el Desarrollo GRADE.

Rojas, Vanessa, and Tamia Portugal. 2010. "¿Educación para el desarrollo rural o para dejar de ser rural? Percepciones y proyectos de pobladores rurales andinos y amazónicos." In *Perú: el problema agrario en debate. SEPIA XIII*, edited by Patricia Ames and Víctor Caballero. Lima: Seminario Permanente de Investigación Agraria SEPIA.

Ruddick, Sara. 1984. "Maternal Thinking." In *Mothering: Essays in Feminist Theory*, edited by Joyce Trebilcot, 213–230. Totowa, NJ: Rowman & Allanheld.

Sahlins, Marshall. 1972. *Stone Age Economics*. Chicago: Aldine—Atherton, Inc.

Salas, Guillermo. 2019. *Lugares parientes: Comida, cohabitación y mundos andinos*. Lima: Pontificia Universidad Católica del Perú.

Saldaña, Johnny. 2009. *The Coding Manual for Qualitative Researchers*. Thousand Oaks, CA: Sage.

Salmón, Elizabeth and Renata Bregaglio, eds. 2015. *Nueve conceptos claves para entender la Convención sobre los Derechos de las Personas con Discapacidad*. Lima: Pontificia Universidad Católica del Perú IDEHPUCP.

Salomon, Frank. 1982. "Andean Ethnology in the 1970s: A Retrospective." *Latin American Research Review* 17:75–128.

———. 2016. "Long Lines of Continuity: Field Ethnohistory and Customary Cultivation in the Sierra de Lima." In *A Return to the Village: Community Ethnographies and the Study of Andean Culture in Retrospective*, edited by Francisco Ferreira, 169–197. London: Institute of Latin American Studies.

Sánchez, Rodolfo, and Gustavo Valdivia. 1994. *Socialización infantil mediante el juego en el sur andino: Estudio de casos en diez comunidades campesinas de Andahuaylas*. Lima: Fundación Bernard Van Leer/Ministry of Education, Government of Peru.

Sautier, Denis, and Isabel Amemiya. 1988. "Sistemas alimentarios y estado nutricional en comunidades campesinas de Yauyos." In *Políticas agrarias y estrategias campesinas en la Cuenca del Cañete*, edited by Michel Eresue and Anne Marie Brougère, 99–132. Lima: Universidad Nacional Agraria/Instituto Francés de Estudios Andinos IFEA.

Scartascini, Carlos, and Juana Valle Luna. 2020. *The Elusive Quest for Growth in Latin America and the Caribbean: The Role of Trust*. Policy Brief No. IDB-PB-341. Washington, DC: Inter-American Development Bank.

Schatzki, Theodore, Carin Knorr Cetina, and Eike von Savigny, eds. 2001. *The Practice Turn in Contemporary Theory*. New York: Routledge.

Scheper-Hughes, Nancy. 1992. *Death without Weeping: The Violence of Everyday Life in Brazil*. Berkeley: University of California Press.

Scheper-Hughes, Nancy, and Carolyn Sargent, eds. 1998. *Small Wars: The Cultural Politics of Childhood*. Berkeley: University of California Press.

Seaman, Aaron T., Jessica C. Robbins, and Elana Buch. 2019. "Beyond the Evaluative Lens: Contextual Unpredictabilities of Care." *Journal of Aging Studies* 51 (100799).

Seligmann, Linda, and Kathleen S. Fine-Dare. 2019. *The Andean World*. New York: Routledge.

Serpell, Robert. 1993. *The Significance of Schooling*. Cambridge, UK: Cambridge University Press.

Shanahan, Michael J. 2000. "Pathways to Adulthood in Changing Societies: Variability and Mechanisms in Life Course Perspective." *Annual Review of Sociology* 26:667–692.

Shepherd, Christopher, and Carmen Barrantes. 2023. "Sex Trafficking by Consent? Andean Padrinazgo, Illegal Mining in Amazonia, and State Intervention." *The Journal of Latin American and Caribbean Anthropology* 28 (1):9–20.

REFERENCES

Singleton, Vicky. 2010. "Good Farming: Control or Care?" In *Care in Practice: On Tinkering in Clinics, Homes and Farms*, edited by Annemarie Mol, Ingunn Moser, and Jeannette Pols, 235–256. Bielefeld, Germany: Transcript.

Skrabut, Kristin. 2018. "Housing the Contingent Life Course: Aspiration and Extreme Poverty in Peruvian Shantytowns." *City and Society* 30 (1):1–26.

Smith, Dorothy. 1987. *The Everyday World as Problematic: A Feminist Sociology*. Boston: Northeastern University Press.

Smith, Linda Tuhiwai. 2006. *Decolonizing Methodologies: Research and Indigenous Peoples*. London: Zed Books Ltd.

Sørensen, Ninna Nyberg. 2002. "Representing the Local: Mobile Livelihood Practices in the Peruvian Central Sierra." In *Work and Migration: Life and Livelihoods in a Globalizing World*, edited by Ninna Nyberg Sørensen and Karen Fog Olwig, 23–44. London: Routledge.

Spray, Julie. 2020. *The Children in Child Health: Negotiating Young Lives and Health in New Zealand*. New Brunswick, NJ: Rutgers University Press.

Starn, Orin. 1991. "Missing the Revolution: Anthropologists and the War in Peru." *Cultural Anthropology* 6:63–91.

———. 1994. "Rethinking the Politics of Anthropology: The Case of the Andes." *Current Anthropology* 35 (1):13–38.

Starn, Orin, and Miguel La Serna. 2019. *The Shining Path: Love, Madness, and Revolution in the Andes*. New York: W. W. Norton & Company.

Strauss, Anselm, and Juliet Corbin. 1990. *Basics of Qualitative Research: Grounded Theory Procedures and Techniques*. Newbury Park, CA: Sage.

Tanaka, Martin, ed. 1999. *El poder visto desde abajo: Democracia, educación y ciudadanía en espacios locales*. Lima: Instituto de Estudios Peruanos.

Theidon, Kimberly. 2004. *Entre prójimos: El conflicto armado interno y la política de reconciliación en el Perú*. Lima: Instituto de Estudios Peruanos.

Thelen, Tatjana. 2015. "Care as Social Organisation: Creating, Maintaining and Dissolving Significant Relations." *Anthropological Theory* 15 (4):497–515.

Thomas, Carol. 1993. "De-constructing the Concept of Care." *Sociology* 27 (4):649–669.

Thomas, R. Brooke. 1997. "Wandering Toward the Edge of Adaptability: Adjustments of Andean Peoples to Change." In *Human Adaptability Past, Present, and Future*, edited by Stanley J. Ulijaszek and Rebecca Huss-Ashmore, 183–232. New York: Oxford University Press.

Ticktin, Miriam. 2011. *Casualties of Care: Immigration and the Politics of Humanitarianism in France*. Berkeley: University of California Press.

Trinidad, Rocío. 2005. *Entre la ilusión y la realidad: Las nuevas tecnologías en dos proyectos educativos del estado*. Lima: Instituto de Estudios Peruanos.

Trivelli, Carolina, and Rodrigo Gil, eds. 2021. *Caminantes: oportunidades, ocupaciones, aspiraciones e identidades de los jóvenes rurales peruanos*. Lima: Instituto de Estudios Peruanos.

Tronto, Joan C. 1993. *Moral Boundaries: A Political Argument for an Ethic of Care*. London: Routledge.

Tucker, Joshua. 2019. *Making Music Indigenous: Popular Music in the Peruvian Andes*. Chicago: University of Chicago Press.

Turino, Thomas. 1993. *Moving Away from Silence: Music of the Peruvian Altiplano and the Experience of Migration*. Chicago: University of Chicago Press.

Turner, Victor. 1974. *The Ritual Process: Structure and Anti-structure*. Ithaca, NY: Cornell University Press.

———. 2001. *From Ritual to Theater: The Human Seriousness of Play*. New York: PAJ Publications.

Uccelli, Francesca, and Mariel García Llorens. 2016. *Solo zapatillas de marca: Jóvenes limeños y los límites de la inclusión desde el mercado*. Lima: Instituto de Estudios Peruanos.

Urrutia, Jaime, and Alejandro Diez. 2016. "Organizaciones y asociatividad: hacia las lógicas de la gobernanza rural." In *Perú: el problema agrario en debate*, edited by José Francisco Durand, Jaime Urrutia, and Carmen Yon, 233–294. Lima: Seminario Permanente de Investigación Agraria SEPIA.

Valle Luna, Juana, and Carlos Scartascini. 2020. "¿En quién confiamos? Una cuestión de percepciones y desigualdad." In *La crisis de la desigualdad: América Latina y el Caribe en la encrucijada*, edited by Matías Busso and Julián Messina, 348–372. Washington, DC: Interamerican Development Bank.

Van Vleet, Krista E. 2008. *Performing Kinship: Narrative, Gender, and the Intimacies of Power in the Andes*. Austin: University of Texas Press.

———. 2019. *Hierarchies of Care: Girls, Motherhood, and Inequality in Peru*. Champaign: University of Illinois Press.

Varillas, Brígido. 1965. *Apuntes para el folklore de Yauyos: mitologías, leyendas, cuentos y fábulas, canciones populares, danzas, costumbres y fiestas, comidas y bebidas, creencias, supersticiones, medicina popular y adivinanzas de la región de Yauyos*. Lima: Huascarán.

Villapolo, Leslie, and Norma Vásquez. 1999. *Entre el juego y la guerra*. Lima: Centro Amazónico de Antropología y Aplicación Práctica.

Vincent, Susan. 2021. "Planning for Old Age in Peru: Count on Kin or Court the State?" *Anthropology & Aging* 42 (2):52–67.

Walker, Margaret Urban. 1998. *Moral Understandings: A Feminist Study in Ethics*. New York: Routledge.

Weismantel, Mary J. 1988. *Food, Gender, and Poverty in the Ecuadorian Andes*. Philadelphia: University of Pennsylvania Press.

———. 2001. *Cholas and Pishtacos: Stories of Race and Sex in the Andes*. Chicago: University of Chicago Press.

Whiting, Beatrice B., and Carolyn Pope Edwards. 1988. *Children of Different Worlds: The Formation of Social Behavior*. Cambridge, MA: Harvard University Press.

Wiley, Andrea S. 2004. *An Ecology of High-Altitude Infancy: A Biocultural Perspective*. Cambridge, UK: Cambridge University Press.

Williams, Fiona. 1997. "Anthology: Care." In *Community Care: A Reader*, edited by Bornat, Joanna, Julia Johnson, Charmaine Pereira, David Pilgrim, and Fiona Williams, 81–95. Basingstoke: Macmillan/Open University.

Wolcott, Harry. 1994. *Transforming Qualitative Data: Description, Analysis, and Interpretation*. Thousand Oaks, CA: Sage.

Yamada, Gustavo. 2010. *Migración interna en el Perú*. Lima: Universidad del Pacífico.

Yarris, Kristin. 2017. *Care Across Generations: Solidarity and Sacrifice in Transnational Families*. Stanford, CA: Stanford University Press.

Yeates, Nicola. 2009. *Globalizing Care Economies and Migrant Workers: Explorations in Global Care Chains*. New York: Palgrave Macmillan.

Yon, Carmen. 2000. *Hablan las mujeres andinas: Preferencias reproductivas y anticoncepción*. Lima: Movimiento Manuel Ramos.

———. 2014. "Vulnerabilidad social, salud y derechos sexuales de adolescentes ayacuchanos." In *Salud, vulnerabilidades, desigualdades*, edited by Roxana Barrantes and Peter Busse, 115–140. Lima: Instituto de Estudios Peruanos.

———. 2016. "Salud, nutrición, medio ambiente y desarrollo rural: Cambios, continuidades y desafíos." In *Perú: el problema agrario en debate*, edited by José Francisco Durand, Jaime Urrutia, and Carmen Yon, 485–574. Lima: Seminario Permanente de Investigación Agraria SEPIA.

Zarger, Rebecca K. 2010. "Learning the Environment." In *The Anthropology of Learning in Childhood*, edited by David F. Lancy, John Bock, and Suzanne Gaskins, 341–369. Walnut Creek, CA: AltaMira Press.

REFERENCES

Zegarra, Eduardo. 2015. "Estructura y dinámica del consumo alimentario de las familias peruanas: análisis desde una perspectiva de seguridad alimentaria." *Debate Agrario: Análisis y Alternativas* 47:29–47.

Zegarra, Eduardo, Jeanine Anderson, Diego Geng, and Fernando González. 2023. "Movilidad y dinámicas socio-económicas en la Provincia de Yauyos: Evidencia sobre impactos de la pandemia COVID-19 y sus secuelas en la población rural." Paper presented at the XX edition of the Seminario Permanente de Investigación Agraria SEPIA, Lima, Peru, 7 November 2023.

Zegarra, Eduardo, Angie Higuchi, and Ricardo Vargas. 2018. "Assessing the Impacts of Peer-to-Peer Training Programme for Women in Peru." *Development in Practice* 28 (6):754–763.

Zegarra, Eduardo, and Verónica Minaya. 2007. "Gasto público, productividad e ingresos agrarios en el Perú: avances de investigación y resultados empíricos propios." In *Investigación, políticas y desarrollo en el Perú*, edited by Grupo de Análisis para el Desarrollo, 27–66. Lima: GRADE.

Zegarra, Magdalena. 2022. "Remaining, Vital Acts, and Possibility: The Exercise of 'Sustaining Oneself' in a Residential Care Center for the Elderly in Lima, Peru." *Anthropology and Humanism* 47:297–311.

Zelizer, Viviana A. 1985. *Pricing the Priceless Child: The Changing Social Value of Children*. Princeton, NJ: Princeton University Press.

———. 2005. *The Purchase of Intimacy*. Princeton, NJ: Princeton University Press.

INDEX

Page numbers in italics refer to illustrations.

adolescents, 160n4; farm work and, 70–72; sexuality and, 50, 116. *See also* children
adoption, 56–57
Aventura Andina, 19
agency: children's, 141–43; concepts of, 6–10; emplacement and, 43; health, hygiene and nutrition and, 90; movement of children and, 56; recognizability of, 3. *See also* child development; children; flourishing; work
agriculture, 12, 59–60, 70–71, *71*, 144
alcohol consumption, 82, 98, 100–101, 103, 110, 114, 119, 136
Alejandra (9), 68, 74
Andean region: biological challenges of, 78–79; community and, 7–10, *8*; demanding environment of, 1–2, 147; emplacement and, 143–45; entrepreneurship and, 148–50; food production and adulthood in, 70; hotels/hostels and, 158n18; marriage and, 45–47; parental practices and, 2; Yauyos region and, *11,* 12–13, *14, 18,* 157n9. *See also* Peru; Yauyos Province
Anderson, Jeanine, 25–26, 30, 33
animal care, 68–70, 86, 140
Anita (19), 54
art. *See* flourishing
atender. See care
attentive experimentation, 139. *See also* care
Aurora (13), 49–50, 65, 76, 132, 161n5

Bellavista, 17, 19
Berman, Elise, 25
Berta (9), 74
Betty (14), 54, 127
biographies sample and analysis, 27–34, *29. See also* research and theoretical framework
Bobby (7), 95
bodegas, 72–73, *73*
Bodenhorn, Barbara, 142, 144
Boris, Eileen, 3
Braulio (15), 52, 98, 129, 131, 160n2
bread, 80–81
Buch, Elana, 3
buen vivir, 6

Camila (8), 41–42, 55–56, 132
Candelaria (6), 120

Cánepa, Gisela, 148–49
Canessa, Andrew, 141
Cañete, 17, 37, 63, 87, 158n10, 161n1
Cañete River system, 12–13. *See also* Yauyos Province
care: among the community, 109–13, *110,* 143, 163n1–163n2; *atender* (tending to) and, 98–101; caregivers and, 91–96, *93, 95*; concepts of, 2–6; gender and, 4, 91–92, *93,* 93–95; household income and, 60–61; loss of caregivers and, 97–98; *preocuparse* (concern for) and, 101–2; self care, 96–97; solicitous, 99–101; sphere of, 108–9, 119; as tinkering, 139–41. *See also* children; emplacement; flourishing; special needs children
Cáritas, 159n8
cemeteries, 117
charitable care, 5
Charo (7), 69–70, 95
cheese/cheesemaking, 60, 68, 79, 83
child abuse. *See* domestic violence
child circulation. *See* adoption; agency
child development: child nutrition and, 79–81, *81,* 161n1–161n3; chore curriculum and, 58–59; developmental psychology and, 157n2; health and illness and, 79, 85–89, 161n7–161n8, 162n12; health and nutrition programs and, 84–85, 161n5; luck and, 140; malnutrition and, 81–83; nutritional windfalls and, 83; special needs children and, 117–20, 140. *See also* care; emplacement; special needs children
children: adoption and, 56–57; agency and, 141–43; Andean childhoods and, 9–10, 138; animal care and, 68–70, 86, 140; bullying and, 119–20; costs of, 61–63, *62*; as entrepreneurs, 74–75; farm work and, 70–72, *71*; first children and, 48–50; health and, 63; negligence of, 111, 140; obedience to caregivers and, 102–6; overlapping roles and, 1; parents standing in the community and, 114–17; payment for work and, 74; play and, 124–25, *126,* 141–42, 164n1; self care and, 96–97; siblings and, 50–53, *51,* 66, *95,* 95–96; special needs children and, 117–20, 140; supernatural Andean beings and, 116–17, 141; view of the world

INDEX

children (cont)
by, 145–46; work and, 63–67, *65, 67,* 142;
working in the family business and, 72–74,
73. See also adolescents; care; clothing;
domestic violence; emplacement;
flourishing; special needs children; work
child support, 50, 163n10
Chino (14), 64
chipitaps, 124, 160n1
chore curriculum, 58–59, 64, 70. *See also* work
Cleber (5), 127
clothing, *62,* 62–63, 66–67, *67,* 132
communitas, 134–35
community care, 5
community traditions and, 134–35
compadrazgo. See kinship
comunidades campesinas (peasant communities), 15, 59–60, 158n12
condenados, 117
Consorcio de Investigación Económica y
Social (CIES), 21, 158n1
Consuelo (3), 50, 85, 97, 99
contraceptives, 51, 160n6
Contreras, Carlos, 157n1
controlled comparison, 8–9, 22
cooking, 64–66, 80, 161n1
corruption, 112–13, 160n2
COVID-19, 150
Cueto, Marcos, 157n1
cuidado. See care
curiosas/curiosos, 89

Dalila (child), 51, 98
debilidad, 53
Defensoría Municipal del Niño, Niña y
Adolescente (DEMUNA), 105–6, 145
de la Cadena, Marisol, 9, 14, 17, 22, 53, 79, 89,
116, 130, 149
Diaconía, 30, 35, 116
Diana (2), 95
Díaz, Maritza, 25
Dina (9), 61, 111, 127
Dionisia (12), 21, 51–52, 54, 78, 86, 125, 131–32
disabilities: access to health care and, 90;
rates of, 164n8; special needs children and,
117–20, 140; Vaso de Leche (Glass of Milk)
program and, 84
discipline, 102–6
Dolores (10), 127
domestic service: children and, 54, 75–76, 114;
gender and, 4; rural to urban migration
and, 16; single mothers and, 48–49
domestic violence, 46, 102–6, 147,
163n8–163n9
Dominga (child), 75

ecónomos (guardians), 98, 106
education, 16, 22, 52, 61–63, 132–34
Elisa (6), 64, 69, 102, 142
emplacement: Andean communities and,
143–45; concept of, 42–43; first child and,
48–50; household membership and, 53–54;
households and, 45–48; houses and, 43–45,
44–45; reciprocity and, 54–56; siblings and,
50–53, *51*

emprendedurismo. See entrepreneurship
endogamy, 48. *See also* marriage
entrepreneurship, 148–50
environment/ecology: child health and,
85–87; child nutrition and, 79–81;
demands of, 1–2, 78–79, 147; Yauyos
Province and, *11,* 12–13, *14, 18,* 157n9. *See
also* animal care; farming; water
Erick (3), 89, 96, 99–100
Escuela en Alternancia, 149
Esperanza (13), 69
Estanislao (12), 103
Estela (11), 49, 94, 129

farming, 70–72
fathers and stepfathers, 93–94, 162n1
feeding/food, 81–83; animal care and,
68–70; *atender* and, 99–100; bread and,
80–81; cheese and, 60, 68, 79, 83; child
nutrition and, 79–81, *81,* 161n1–161n3; of
domestic animals, 70; farm work and,
70–72; health and nutrition programs
and, 84–85, 161n5; malnutrition and,
81–83; nutritional windfalls and, 83;
vegetables and, 80
Felicitas (8), 85
Feminist standpoint theory, 37–38, 145
Ferreira, Francisco, 9, 157n5
fish farms, 113–14
Flor (10), 69–70, 95
flourishing: art and song and, 126–28, 164n2;
community traditions and, 134–36;
education and, 132–34; gifts and, 131–32;
nature and, 128–30, 164n3, 165n1; play and,
124–25, *125, 126, 126,* 141–42; spirituality
and, 130–31, 141; in Yauyos, 123–24, 136–37,
146
FONCOMUN (Municipal Compensation
Fund), 16
Fonseca, Claudia, 25
food. *See* feeding/food
FORSUR, 159n7
Franklin (10), 66, 96
friendship. *See* flourishing
fruit, 80

gender: antipoverty programs and, 160n4;
care and, 4, 91–95; entrepreneurship and,
165n4; gender transgressiveness and,
125–26; life course and, 147; play and,
124–26; reputation and, 114–16
gifts. *See* flourishing
Gladis (14), 66, 75, 96, 131
Glenn, Evelyn Nakano, 3
gratitude, 101
Guille (7), 74, 76, 105
Guillermina (approximately 8), 104–5, 123

Hamilton (13), 74
happiness. *See* flourishing
Harbers, Hans, 140
Harriss-White, Barbara, 112
Harvey, Penelope, 134–35
Haydee (6), 60, 87, 98
healing, 85–89

INDEX

health centers, 87–88, 141, 158n11, 160n6, 161n8–161n9. *See also* Serumistas
Henry (14-15), 118–19
herbal medicine, 89
herding. *See* animal care
herranzas, 38, *38*, 39, 69–70, 111, 135
Hilario (14), 50, 88, 118–19
Hogan, Diane, 157n2
household income, 60–61
household membership, 53–54
households, 45–48. *See also* emplacement
houses: design and construction of, 43–45, *44–45*. *See also* emplacement
huancas, 135
Huancayo, 17, 60, 63
Huber, Ludwig, 16, 112
Hughes, Christina, 3

Iglesia del Movimento Misionero Mundial (MMM), 130–31, 143
illness, 85–89
indigenous people, 1–2, 147–48, 150–51, 157n1
indigenistas, 8
inequality, 109
inheritance, 54–55
INRENA, 160n1
Institute of Peruvian Studies, 157n4
intentionality. *See* agency
intimacy, 5
Iris (16), 68, 75
Isaac (12), 75–76, 88
Isbell, Billie Jean, 157n5

Jeferson (10), 47–48, 59, 66, 87, 100, 132
Johnson-Hanks, Jennifer, 43
Junior (8), 68, 86–87, 114–15
Juntos, 165n3

Katherine (11), 68, 110–11, 128
Katya (2), 95
kinship, 3, 8–9

Lamas, Leonor, 148–49
Lancy, David. *See* chore curriculum
Las Cascadas: community traditions and, 135; infrastructure and, 161n6; museum of, 158n20; population and, 17; SAIS Tupac Amaru and, 159n9; scenic reserve and, 19, 158n19
Latin America, 109
Lázaro, 119–20
Lee, Elsa, 142, 144
Leinaweaver, Jessaca B., 25, 101
leishmaniasis, 86–87
Lenin (5), 85
Leoncio (11), 50, 63, 101
Lima: migration and, 17, 144; population and, 17; Region of, 13; Shining Path and, 35
living well, 6. *See also* flourishing
Lizbeth (5), 49–51, 82, 100, 125–26
Los Caminos: land route to, 113; population and, 17

malnutrition, 81–83. *See also* child development

Mariano (11), 74
marriage, 45–50. *See also* single mothers
Maruja (12), 97, 114–15, 123
Máximo (10), 69
Mayer, Enrique, 8, 59, 146, 159n2
methodology. *See* research and theoretical framework
mining, 12–13, 15, 23, 80, 158n14
Mirabel (child), 65
Moisés (11), 132
Morales, Sonia, 127
moral failings, 114–17
mothers. *See* care; gender; marriage; single mothers
music. *See* flourishing

Narciso (7), 116
nearby rich, 112
negligence, 111
neighbors, 109–10, *110*
Nilton (12), 52, 62, 75–76, 99
nuns. *See* Service and Sacrifice congregation
Nussbaum, Martha C., 5
nutrition. *See* child development; feeding/food

obedience. *See* discipline
Opus Dei, 130
Oré, Beatriz, 25
Ortner, Sherry B., 6–7
Oscar (10), 68–69, 72, 87

Palma, Helen, 25
Pamela (9), 66, 68, 102, 117, 125, 142
Parreñas, Rhacel, 3
Pascual (3), 50, 66, 96, 115
Pastizales: community traditions and, 135; fish farms and, 113–14; population and, 17; scenic reserve and, 19
Pepe (14), 71–72, 97, 162n3
Peru: charitable care and, 5; child protection and, 105; churches and, 130; conservatism and, 1–2; corruption and, 112–13, 160n2; entrepreneurship and, 148–50; fertility rate, 160n5; large families and, 51; migration and, 16–19, 144, 149, 158n16, 163n4; 2007 earthquake and, 34–35; views of indigenous people and, 1–2, 147–48, 150–51, 157n1; War of the Pacific and, 164n6. *See also* Andean region; Yauyos Province
Peruvian Ministry of Education, 22, 82
Peruvian Ministry of Health, 87–88
pets, 39–40, *71*, 119, 129, 140. *See also* animal care
petty theft. *See* theft
physical expression, 132
play, 124–25, *125*, 126, *126*, 141–42, 164n1
Ponce, Carmen, 160n4
Ponciano (7), 132
Pontifical Catholic University of Peru (PUCP), 22, 25
Portocarrero, Julio, 25
poverty, 158n15, 160n4
preocuparse. See care
projects. *See* agency
punishment. *See* discipline

Rebeca (18), 92, 99, 114
reciprocity, 54–56, 92
religion, 130–31. *See also* Service and Sacrifice congregation; supernatural Andean beings
Renzo (10), 66, 82, 86–87
reputation, 114–17
research and theoretical framework: agency and, 6–10; biographies sample and analysis and, 27–34, *29*; care and, 2–6; children and, *29*, 37–40; conditioning circumstances and, 34–37; controlled comparison and, 22; organization of the book and, 20; research design and, 23–25, 159n6; research team, 25–27, *26*, *30–32*; the revisit, 22; support for, 21; Yauyos Values Study and, 22–23
Return to the Village, A, 9
the revisit, 22
Ricardina, 115
Rogoff, Barbara, 146
Rojas, Vanessa, 162n6
Rufina (15), 76, 103, 127, 161n7, 162n2

SAIS Tupac Amaru, 159n9
Samuel (5), 50, 82, 92
Sánchez, Rodolfo, 124
San Martín de Porras, 162n7
Sen, Amartya, 5
Sendero Luminoso. *See* Shining Path
Serumistas, 87
Service and Sacrifice congregation, 101, 130, 141, 162n11
Shining Path, 9, 35–37, 117
Shirley (10), 85, 95, 120
Silvia (14), 63, 115
single mothers, 48–50. *See also* marriage
Smith rule, 25
social capital, 109
social reproduction, 4
song. *See* flourishing
Sonia (6), 132
sopa de mantequilla (butter soup), 80
special needs children, 117–20, 163n8
stepfathers. *See* fathers and stepfathers
supernatural Andean beings, 116–17
Susana (child), 96
swaddling, 162n10

team research. *See* research and theoretical framework
Terrazas: corruption and, 112–13; fiestas and, 161n4; fish farms and, 113–14; infrastructure and, 15, 158n14; population and, 17; purchases of medicine and, 162n11; scenic reserve and, 19, 158n19
theft, 110–12
theory. *See* research and theoretical framework
time of hunger *(época de hambruna),* 83
tinkering, 139–41. *See also* care
Tomás (11), 50, 83, 117
tourism, 60

toys, 63
trial marriage. *See* marriage
Tronto, Joan C., 3–4, 6
trout, 113–14
Turner, Victor, 134–35

United Nations Entity for Gender Equality (UNWomen), 5
USAID, 159n8

Valdiva, Gustavo, 124
Valery (17), 131
Valle Grande Institute, 149, 164n4
Vanessa (child), 75
Vaso de Leche program (Glass of Milk), 84
vegetables, 80
Velasco, Margarita, 25, 33
Victor (8), 129
violence. *See* domestic violence
virilocality, 48. *See also* marriage
vital conjuncture, 47, 49, 86–87, 97–98

War of the Pacific, 164n6
water: animal care and, 68, 70; bathing and, 86; children and, 78; clothes washing and, 41; irrigation and, 71–72; sources and infrastructure, 12–14, 158n11; theft of, 112; tourism and, 19
Wenner-Gren Foundation for Anthropological Research, 21
Wilson (child), 73
work: animal care and, 68–70, 86, 140; children and, 63–67, *65, 67,* 142; children as entrepreneurs and, 74–75; economy of Yauyos and, 59–61; in the family business and, *72–74, 73;* farm work and, 70–72, *71;* illegal activities and, 59–60; Yauyos and, 58–59

Yauyos City: population and, 17; tourism and, 19
Yauyos Province: 2007 earthquake and, 34–35, 159n8; economy of, 59–61; entrepreneurship and, 148–50; environment of, *11,* 12–13, *14, 18,* 157n9; free-range animals and, 68; general information on, 10–12, *11;* infrastructure and, 13–15, 150, 158n10–158n11; loans and, 163n4; mayors and, 159n4; migration and mobility in, 16–19, 138, 144, 149, 158n16, 163n5; Opus Dei and, 130; politics of, 15–16; research history and, 159n2; Shining Path and, 35–37; tourism and, 60. *See also* Andean region; Bellavista; child development; children; Las Cascadas; Los Caminos; Pastizales; Terrazas
Yauyos Values Study, 22–23, 109–10, *110,* 119, 122–23
Yeny (11), 74, 83
Yon, Carmen, 48, 88, 160n6
Yovana (5), 51, 100, 126

Zelizer, Viviana A., 4–5
Zenaida (16), 97

ABOUT THE AUTHORS

JEANINE ANDERSON is originally from the Midwestern United States, where her interest in anthropology was piqued by the presence of Native Americans alongside European immigrant communities. A dual citizen, she has lived in Peru since 1970, having arrived with a project for a doctoral dissertation. Over her career she has worked for the Peruvian government, feminist NGOs, international cooperation, and academic institutions. She is currently retired after twenty years as a member of the social science faculty of the Pontifical Catholic University of Peru.

JESSACA B. LEINAWEAVER is a professor of anthropology at Brown University. She has researched children, families, and care in Peru for more than two decades. Her book *The Circulation of Children: Adoption, Kinship, and Morality in Andean Peru* won the Margaret Mead Award. She is also the author of *Adoptive Migration: Raising Latinos in Spain*. Leinaweaver's research has been supported by the Fulbright IIE, the Wenner-Gren Foundation, the National Science Foundation, and the Social Sciences and Humanities Research Council of Canada, among others.

Available titles in the Rutgers Series in Childhood Studies:

Amanda E. Lewis, *Race in the Schoolyard: Negotiating the Color Line in Classrooms and Communities*

Donna M. Lanclos, *At Play in Belfast: Children's Folklore and Identities in Northern Ireland*

Cindy Dell Clark, *In Sickness and in Play: Children Coping with Chronic Illness*

Peter B. Pufall and Richard P. Unsworth, eds., *Rethinking Childhood*

David M. Rosen, *Armies of the Young: Child Soldiers in War and Terrorism*

Lydia Murdoch, *Imagined Orphans: Poor Families, Child Welfare, and Contested Citizenship in London*

Rachel Burr, *Vietnam's Children in a Changing World*

Laurie Schaffner, *Girls in Trouble with the Law*

Susan A. Miller, *Growing Girls: The Natural Origins of Girls' Organizations in America*

Marta Gutman and Ning de Coninck-Smith, eds., *Designing Modern Childhoods: History, Space, and the Material Culture of Children*

Jessica Fields, *Risky Lessons: Sex Education and Social Inequality*

Sarah E. Chinn, *Inventing Modern Adolescence: The Children of Immigrants in Turn-of-the-Century America*

Debra Curtis, *Pleasures and Perils: Girls' Sexuality in a Caribbean Consumer Culture*

Don S. Browning and Binnie J. Miller-McLemore, eds., *Children and Childhood in American Religions*

Marjorie Faulstich Orellana, *Translating Childhoods: Immigrant Youth, Language, and Culture* Don S. Browning and Marcia J. Bunge, eds., *Children and Childhood in World Religions*

Hava Rachel Gordon, *We Fight to Win: Inequality and the Politics of Youth Activism*

Nikki Jones, *Between Good and Ghetto: African American Girls and Inner-City Violence*

Kate Douglas, *Contesting Childhood: Autobiography, Trauma, and Memory*

Jennifer Helgren and Colleen A. Vasconcellos, eds., *Girlhood: A Global History*

Karen Lury, *The Child in Film: Tears, Fears, and Fairy Tales*

Michelle Ann Abate, *Raising Your Kids Right: Children's Literature and American Political Conservatism*

Michael Bourdillon, Deborah Levison, William Myers, and Ben White, *Rights and Wrongs of Children's Work*

Jane A. Siegel, *Disrupted Childhoods: Children of Women in Prison*

Valerie Leiter, *Their Time Has Come: Youth with Disabilities on the Cusp of Adulthood*

Edward W. Morris, *Learning the Hard Way: Masculinity, Place, and the Gender Gap in Education*

Erin N. Winkler, *Learning Race, Learning Place: Shaping Racial Identities and Ideas in African American Childhoods*

Jenny Huberman, *Ambivalent Encounters: Childhood, Tourism, and Social Change in Banaras, India*

Walter Hamilton, *Children of the Occupation: Japan's Untold Story*

Jon M. Wolseth, *Life on the Malecón: Children and Youth on the Streets of Santo Domingo*

Lisa M. Nunn, *Defining Student Success: The Role of School and Culture*

Vikki S. Katz, *Kids in the Middle: How Children of Immigrants Negotiate Community Interactions for Their Families*

Bambi L. Chapin, *Childhood in a Sri Lankan Village: Shaping Hierarchy and Desire*

David M. Rosen, *Child Soldiers in the Western Imagination: From Patriots to Victims*

Marianne Modica, *Race among Friends: Exploring Race at a Suburban School*

Elzbieta M. Gozdziak, *Trafficked Children and Youth in the United States: Reimagining Survivors*

Pamela Robertson Wojcik, *Fantasies of Neglect: Imagining the Urban Child in American Film and Fiction*

Maria Kromidas, *City Kids: Transforming Racial Baggage*

Ingred A. Nelson, *Why Afterschool Matters*

Jean Marie Hunleth, *Children as Caregivers: The Global Fight against Tuberculosis and HIV in Zambia*

Abby Hardgrove, *Life after Guns: Reciprocity and Respect among Young Men in Liberia*

Michelle J. Bellino, *Youth in Postwar Guatemala: Education and Civic Identity in Transition*

Vera Lopez, *Complicated Lives: Girls, Parents, Drugs, and Juvenile Justice*

Rachel E. Dunifon, *You've Always Been There for Me: Understanding the Lives of Grandchildren Raised by Grandparents*

Cindy Dell Clark, *All Together Now: American Holiday Symbolism among Children and Adults*

Laura Moran, *Belonging and Becoming in a Multicultural World: Refugee Youth and the Pursuit of Identity*

Hannah Dyer, *The Queer Aesthetics of Childhood: Asymmetries of Innocence and the Cultural Politics of Child Development*

Julie Spray, *The Children in Child Health: Negotiating Young Lives and Health in New Zealand*

Franziska Fay, *Disputing Discipline: Child Protection, Punishment, and Piety in Zanzibar Schools*

Kathie Carpenter, *Life in a Cambodian Orphanage: A Childhood Journey for New Opportunities*

Norbert Ross, *A World of Many: Ontology and Child Development among the Maya of Southern Mexico*

Camilla Morelli, *Children of the Rainforest: Shaping the Future in Amazonia*

Junehui Ahn, *Between Self and Community: Children's Personhood in a Globalized South Korea*

Francesca Meloni, *Ways of Belonging: Undocumented Youth in the Shadow of Illegality*

Xiaojin Chen, *China's Left-Behind Children: Caretaking, Parenting, and Struggles*

Jeanine Anderson and Jessaca B. Leinaweaver, *Care and Agency: The Andean Community through the Eyes of Children*